Peace Psychology Book Series

More information about this series at http://www.springer.com/series/7298

Mohamed Seedat • Shahnaaz Suffla
Daniel J. Christie
Editors

Emancipatory and Participatory Methodologies in Peace, Critical, and Community Psychology

Springer

Editors
Mohamed Seedat
Institute for Social and Health Sciences
University of South Africa
Johannesburg, South Africa

South African Medical Research Council-
University of South Africa Violence
Injury and Peace Research Unit
Cape Town, South Africa

Daniel J. Christie
Department of Psychology
The Ohio State University
Columbus, OH, USA

Institute for Social and Health Sciences
University of South Africa
Johannesburg, South Africa

South African Medical Research Council-
University of South Africa Violence
Injury and Peace Research Unit
Cape Town, South Africa

Shahnaaz Suffla
South African Medical Research Council-
University of South Africa Violence
Injury and Peace Research Unit
Cape Town, South Africa

Institute for Social and Health Sciences
University of South Africa
Johannesburg, South Africa

ISSN 2197-5779 ISSN 2197-5787 (electronic)
Peace Psychology Book Series
ISBN 978-3-319-63488-3 ISBN 978-3-319-63489-0 (eBook)
DOI 10.1007/978-3-319-63489-0

Library of Congress Control Number: 2017952603

Printed on acid-free paper

This Springer imprint is published by Springer Nature
The registered company is Springer International Publishing AG
The registered company address is: Gewerbestrasse 11, 6330 Cham, Switzerland

Acknowledgments

This text was borne out of our respective scholarly dedications and passions; the myriad inspirations that we draw from our participatory research pursuits; and the compelling, disrupting, and prompting praxis that animated the 6th International Conference on Community Psychology, held in Durban, South Africa, in May 2016, that we had the privilege to chair.

Equally, the genesis of the book is a tale of the creative, productive, and warm collaboration that we share with our colleague and friend, Daniel Christie. We are deeply appreciative to Dan who, as editor of the *Peace Psychology Book Series*, invoked nothing less than enthusiasm and support for the bricolage of praxical contributions contained in the chapters that comprise this publication. Dan's vision for the book series nurtures a knowledge space that authenticates its origins yet is always open to challenging and expanding knowledge horizons in service of epistemic and social justice.

Our sincere gratitude to the chapter authors who contributed their expertise and time to this book. The pages of this book are enlivened by a stimulating blend of innovation, epistemic disobedience, and incitement toward transformative modes of research engagement. The chapters invite engagement with the questions of "what", "why", "how," and "who" of knowledge-making that will undoubtedly serve readers' critical, resistant, generative, and inventive sensibilities. We also acknowledge the communities of people, on whose participation many of the chapters draw and who have informed, impugned, and improved our scholarship. Of course, we thank the reviewers for their constructive interventions, which were invaluable in enhancing the quality and coherence of the book.

A special thanks to our colleague Nick Malherbe for his efficient management of the administrative tasks associated with the book, undertaken with utmost helpfulness, and also to Josephine Cornell for her meticulous support on the technical aspects of the book. Finally, we thank the wonderful Morgan Ryan, editor of Behavioral Sciences at Springer, for her sturdy support on the book project from its inception, for her investment in and appreciation of the book's metamessage, and for facilitating our interaction with Springer. Our appreciation is also extended to the Springer team that has worked steadfastly behind the scenes so that the critical and emancipatory voices of our colleagues and their community collaborators are now etched in the pages that follow.

Mohamed Seedat & Shahnaaz Suffla
Co-editors

Contents

Contributors

Umesh Bawa Department of Psychology, University of the Western Cape, Cape Town, South Africa

Institute for Social and Health Sciences, University of South Africa, Johannesburg, South Africa

Deanne Bell School of Psychology, University of East London, London, UK

Rezarta Bilali Department of Applied Psychology, New York University, New York, NY, USA

Daniel J. Christie Department of Psychology, The Ohio State University, Columbus, OH, USA

Institute for Social and Health Sciences, University of South Africa, Johannesburg, South Africa

South African Medical Research Council-University of South Africa Violence, Injury and Peace Research Unit, Cape Town, South Africa

Brittany Everitt-Penhale Institute for Social and Health Sciences, University of South Africa, Johannesburg, South Africa

South African Medical Research Council-University of South Africa Violence, Injury and Peace Research Unit, Cape Town, South Africa

Michelle Fine The Graduate Center, City University of New York, New York, NY, USA

David Fryer School of Education, University of Queensland, Brisbane, QLD, Australia

Institute of Social and Health Sciences, University of South Africa, Johannesburg, South Africa

South African Medical Research Council-University of South Africa Violence Injury and Peace Research Unit, Cape Town, South Africa

Sindi F. Gordon Department of Education, University of Sussex, Brighton, UK

Yeshim Iqbal Department of Applied Psychology, New York University, New York, NY, USA

Pilar Kasat Sustainability Policy Institute, Curtin University, Perth, WA, Australia

Lesego Bertha Kgatitswe Sociology Department, University of the Witwatersrand, Johannesburg, South Africa

Ursula Lau Institute for Social and Health Sciences, University of South Africa, Johannesburg, South Africa

South African Medical Research Council-University of South Africa Violence, Injury and Peace Research Unit, Cape Town, South Africa

Institute for Dispute Resolution in Africa, University of South Africa, Pretoria, South Africa

Siew Fang Law College of Arts and Education, Victoria University, Melbourne, VIC, Australia

Institute for Social and Health Sciences, University of South Africa, Johannesburg, South Africa

South African Medical Research Council-University of South Africa Violence, Injury and Peace Research Unit, Cape Town, South Africa

Sandy Lazarus Institute for Social and Health Sciences, University of South Africa, Johannesburg, South Africa

Violence Injury and Peace Research Unit, South African Medical Research Council-University of South Africa, Cape Town, South Africa

Nick Malherbe Institute for Social and Health Sciences, University of South Africa, Johannesburg, South Africa

South African Medical Research Council-University of South Africa Violence, Injury and Peace Research Unit, Cape Town, South Africa

Anthony V. Naidoo Department of Psychology, Stellenbosch University, Stellenbosch, South Africa

Shaun Philips Building Bridges, Cape Town, South Africa

Amy F. Quayle College of Health and Biomedicine, Victoria University, Melbourne, VIC, Australia

Jose Ramos Center for Cultural Diversity and Wellbeing, Victoria University, Melbourne, VIC, Australia

Mohamed Seedat Institute for Social and Health Sciences, University of South Africa, Johannesburg, South Africa

South African Medical Research Council-University of South Africa Violence, Injury and Peace Research Unit, Cape Town, South Africa

Puleng Segalo Department of Psychology, University of South Africa, Pretoria, South Africa

Christopher C. Sonn College of Health and Biomedicine, Victoria University, Melbourne, VIC, Australia

Garth Stevens Department of Psychology, University of the Witwatersrand, Johannesburg, South Africa

Shahnaaz Suffla South African Medical Research Council-University of South Africa Violence, Injury and Peace Research Unit, Cape Town, South Africa

Institute for Social and Health Sciences, University of South Africa, Johannesburg, South Africa

Naiema Taliep South African Medical Research Council-University of South Africa Violence, Injury and Peace Research Unit, Cape Town, South Africa

Institute for Social and Health Sciences, University of South Africa, Johannesburg, South Africa

Conrad Zygmont Department of Psychology, Stellenbosch University, Stellenbosch, South Africa

Department of Psychology, Helderberg College, Somerset West, South Africa

Chapter 1
Pluriversal Readings of Emancipatory Engagements

Mohamed Seedat, Shahnaaz Suffla, and Daniel J. Christie

This volume brings together pluriversal readings of emancipatory approaches to community and other reflexive engagements. In so doing, the book recognises the confluences between critical peace psychology and other critically derived psychologies. For instance, the chapter by Siew Fang Law and Jose Ramos is placed at the peace psychology–community psychology interface; Anthony Naidoo, Conrad Zygmont and Shaun Philips draw on ecopsychology; and Sindi Gordon invokes cultural studies, critical thought and psychodynamic theory in her elucidation of creative life writing as emancipatory. As an intersected collection of chapters on emancipatory engagements, the volume evokes what Pelias (2004) terms the "methodology of the heart", that is, the authors—conscious of the epistemic pitfalls inherent to detached expert formulaic pronouncements—are present in their work as embodied activist writers and reflexive analysts. Through their respective probing voices, the authors of these chapters occupy the interdiscursive realm of meaning and experience that interrogates what it means to engage in emancipatory work and build compassionate critical connections, while accompanying the subaltern through moments of destabilising dominant discourses and inscribing generative spaces. All of the

M. Seedat (✉) • S. Suffla
Institute for Social and Health Sciences, University of South Africa, Johannesburg, South Africa

South African Medical Research Council-University of South Africa Violence, Injury and Peace Research Unit, Cape Town, South Africa
e-mail: Seedama@unisa.ac.za

D.J. Christie
Institute for Social and Health Sciences, University of South Africa, Johannesburg, South Africa

South African Medical Research Council-University of South Africa Violence, Injury and Peace Research Unit, Cape Town, South Africa

Department of Psychology, The Ohio State University, Columbus, OH, USA

M. Seedat et al. (eds.), *Emancipatory and Participatory Methodologies in Peace, Critical, and Community Psychology*, Peace Psychology Book Series, DOI 10.1007/978-3-319-63489-0_1

contributors, without exception, locate themselves within their respective texts; they are sensitive to the traps of the narcissistic researcher-writer and yet astutely aware of the significance of positioning themselves as engaged subjects, immersed in the messiness and complexities of community and other reflexive engagements.

In the opening chapter, Sindi Gordon, drawing from critical social thought, psychodynamics and cultural studies, reflects on participatory creative writing as a conjunctural moment of engagement where self, family, community and society interface. She offers us textured insights into "what happens when writers enter into a creative relationship with their life stories". For Gordon, creative life writing as liberatory engagement is a journey of self-discovery that is multiple and embodied. David Fryer, assuming a Foucauldian perspective, follows on from Gordon to present academic writing as an engaged form of resistance and liberation. The Gordon and Fryer chapters are embodied performances of writing to both resist and liberate. The authors illustrate the complexities and obscurities inherent to writing as an unconventional methodology of engagement, and inscribe the practices of writing that they consider in their respective chapters as emancipatory engagement.

Several chapters construct community engagement as a transformative process of participatory knowledge co-creation. These chapters compose methodologies that support emancipation, redraw power boundaries, and encourage a sense of belonging and connections within and across geographical and sociological communities and larger environments. The chapters offer situated accounts of community engagement. The work of Yeshim Iqbal and Rezarta Bilali in the Great Lakes Region of Africa, including Burundi, Rwanda and Democratic Republic of Congo, focuses on community radio education-entertainment campaigns as community engagement, and highlights the influences of context in forging participatory relations for social change. The chapter by Sandy Lazarus, Naiema Taliep and Anthony Naidoo considers community asset mapping as inherent to liberatory engagement. Together with the case study by Siew Fang Law and Jose Ramos on the Maribyrnong Maker Map, these authors represent voices that resist neo-liberal forms of knowledge-making, and demonstrate collaborative forms of action inquiry that draw on cross-disciplinary traditions. The authors of these two chapters offer methodologies for building connections, critical knowledge traditions, and grounded approaches to knowledge construction. Resonant with the ideals of community groundedness and cross-disciplinary enquiry, the work of Anthony Naidoo, Conrad Zygmont and Shaun Philips is framed by concepts inherent to community psychology, adventure programming and ecopsychology. Through the lens of a community-based participatory research framework, Naidoo and his associates showcase the liberation capacities of a wilderness-based intervention.

In other compelling chapters, Christopher Sonn, Pilar Kasat and Amy Quayle, situated in Australia, and Puleng Segalo and Michelle Fine, writing as Africa-centred engaged researchers, bring a nuanced focus to the creative arts as a methodological resource that enables community engagement as forms of emancipatory knowledge-making and sociopolitical solidarity. Sonn and his co-authors offer us a theoretically grounded and indigenous situated analysis of community arts and cultural development. The contribution by Segalo and Fine provides a colourful analysis of the "power of embodied sharing through embroideries as a form of artistic expression". Also in the tradition of critical creative methodology, Deanne Bell describes how oral history may contest methods that fabricate engagement as a mere rational-empirical process and, in contrast, facilitate community engagement that breaks silences, reconstructs social memories, and generate forms of social awakening that movingly support social transformation. Assuming a similar critical thrust, Nick Malherbe and Brittany Everitt-Penhale elucidate the liberatory nature and capacity of participant-led film-making. Representing insightful voices, Malherbe and Everitt-Penhale guide readers through the intricate processes inherent to participant-led film-making: processes that enable youth to resist socially imposed limits to their agency and social power, and creatively engage in action, reflexivity and criticality through multimodal language. Continuing with the idea of engagement as messy, contradictory and complex, Ursula Lau, Shahnaaz Suffla and Lesego Bertha Kgatitswe skillfully describe how the processes of group storytelling may both enhance sense of agency, voice and mutual recognition, and yet trigger community chasms and dividing othering processes. Lau and her colleagues offer thought-provoking commentary on the tensions and dilemmas accompanying the community-engaged researcher's imperative to validate struggle and pain on the one hand, and stimulate agentic possibilities for hope and change on the other in community settings characterised by structural violence. Building on some of the aforementioned themes, the chapter by Nick Malherbe, Shahnaaz Suffla, Mohamed Seedat and Umesh Bawa considers Photovoice "as a praxis of epistemic correction and agency within contexts of dominant knowledge claims". The authors adeptly employ an instance of epistemic disruption within an Africa-centred case illustration to reflexively analyse the liberatory performances and limits of Photovoice methodology. The contributions of these six chapters show how rearticulating stories of oppression, pain, loss, agency, generativity and hope opens up spaces for creative and emancipatory forms of social engagement.

In the last chapter of the volume, Garth Stevens offers a complex meta-analysis of community engagement. Drawing on his work on the Apartheid Archive Project and recognising archives as sites of contestation, Stevens shifts our conceptualisations of community engagement. For Stevens, community engagement as critical psychosocial mnemonics is in part a disruption of assumed understandings of the world, a dislocation of the grand narratives of history, and the inscription of ordinary peoples' experiences of oppression. The chapter constructs critical community engagement as subversion of prevailing hierarchical power relations and assertion of epistemic justice, namely inventing spaces in which the subaltern may insert their stories and narratives of oppression and hope.

A comprehensive reading of this volume and its pluriversal voices embodies enactments of generative-disruptive community engagement, and the spirit of social justice oriented scholarship. The contributors seek to disrupt orthodox, received and presumed knowledges, encouraging us as readers to reconstitute—generatively—the boundaries, horizons and scope of what we have come to cognise as community engagement. Across the chapters, the contributors invite readers to disobey and rearrange conformist and formulaic notions of community engagement; the contributors move us to consider engagement as more than instrumental action.

Engagement as action is exemplified as professional exchanges between "communities in need" on the one hand, and activists, consultants, university-based researchers or NGO-based workers on the other hand. The denotation of engagement as action produces a binary between reflexivity and action, assuming a linear logic (see Bowen, Newenham-Kahindi, & Herremans, 2010), and tends to obscure the fabricated exercise of power in both the discourses and the practices of community engagement (see Cooke & Kothari, 2004; Kothari, 2004). Resisting orthodox notions, the contributors to this volume echo Seedat's (2012) reading of community engagement as an animated, fluctuating, messy and intricate process of praxis, that is sculpted and resculpted by inspired social forces, knowledge traditions, emancipatory philosophical thought, and social actor persuasions that are dialectically interlocking. Read together, the authors assume praxis as comprising imagination, innovation, critical reflexivity and emancipatory action, and a site for the formation of community relationships. This volume succeeds in imprinting community engagement as praxis that is messy, situated and dynamic, and that evokes the methodology of the heart (see Pelias, 2004; Seedat, 2012).

References

Bowen, F., Newenham-Kahindi, A., & Herremans, I. (2010). When suits meet roots: The antecedents and consequences of community engagement strategies. *Journal of Business Ethics, 95*, 297–318.

Cooke, B., & Kothari, U. (2004). The case for participation as tyranny. In B. Cooke & U. Kothari (Eds.), *Participation. The new tyranny* (pp. 1–15). London, England: Zed.

Kothari, U. (2004). Power, knowledge and social control in participatory development. In B. Cooke & U. Kothari (Eds.), *Participation. The new tyranny* (pp. 139–152). London, England: Zed.

Pelias, R. J. (2004). *A methodology of the heart. Evoking academic and daily life*. Walnut Creek, CA: Altamira Press.

Seedat, M. (2012). Community engagement as liberal performance, as critical intellectualism and as praxis. *Journal of Psychology in Africa, 22*(4), 489–498.

Chapter 2
The Potential of Creative Life Writing as a Liberatory Practice

Sindi F. Gordon

Renewal begins in the imagination
(Chandler, 1990, p. 70)

This chapter discusses a narrative study as a community-based participatory research method. It is a critical and creative investigation into the dialogic relationship between memory and imagination through creative life writing and its potential for personal freedom. It looks at what happens when people enter into a creative relationship with their life stories, focusing on the potential of creative life writing for loosening personal and collective narratives and self-conceptions that mould identity.

The starting point for my research topic was where I was born, a place that neither parents called "home". I grew up in one of the largest migratory communities in England, also the proud home of the far-right National Front. Neighbours of Indian, Jamaican, Pakistani, Polish, Irish and Ugandan origins lived next to one another in tightly packed rows of pre-war terraced houses. It was from here that I inherited a residue of displacement and "otherness", oscillating between conflicting positions of insider and outsider, but where I was also introduced to the necessity of story-making and how stories travelled through memory, generations and play.

My desire to explore story-making led me to become a documentary filmmaker and work across three continents, listening to people's stories. However, it was in my last job in the USA that I began to take a further interest in the stories we told and how they impacted the lives we lived. I was working on a television series in New York with a team of experts: filmmakers, scholars, artists and community activists brought together to explore contemporary issues regarding racial politics in

S.F. Gordon (✉)
Department of Education, University of Sussex, Brighton, UK
e-mail: sindi.gordon@sussex.ac.uk

M. Seedat et al. (eds.), *Emancipatory and Participatory Methodologies in Peace, Critical, and Community Psychology*, Peace Psychology Book Series,
DOI 10.1007/978-3-319-63489-0_2

the twenty-first century, with the objective of offering a new insight into the existing dialogue. One of the concerns for the series was that the discussion of racial politics was still being discussed within a black and white paradigm and therefore failed to reflect the complex realities and voices of a contemporary multicultural nation. The filmmakers and production crew were racially diverse and highly qualified, but for the most part I felt the series did not challenge the racial discourse to the extent that had been premised. I felt that we had fallen into a familiar pit where new initiatives were drawn from old formulas and consequently little change was made. In my view this was because we as storytellers had not fully acknowledged and challenged our own internalisation of the racial paradigm and dominant discourses we were aiming to dismantle. It therefore proved difficult for new insights and questions to surface, and new possibilities to be unearthed.

I wanted to know if it was possible—if we needed to—could we distance ourselves from the stories we told, in order to ask: "What might this situation look like from a different angle" (Chandler, 1990, p. 41). Narratives are crucial to the way we see ourselves and relate to others. I wanted to see whether, if we changed the narratives we lived by, could we give new meaning to our past and current experiences? I was particularly interested in the notion of "living in the wrong story", the implication being that the stories we tell may have little connection with the narratives that currently govern our lives.

I decided to use the genre of creative life writing because, unlike conventional autobiography or life writing where the writer "may not be aware of the extent, to which she is fictionalizing, in creative life writing—also known as fictional autobiography—she has given herself permission to fictionalize herself" (Hunt, 2000, p. 12). In creative life writing the writer takes a step further and is not so occupied with factual accounts of past or present but with expressing personal memories and experiences through feelings and emotions associated with them. For this purpose the writer makes a "pact" with herself that she will "allow [her] material to emerge as freely as possible" (Hunt, 2000, p. 163). Liz Stanley suggests that "fictions may actually hold more truths about the past than a factual account" (Stanley, 1992, p. 64).

Underlying the exploration of imaginative space(s) in my research is the understanding that memory is reconstructed: "the past is continuously modified by the experiences of the present and the "self" who is doing the remembering" (King, 2000, p. 32) and therefore memory is always using imagination. Author Toni Morrison states that "the act of imagination is bound up with memory" (Morrison, 1995, p. 98). The fictionalising of our life story allows us to excavate and explore conscious and unconscious material, memories that have been hidden or previously unavailable. My research explores how the imagination impacts the telling of memories; stories that "make sense of our lives". I refer to memories that appear fixed and prevailing as life-held narratives, or "life narratives", deemed to be critical as they become significant memories and a "way of defining ourselves" (Neisser & Fivush, 1994, p. 1). The problem is that life narratives are often presented as "if they were the chief or even the only ingredient of the self", which are very difficult to change (Neisser & Fivush, 1994, p. 1).

The work of creative life writing for personal development was mainly based in individual psychology and did not look at the wider sociopolitical perspective. Thus, by locating my study in a specific sociocultural location, a hair salon/barbershop in the UK catering for people of African, Caribbean and Asian heritage, I opened the discussion of the practice and potential of creative life writing. The salon is a microcosm of a contemporary urban British society, a setting where boundaries such as gender, race, religion and other signifiers are crossed and intertwined. It is an English community that challenges the deeply held hegemonic claims of Englishness/Britishness, representing a new generation of Europeans. The salon is the "hub" of the community, a place of collective activities and a natural setting for the telling and sharing of stories.

It was also important for my study that I addressed what bell hooks refers to as "the gap between theory and practice" (hooks, 1994, p. 65). This ethos and engagement—mindfully placing theory at the centre of the lives of "ordinary people", making genuine connections and critical analysis—served as salient founding blocks for my research.

The Salon: Creative Life Writing as a Method

I was involved in the hair salon/barbershop community as a client before I decided to locate my research in this location. I spoke with other clients from the salon about my idea of teaching a creative writing workshop and soon became aware that the exploration of personal memories and experiences were at the core of their interests. The idea of using fictional and poetic techniques to engage with personal memories offered a different approach for the clients to explore their life-stories. Locating the creative life writing workshops in a salon, a non-traditional learning space, allowed for a more collaborative design and development of the research inquiry with the salon community. I was invariably led to participatory action research (PAR), particularly community-based participatory research (CBPR), as it offered a flexible and sustainable framework for an alternative research inquiry that brought together practice, theory and experience. Using a participatory method was a way of engaging with the community, with creative life writing as a guide for allowing people to work both on their own and with each other. Also contrary to conventional research, in CBPR the researched are positioned as partners in the entire research process, which was critical in a study that was located in the community and committed to generating knowledge from collaborative and equitable partnerships.

All the participants were clients of the salon and were recruited to the project via flyers or word of mouth. For 2 h every Saturday morning over 10 weeks I ran a creative life writing workshop in the basement of the salon. The participants were women and men; from the African and Asian diaspora, their cultural heritage included Liberian, Jamaican, German, Barbadian, Indian, Nigerian, Scottish, English, Brazilian and Chinese. We sat around a table with snacks and drinks, introducing an element of informality to diminish negative classroom experiences of writing which many of the participants referred to, and also to demystify the idea of "a writer". My facilitation aimed to install the belief that everyone was equipped to participate fully in the workshop and to become authors of their own stories.

By introducing the participants to poetic and fictional exercises, oral storytelling techniques and a range of literary texts, I was offering the group ways of thinking about their own experience from different perspectives. Selected writers were chosen for discussion that crossed cultural and literary boundaries, including Sathnam Sanghera, John Agard, Ishle Parke, Rayda Jacobs, Ted Hughes and Prince Massingham. Using exercises and texts that were culturally diverse and a range of genres helped the writers to have a better understanding of the creative process and nurtured their willingness to engage. As Linda Christensen says:

> The books we choose to bring into the classroom say a lot about what we think is important, whose stories get told, whose voices are heard, whose are marginalised (Christensen, 2009, p. 6).

The creative practice for many of the participants opened up an imaginative space for a story they "had not set out to write",[1] which allowed them to see themselves from a different perspective. All were keen to explore a broader narrative that shaped their lives, as reflected in one of the list poems, where the writer begins each line with the same words.

> I wish I could skate
> I wish I could tell people what I really think
> I wish I could live in a white skin for a day
> I wish I could live as a man for a day ...
> I wish I could not be so fearful at times
> I wish I could wrap protective bubble round my daughter

In this exercise the aim for the writer is to not think about spelling or grammar, thereby transcending the inner critic and entering a place "where you are writing what your mind actually sees and feels, not what it *thinks* it should see or feel" (Goldberg, 1986, p. 7). Manjusvara suggests the list poem is a good exercise to approach core beliefs. He claims that "the momentum to keep adding to the list is often enough to overrule what we consider to be a more acceptable voice" (Manjusvara, 2005, p. 26). The above poem also served as a catalyst for other writers in the group, as they responded saying that they wanted to explore the idea of living in someone else's skin. The following week I devised a writing exercise called "Walking in Someone Else's Moccasins". The idea was to write from a completely opposite perspective, for example if they were female, to write from a male perspective, or if they were young, to write from an older voice, etc. By occupying "someone else's skin", the writers explored feelings and emotions outside their own autobiographical framework. The formulation of this exercise also demonstrates the reciprocal relationship between facilitator and writers in the group, a relationship that allowed all of us to feel engaged in the story-making process of the workshop.

---

[1] Unascribed quotations are drawn from the research participants' interviews and creative writing, with their permission.

In the process of these seemingly simple writing exercises participants began to understand their own creative writing process and the impact that it had on the telling of their stories. One of the participants referred to the writing as a method for how "we can unseat our narratives because you have a narrative of yourself … and it is about how you unlock yourself out of that narrative".

The Liberatory Role of Creative Life Writing in the Workshop

> It's on the page, you have truly liberated yourself and since then I never think of it again, and if I think of it, I feel very differently. I feel it's an old landscape; it's no longer in me (a workshop participant).

I was struck by the immediacy and willingness of the participants to "let go" into the creative process and embark on a journey across unknown territories. One of the reasons they were able to do this was because they felt safe and comfortable in the workshop space, but they also expressed a pressing need to tell their stories: "I let myself go"; "It was like a floodgate that was opened. It was all packed in there ready to go"; "There is something that is dying to emerge". According to Marilyn Chandler, "making experience into story fulfils a variety of human needs" (Chandler, 1990, p. 3). She observes that we have a need to become the "authors of our own stories" (Chandler, 1990, p. 3) as a way of reclaiming control of our lives, and that we also need to assert our differences and similarities to one another. The group work exemplified such explorations and expressions. One of the participants wrote an autofictional piece called "Twenty Three Minutes" about a 15-year-old girl going to a party in a car with American GIs. When she wrote the story she felt she had acquired "the freedom to imagine being powerful". She spoke of regaining control of her life by "taking it [memory] out of your head and bringing it to the page":

> Georgia was very clear in her head, crisp, cold, alert and awake …. You could say in the last seconds Georgia was never clearer and more in control.

Writing her story was an empowering process, as she was able to gain distance from a painful experience she had been carrying for a long time: "I wanted to explore fiction and that freedom, if the girl has that freedom to go all the way … what would she do?" The story reveals a personal journey of moving from powerlessness to empowerment, which allows the protagonist to become an agent of change of her circumstances. Creative life writing is a "deeply personal, deeply connected with the writer's self, but it also involves moving away from the self and becoming impersonal" (Hunt & Sampson, 2006, p. 2). The writers at times engendered their characters to act and speak in circumstances that in real life they themselves may have found difficult; as a result, they entered terrain of the self they had not dared explore before.

Creative life writing provided an important opportunity for people to reflect on their sense of self and how dominant discourses and self-concepts construct them. As the participants began to pay attention to their feelings and emotions, they explored stories that stretched far beyond implicit narratives. One participant felt a "release" when her stories revealed: "how funny she [her mother] was. I completely forgot. I've been angry with her for so long"; without warning her words gave light to a relationship darkened by sorrow and pain. Jill Kel Conway says of her experience of recollecting her memories: "I found that my memory was all the painful things. But in the process of telling that story I rediscovered so much that was beautiful about my childhood" (Conway, 1995, p. 172). Similarly to Conway, the writing process for the participants was also at times able to give "back the good things that [they] had forgotten" (Conway, 1995, p. 172).

It is not easy to determine the experience of change for the participants, but one of the changes that unquestionably did occur was that through the writing, group work and facilitation, a safe space was held for imaginative explorations, a space that allowed for engagement of the known and, even more, unknown material of the self. There was also something in this process that was fluid as well as focused, which allowed the participants to capture and convey stories that felt authentic to them.

Generating Psychic Space for Thinking Differently

What I found from the writers' experience in the workshops was the invaluable process of being able, on the one hand, to gain closer access to their deeply felt memories and experiences and, on the other hand, to gain sufficient creative distance from them to transform them into creative writing. Hunt calls this "accessing and objectifying personal material" (Hunt, 2001, p. 30); writers are able to distance themselves from life-held narratives and open up psychic space for looking at themselves from different perspectives. As one participant said: "It's like looking at the same thing but twisting it a bit in the light and being able to see it differently". This allows new stories to emerge which can bring insight into the self.

Relevant here is Stuart Hall's notion of the "gaze of the Other" (Hall, 2000, p. 202), as the starting self-perceptions for most of the participants were rooted in racial and cultural identities, which produced feelings of otherness and difference within mainstream society. Since W.E.B. Dubois and Simone de Beauvoir, attention has been given to how we come to experience ourselves through the eyes of others, the internalisation of racialised and gendered agendas from the outside world (Beauvoir, 1953; Dubois, 1903). Creative life writing enables writers to engage in a process that creates a fundamental shift in the relationship to the other; by fictionalising our memories we are able to be "both 'inside' and 'outside' ourselves simultaneously and able to switch back and forth fluidly" (Hunt & Sampson, 2006, p. 4), and thus the writer is able to be the "eyes of another" for herself (Bakhtin, 1984, p. 287). The writer actively becomes the gaze of the other; the story offers a new awareness from the point of view of the narrator. The work of creative life writing presents the possibility for the writer to create a shift from a gaze which *disparages* to one that is *deferential*. Seeing stories through the eyes of another was invaluable in the participants' process of renewing stories that were embedded and unchanging. The workshops created the possibility for them to suspend, if only temporarily, less helpful narratives, as they redirected their attention to stories that resonated deeply with them.

For one participant, writing about himself as a racing car driver became a catalyst in his writing practice and personal growth:

> As I watch him approach his racing car I could see the beam, the happiness in his flow, the eagerness in his stride, the command in his movement …

The participant had previously written in an impersonal first person, but this time he shifted to a point of view in which he was both the narrator and a third person character. This helped him to create a distance from more dominant narratives that shaped how he saw himself. He recognised the importance of his identity rooted in his heritage, but his story offered a new awareness, another side of himself that emerged in the objectified self-character: "It struck me, this man loves to be free to flow without boundaries". Being able to objectify himself in this way enabled the writer to explore and release feelings and emotions that lay on the margins of his awareness. This was particularly relevant for a writer who oscillated between life narratives rooted in tradition and culture and his own individual aspirations. In his creative life writing he was able to bring together two worlds of himself that he did not think could coexist.

The idea of creating an internal distance from our personal memories and experiences fosters a position of outsideness to our stories, which enables us to develop a reflexive dialogue that offers greater understanding of the self and opens up the ability to step outside existing conceptual frameworks and view the self and the world through a broader lens. There was something undoubtedly empowering for the participants to bring what was going on inside them onto the page. The ability to objectify their felt experience was an essential step towards personal freedom.

Developing a Multiple and Embodied Sense of Self

Regardless of our many identities, whether engendered by family or society, there are elements of identity which tend to drive us towards fixity; this impacts our development of self-understanding and in the process we lose our fluidity and our ability to be multiple. The cultural identities of the participants were multiple, yet most experienced themselves in a way that Hall describes as comprised of the acknowledgment of self through *difference* (Hall, 1987). As one participant shared: "I don't think that you ever get used to never being in the majority". The idea that we have a self which is a fixed thing is experiential. The fact that we are now discovering that our sense of self is a process rather than a thing (e.g. Damasio, 2000) does not change the fact that most people experience it as a thing and will continue to do so. The participants in the workshop experienced a process of trying to understand how a self is not fixed, but fluid and constantly in process. One spoke candidly about the difficulties of being of dual-heritage growing up in a working class community in Scotland and living in a care home. She saw her writing practice as allowing her to take ownership of her life: "I discovered that I was meant to be a bridge between all these different worlds that I was to inhabit".

Creative life writing provides a space for the imagination that enables writers to engage with the many sides of their personalities and identities that shape their lives. My study explored the idea that the self has multiple dimensions but there is nevertheless a possibility of feeling whole and grounded. That sense is also developed through the writing exercises, as it redirected participants' attention towards the feelings and emotions attached to their memories. They began to pay attention to their bodies and to listen to how they were feeling.

Focusing more on their bodily feelings allowed the writers to open space for the imagination, creating generative space in the psyche where language could come together with both conscious and unconscious material. This allowed them as writers to increasingly trust bodily feeling as the core of who they are, and therefore identity becomes a fluid process as they become less reliant on identities embedded in social discourses. Eugene Gendlin (1996) refers to the bodily felt sense, a physical feeling that carries deep embodied knowledge and can bring personal meaning. He sees this felt sense as those feelings that are often not given much attention, a "gut feeling", a sensation that "begins in the body and occurs in the zone between the conscious and the unconscious" (Gendlin, 1996, p. 1). He points out that at first the feeling can be "unclear, murky, puzzling, not fully recognizable" (Gendlin, 1996, p. 26), but in time it can reveal experiences and memories that would otherwise be missed. Gendlin's (1996) notion of the bodily felt sense that precedes language supports the idea that we are not just discourse and that the body plays an important role in our search for identity and sense of self.

Honor Ford-Smith (2005) offers another way to think about the role of the body within emancipatory processes. She draws from a Caribbean legacy of passing on tales of freedom found in the lives of ordinary women. These stories themselves hold a creative power of rebel consciousness, a hidden power that can enable us to fight oppression and acquire freedom. She claims the body holds knowledge that has been suppressed and that this knowledge is essential for liberatory action. She draws from tales such as that of priestess Ni, which speaks of hidden powers within a woman's body. For Ford-Smith (2005), bodily knowledge induces both thought and feeling, and as the stories are passed through generations, they release a power that can serve as a basis to reinvent possibilities and redefine liberatory action.

The Liberatory Role of Finding a Writing Voice

The salon represents a community of people, many of whom felt their voices were not heard or authorised in mainstream society. The workshops focused on helping people to find a voice on an individual level and engaging with discourses that shaped their identities and sense of self. The participants spoke about "the ability to talk about anything, there was freedom, it was liberating"; "I have found my voice … own unique voice"; "I experienced freedom because of digging, I excavated what

I found so hard to express"; "when it is your voice on the page you have liberated yourself".

I was particularly interested in the notion of voice in relationship to identity. Peter Elbow refers to having a voice, which is traditionally associated with "having the authority to speak" (Elbow, 2000, p. 204). Voice in relation to identity often refers to an identity which is officially not recognised, and therefore the process of finding a voice involves the recovery of hidden, suppressed or forgotten identities. Poet-activist Audre Lorde says: "I have come to believe over and over again that what is most important to me must be spoken, made verbal and shared" (Lorde, 1984, p. 41), confirming the notion that "there is something important and political at stake in being able to use a voice that you experience as yours" (Elbow, 2000, p. 192).

Zadie Smith explores the relationship between the singularity and plurality of voice and identity. She speaks of her experience of oscillating between different voices: her old voice which represented Willesden where she grew up, "a big colourful working class sea", and her Cambridge voice, where she studied, which was a "smaller, posher pond and almost univocal" (Smith, 2009, p. 134). As time progressed Smith says regrettably she lost her double voice for a single one, the voice she picked up at college. She suggests that society requires that we sacrifice one voice for another; our voice like our identity is presented as fixed and singular, which is an "illusion" (Smith, 2009, p. 134).

Elbow's concept of resonant voice is particularly valuable for my study as it refers to the relationship between social discourse and the unconscious. He suggests that the voice that resonates is the voice that is closest to a whole person because it connects to the unconscious. He emphasises that resonant voice is connected to the body: "the body shows more of ourselves than the conscious mind does" (Elbow, 2000, p. 208). He claims that resonance occurs more in artistic discourse; there is more of the unconscious in discourse when "we make up things, tell stories, use metaphors and exploit the rhythm and sounds of language" (Elbow, 2000, p. 207). Fiction allows the conscious and unconscious voices to come together; as Bakhtin (1981) says of the heteroglossia of the novel, when the page serves as the space for the many voices of the writer.

Through the characters in her story one participant brought together different strands of her African-European identity that had previously felt disconnected. She is reminded of her Germanness when her character is asked if she speaks German, "Spreken Zi Deutsch?" This reminder connects her to a part of herself she had denied and kept hidden: "it came as a shock to feel it so deeply". She realised at this point the importance of accepting the complexity of her identity and history. Writing about herself in third person she says: "she almost eradicated her German accent, almost fooled her to be what she wasn't".

The writers excavated their memories and by doing so discovered subtle voices and experiences that often lay in the shadows of implicit discourses.

Creative Playing in a Safe Environment

The environment of the salon and the facilitation of the workshops played a far more significant role in my research inquiry than I had anticipated, reinforcing Winnicott's view of the importance of creating a safe-enough holding space for creativity to take place (Winnicott, 1971). It was essential to enable participants to move with confidence into their own personal space and writing and therefore I built on the safe space that the salon had already established. There were strong ties and intimacy between the clients and the salon staff due to the longevity of the relationships, which for most had extended over several years. The writers discussed their familiarity and comfort with the salon and spoke of the workshop as a space that enabled them to "belong"; "feel heard"; "feel free to say anything and not be judged". This connection between the participants and the salon was a major influence on the group dynamics and the creative process and outcome of the workshop. There was interdependence, one could not happen without the other, as they nurtured and sustained each other.

I had intentionally wanted to create a playful environment for the workshops, with the aim of creating a space that helped people explore outside their comfort zone. The participants expressed their experience of the workshops as: "funny and silly, it took away my fear of anxiety"; "I just think we laughed a lot so the ego of people trying to impress was just not there, we were just enjoying being together"; "I had so much fun, I didn't feel embarrassed".

It is in the playing and only in the playing that the individual child or adult is able to be creative and to use the whole personality, and it is only in being creative that the individual discovers the self (Winnicott, 1971, p. 73). I drew from Winnicott's idea that playing facilitates growth and is intrinsic to the creative process. He describes the preoccupation that typifies the playing as the moment when a person becomes absorbed in play (Winnicott, 1971). In the context of my research, I understand this as an experience that allows the participants to lose themselves, as they become immersed in the creative process. The writers spoke of their experience of their writing process as being: "immersed in what's going on rather than slightly holding back"; "feeling relaxed is what I feel certainly has led me to my breakthrough"; "it's a space that you occupy, fully". There was a shared experience between the participants of feeling absorbed into the creative process which allowed them to enter into unfamiliar memories: "a bit like going into a trance and going quite deep".

For Winnicott (1971) the notion of creative playing is established during the early stages of a child's life; the child is gradually able to be alone because the unconscious has become imbued with the presence of the mother; the child has gained a sense of benign inner presence. The mother's presence exists particularly in transitional objects, such as toys, blankets and teddy bears which have been important parts of the relationship between them. The holding environment is critical during this transitional stage: if the child does not feel safe, the experience of playing can be frightening and chaotic. This notion of creative play is located in a therapeutic context but is still pertinent to a group learning environment.

In the context of my research the salon could be seen as a maternal presence for the participants' learning process and the workshop space as a holding environment. When I presented the exercise of "introducing yourself through a favourite item of clothes", participants included their favourite boots, necklaces and a charm bracelet, most of them were wearing their chosen item in the workshop, and some of the items continued to be worn throughout the series. The reasons offered included: "it's my favourite"; "it makes me feel good"; "I wear it for good luck". It was here that I began to see Winnicott's transitional objects in a different context. The participants had brought into the workshop their own transitional objects, which enabled them to feel safe enough to explore their inner worlds and outer realities. From there I began to see the collective identity also like a transitional object, something that members of the group brought into the workshop; the racial and cultural identity, as well as their "client" identity installed a collective sense of safety and belonging. In the early stages of the workshop the shared narrative between the participants provided a key component in their ability to let go in the creative process.

Conclusion: Creative Writing as a Liberatory Method in a Community Setting

The most important factor in the success of the project was establishing an environment where participants felt safe enough to engage with the creative writing process. However, at the beginning I had no idea of the difficulties of establishing and maintaining a secure space. I had focused on the workshop but I had not paid attention to the introductory meeting which took place a week before. I soon began to realise that this meeting was the starting point for establishing the group dynamics between the facilitator, participants and environment. The introductory meeting offered structure, information and clarity to the clients, all of which reinforced a feeling of safety within the group. During the meeting prospective participants spoke of the work of artists they liked. One referred to Bob Marley, which was greeted with an enthusiastic approval from other people, including myself. But after the meeting one client spoke to me of a specific moment when she felt estranged from the group. This was the discussion of Marley; she did not like his music and therefore felt at odds when the rest of the group, including me the facilitator. She felt marginalised.

The participants spoke of their challenge of being the only black person in other writers' groups, but locating a creative life writing workshop in a space where black people are the majority has its own challenges. I thought of Zadie Smith when she wrote about the concept of blackness being "too narrow ... It made the blackness a quality each individual black person was constantly in danger of losing" (Smith, 2009, p. 143). When the client raised the issues of Bob with me, it was a reminder of the tenuousness of our identity, particularly where the issue of identity is heavily woven into a collective narrative which offers a sense of belonging to a group.

It also reminded me of my role as facilitator and to be cautious of revealing my own preferences and choices which may inhibit or distance participants' involvement in the group. It was an invaluable lesson for forthcoming workshops.

Within the creative life writing process difficult emotions and experiences can emerge, such as grief, loss, pain, regret, beating oneself up for not having achieved this or that, or for not being a good person. The space is important, but the space is difficult and that is why it was important for me as the facilitator that the writers trusted my ability to hold the group, to contain and navigate emotional tensions within individuals and the group, as they chose the uncertain path of self-exploration: "It was the trust you had with the tutor; the way you [facilitator] were in the group, I felt I could write anything".

It is important that the holding framework is not solely dependent on the facilitator and that group members also participate in this process. Each participant had to assume responsibility for how much of their personal material they felt comfortable to share. The group dynamic created an atmosphere in which participants felt accepted and not judged: "Whatever you came in with and whatever was going on for you, you would be accepted", enabling them to explore differences, contradictions, ambiguities and uncertainties that existed within themselves individually, within the group and outside the group.

The strength of my research is found in its practice, which demonstrates that having a voice is critical to an empowering process. Participants' writing practice and the group discussions revealed complex, multidimensional lives, challenging single identities and hegemonic agendas, offering a new "consciousness of expansiveness" from a "cross cultural, transnational, translocal, diasporic perspective [that] redefines identity away from exclusion and marginality" (Boyce-Davies, 1994, p. 4). I contend that creative life writing that engages with a sociopolitical context is a valuable tool of renewal, reconstruction and transformation. The research from which this chapter draws shows how creative life writing presents the possibilities of enabling us to become agentic in our own emancipatory processes; introducing the understanding and necessity for "new analyses, new questions and new understandings [as we] unlock some of the narrow terms of the discourses in which we are inscribed" (Boyce-Davies, 1994, p. 5).

One of the most liberating aspects of the participants' learning was the very simple recognition and acceptance that our lives did not fit into a tidy box. Such workshops allow us to unlock the creative power of rebel consciousness buried deep within our own stories (Ford-Smith, 2005). As we learn to express our silences, feelings and emotions on the page, we begin to take those personal tiny and titanic steps towards freedom:

> You're never really a whole person if you remain silent, because there's always that one little piece inside of you that wants to be spoken out, and if you keep ignoring it, it gets madder and madder and hotter and hotter, and if you don't speak it out one day it will just up and punch you in the mouth from the inside (Lorde, 1984, p. 42).

References

Bakhtin, M. (1981). *The dialogic imagination: Four essays*. Austin: University of Texas Press.

Bakhtin, M. (1984). *Problems of Dostoevsky's poetics*. Minneapolis, MN: Bloomsbury.

Beauvoir, S. D. E. (1953). *The second sex*. London: Vintage.

Boyce-Davies, C. (1994). *Black women, writing and identity: Migrations of the subject*. London: Routledge.

Chandler, M. (1990). *A healing art: Regeneration through autobiography*. London: Garland Publishers.

Christensen, L. (2009). *Teaching for joy and justice: Re-imagining the language arts classrooms*. Milwaukee, WI: A Rethinking Schools Publications.

Conway, J. K. (1995). The site in memory. In W. Zinseer (Ed.), *Inventing the truth: The art and craft of memoir* (pp. 41–60). New York, NY: Houghton Mifflin Company.

Damasio, A. (2000). *The feeling of what happens: Body, emotion and the making of consciousness*. London: Vintage.

Dubois, W. E. B. (1903). *The souls of black folks*. Boston, MA: Bedford Books.

Elbow, P. (2000). *Everyone can write: Essays toward a hopeful theory of writing and teaching writing*. New York, NY: Oxford University Press.

Ford-Smith, H. (2005). *Lionheart gal: Life stories of Jamaican women*. Kingston: University of West Indies Press.

Gendlin, E. (1996). *Focusing-orientated psychotherapy: A manual of the experiential method*. New York, NY: Guildford Press.

Goldberg, N. (1986). *Writing down the bones: Freeing the writer inside*. Boston, MA: Shambhala.

hooks, b. (1994). *Teaching to transgress: Education as the practice of freedom*. New York: Routledge.

Hall, S. (2000). Old and new identities, old and new ethnicities. In L. Back & J. Solomous (Eds.), *Theories of race and racism: A reader* (2nd ed.). London: Routledge.

Hall, S. (1987). Minimal Selves'. In: *ICA (Institute of Contemporary Arts), documents 6, identity the real*. London: ICA.

Hunt, C. (2000). *Therapeutic dimensions of autobiography in creative writing*. London: Jessica Kingsley.

Hunt, C. (2001). Assessing personal writing. *Auto/Biography, 9*(1–2), 89–94.

Hunt, C., & Sampson, F. (2006). *Writing: Self and reflexivity*. London: Palgrave.

King, N. (2000). *Memory, narrative, identity: Remembering the self*. Edinburgh: Edinburgh University Press.

Lorde, A. (1984). *Sister outsider: Essays and speeches from Audre Lorde*. Berkeley, CA: Cross Press.

Manjusvara, A. (2005). *Writing your way*. Birmingham: Windhorse.

Morrison, T. (1995). The site of memory. In W. Zinseer (Ed.), *Inventing the truth: The art and craft of memoir*. New York: Houghton Mifflin Company.

Neisser, U., & Fivush, R. (1994). *The remembering self: Construction and accuracy in the self-narrative*. Cambridge: Cambridge University Press.

Smith, Z. (2009). *Changing my mind: Occasional essays*. London: Hamish Hamilton.

Stanley, L. (1992). *The auto/biographical I: The theory and practice of feminist auto/biography*. Manchester: Manchester University Press.

Winnicott, D. (1971). *Playing and reality*. London: Routledge.

Chapter 3
Writing as an Engaged Method of Resistance and Liberation

David Fryer

> *"Those who are separated from what they can do, can, however, still resist; they can still not do"*
>
> (Agamben, 2011, p. 45).

Any attempt to engage in resistance and liberation through writing immediately raises the questions: resistance to what? Liberation from what? Resistance and liberation in which ways? In this chapter, explication of resistance starts with critical exploration of some attempts at resistance to the deployment of key performance indicators (KPIs) in relation to academic publishing as a means of surveillance, policing and government within contemporary neo-liberalised academia. This involves resisting writing within the neo-liberalised academic frame of reference. The chapter continues with scrutiny of academic writing which is positioned, within one critical frame of reference, as resistance to and liberation from oppressive forces, for example the political use of unemployment as an instrument of economic control, through critical review and theorisation which, upon examination within a different critical frame of reference, is found to re-inscribe problematic discourses which are deployed oppressively by the status quo. The chapter continues with explication of non-normative resistance through critique which "refuses to develop a framework of normative standards with which to evaluate the desirability of power relations, institutions, structures and … refuses to take up the role of reform

D. Fryer (✉)
School of Education, University of Queensland, Brisbane, QLD 4072, Australia

Institute for Social and Health Sciences, University of South Africa, Johannesburg, South Africa

South African Medical Research Council-University of South Africa Violence, Injury and Peace Research Unit, Cape Town, South Africa
e-mail: drdavidfryer@yahoo.co.uk

M. Seedat et al. (eds.), *Emancipatory and Participatory Methodologies in Peace, Critical, and Community Psychology*, Peace Psychology Book Series,
DOI 10.1007/978-3-319-63489-0_3

designer" (Triantafillou, 2012 as cited in Hansen, 2016, p. 127). Resistance through critique in this sense involves resisting governmentality through engaging in "critical practices understood in the broadest possible way as related to doubt, pointing to the possibility of 'otherness'" (Hansen, 2016, p. 127). The chapter concludes by positioning resistance as also including liberation from the potential coercive power over the reader of the handbook apparatus which includes the handbook chapter author, reviewers, editors, publishers and so on, which constitute the authority of the chapter. A central message to the reader of this chapter is: do not do what the author has done, nor do what the author or handbook recommends.

Writing for publication within the dominant neo-liberal academic frame of reference is discursively positioned as: "a good thing", a quality-controlled contribution to knowledge, the result of sustained, painstaking, individual, agentic, intellectual work independent of political and economic agendas in contemporary neo-liberalised academia. At least in the metropole as opposed to the periphery, a useful binary distinction is made by Connell (2007) to call up "the long-lasting pattern of inequality in power, wealth and cultural influence that grew historically out of European and North American imperialism" (Connell, 2007, p. 212).

Writing publications in peer-reviewed journals may indeed be "a good thing" for: orthodox career academics, whose writing ticks contemporary key performance indicators in their disciplines and thereby assists them in gaining status, promotion and a disproportionate share of resources; a good thing for those who manage academics providing, superficially legitimate, means to justify the subjection of academics to surveillance, governmentality and policing to render them compliant with paradigmatic, methodological and political status quos; a good thing for the commercial publishing companies which make huge profits out of the publication of academics' writing; and a good thing for industries which use academic publications as marketing devices to increase their profits.

However, writing for publication is *not* "a good thing" for the well-being of those writers working from critical, decolonising, feminist, liberation, queer or other radical standpoints whose teaching, scholarship and research is constantly at risk of being shut down (Fryer & Duckett, 2014). Critical academic writers are systematically culled from the academies of the metropole, but perhaps the most shocking case was that of Ignacio Martin-Baro. "In your country", Martin-Baro once quipped to a North American colleague, "it's publish or perish. In ours it's publish and perish" (Aron & Corne, 1994, p. 2). This was not mere hyperbole: "It was the middle of the night of November 16th, 1989. It had been quiet on the UCA[1] campus. Until the soldiers stormed into the Jesuit residence, only Martin-Baro had been awake, putting some finishing touches on a manuscript. Forced out to a courtyard, the scholar was to be left there as a crumpled corpse, together with Ellacuria,[2] four of their Jesuit brothers, and their housekeeper and her teenage daughter, who had come to stay with the priests thinking they would be safe there. The US-trained troops of the elite Atlacatl Battalion

[1] UCA in the above quotation is an acronym for Universidad Centroamericana Jose Simeon Canas.

[2] Ignacio Ellacuria, Rector of the Universidad Centroamericana Jose Simeon Canas.

had aimed their weapons at the Jesuits heads and blown their brains out. This was more than a mass murder, it was an attempted sophiacide" (Aron & Corne, 1994, p. 1).

Moreover, academic writing is certainly not a good thing for oppressed people who are written about and intervened into. Smith (1999, p. 20) wrote of: "imperialism, history, writing and theory" that she "selected these words because from an Indigenous perspective they are problematic. They are words … which draw attention to the thousands of ways in which indigenous languages, knowledges and cultures have been silenced or misrepresented, ridiculed or condemned in academic and popular discourses". Smith (1999) later continued in relation to academic writing: "Much of what I have read has said that we do not exist, that if we do exist it is in terms which I cannot recognise, that we are no good and that what we think is not valid" (p. 35).

A key problem with metropolitan academic writing whose authority derives, within the metropolitan academic frame of reference, from claimed warranting through research and or scholarship, according to Linda Tuhiwai Smith, is that the warranting is based upon others' research, which others own, which serves others' interests; which benefits others, which others write up, disseminate and deploy for their own ends. Linda Tuhiwai Smith identifies the knowledges others construct and legitimise as the battle grounds for colonisation in particular and oppression in general: "Indigenous communities … are not only beginning to fight back against the invasion of their communities by academic, corporate and populist researchers, but to think about, and carry out research, on their own concerns" (Smith, 1999, p. 39). But they are not alone. Like indigenous people in New Zealand, working class people in Scotland often regard themselves as the most research-written about people on earth. Mrs. Cathy McCormack, an extraordinary Scottish community activist, author (McCormack, 2009), documentary film maker (http://truetvandfilm.co.uk/product/at-the-sharp-end-of-the-knife/) and blogger (http://cathysblogstogod.org/), once joked with me that the public housing scheme where she lived had two rush hours: one when the academics, students, journalists, social workers and other scribes drove in in the morning and another when they drove out again to their homes in the leafy suburbs at the end of the working day. Many people in such communities feel invaded by, intruded upon and resentful of the legions of paid and unpaid wielders of pens who regard members of their communities as a pool of people with nothing better to do than take part in their knowledge-projects, which are used by the authors to generate articles, reports and papers to gain qualifications, build CVs and contribute to policy developments, which are at best irrelevant or at worst part of the problem, from the perspectives of community members.

Cathy McCormack and I have worked together for over a quarter of a century, sometimes in parallel, sometimes together but always in mutually supportive and stimulating ways, as allies, trying to bring critical activism and critical psychology productively together try to understand socio-structural violence and progressively deploy that understanding. Each of us has attempted to do so by focusing critically, albeit in different ways, on interconnections between material poverty, societal inequality, socio-economic policy and psychosocial violence. Cathy discursively positioned the carnage in her community as the consequences of a war without bullets and we have together deployed that discourse to articulate new questions and write new answers. The "enemy" within the war without bullets have been positioned in our writing as non-producers/consumers surplus to contemporary market requirements. The means of waging the war without bullets has been positioned in our writing as "weapons of mass demoralisation" which generate toxic inequality; poverty; unemployment; insecure, part-time, temporary, dissatisfying, poorly paid jobs; substandard housing; stigma; social apartheid; and miseducation to produce critical illiteracy. The scale of the war without bullets has been positioned in our writing as all-out—the chances of surviving the oppressive policy blitz in parts of the neo-liberal world are far less than the chances of surviving whilst walking through a war zone minefield. The goal of the war without bullets has been positioned in our writing as "full spectrum governmentality". The weapons of resistance have been positioned in our writing as critique; answering back; subversion; solidarity; conscientisation; and praxis. Those from whom we can learn effective resistance skills have been positioned in our writing as decolonisers, emancipatory disability activists, community activists, critical theorists, feminists, queer theorists, trades unionists, anti-capitalists, anti-globalisation activists, green activists, popular educators, progressive journalists and anti-imperial intellectuals. Those who are waging the war without bullets have been positioned in our writing as those drafting and enacting policy, inscribing and relaying problematic discourses, including politicians, policy makers, bureaucrats, researchers, teachers, lecturers, psychiatrists, psychologists, therapists, counsellors, social workers, journalists, street level bureaucrats and authors.

In our writing, Cathy and I have tried to avoid default back to psychologism or individualism in the form of positioning the war without bullets as being intentionally waged by malevolent individual agents. However, the more interesting thing about this writing in the context of this handbook chapter is that our writing has largely eschewed the neo-liberal academy's preferred forms and forums. Cathy and I have engaged in diverse forms of inscription, together communicating through podcast, through conversations interspersed with music on local radio, through discussing books at the Edinburgh Radical Book Fair, and participating in the Church of Scotland Poverty Commission in addition to conventional activity writing (for example, Fryer & McCormack, 2011, 2012, 2013). However, although we have used different means and locations for delivering the words, written or spoken, my own writing with Cathy at least, whilst intended to resist and liberate, is—within the critical frame of reference in which I currently locate my work—in many respects problematic.

The chapter continues with explication of writing "by the author"[3] which is now discursively positioned as problematic. It is intended that clarification of why and how it was problematic will increase the possibility of others avoiding reinscribing the same problematic positions and demonstrate that resistance is never finished and what seems like resistance within one frame of reference seems like compliance in

[3] The scare quotes are an acknowledgement of the troubling of the notion of "author" by Foucault (1984, pp. 101–120).

another frame of reference. Community psychology was positioned by some of its advocates as a form of resistance to mainstream psychology, but is turning out to be the mainstream psychology of our times. Qualitative research was positioned by some of its advocates as a form of resistance to quantitative research, but is becoming the new orthodoxy (Fryer, 2013). More recent and contemporary writing "by the author" intended to resist and liberate will undoubtedly be discursively positioned as problematic too in due course. It is certainly to be hoped so: critique is never finished or complete.

One of my first tasks as a postdoctoral researcher in a research unit was to read a vast number of research publications about unemployment and mental health and to write a review which would help lay the foundations for future research. It was assumed by research unit staff that there was a huge gulf between the "knowledge" of politicians and opinionated pundits and the "knowledge" of researchers. Whilst not precisely formulated, a key assumption with regard to writing a review of "the literature" was that more confidence should be accorded to knowledge claims warranted by "research" than to the "politically motivated" knowledge claims of politicians and policy makers or to quotidian knowledge claims based on "anecdotal evidence". In line with modernist "Enlightenment" thinking, it was also taken for granted in that context that policy change could be brought about by persuasive reasoned presentation of evidence. Two examples of review papers from this period include my first published review of the psychology of unemployment (Hartley and Fryer, 1984) and, 2 years later, a fuller review (Fryer & Payne, 1986). Many other reviews followed whose central thrust was repeated, albeit updated in content and written slightly differently for different groups of readers. Verbal versions of the review were also presented to bureaucrats attached to the UK's Department of Employment, to trades unionists, as well as to other academics and researchers.

A key controversy addressed by many of the publications reviewed in the mainstream unemployment research literature spanning over 8 decades was whether the consensually agreed "poor mental health" of "unemployed" people was a result of people with poor mental health being disproportionately likely to become and remain unemployed (selection/individual drift) or whether becoming and remaining unemployed was likely to result in (cause) poor mental health ("social causation"). Although, in my writing at that time, discursively positioning poor mental health as the result of the mass unemployment, which was a deliberate outcome of politico-economic policy, was taken for granted as progressive. In my contemporary writing, that writing is discursively positioned as functioning, not as an engaged method of resistance and liberation, but rather as a disengaged method of fostering compliance and intellectual enslavement.

In attempting to resist and liberate through writing, these reviews, naively assumed to encourage "evidence-based policy", actually reproduced and reinforced discourses which had already achieved dominance by reviewing what had already been warranted as (given the status of) "knowledge" in order to appear in "the literature" being reviewed. These dominant discourses had already been active in the construction of research problems, in programmes of, and fashions in, research funding, in the operations of Human Research Ethics committees and gatekeepers of research access and in the refereeing process following submissions to journals. The problematic nature of literature reviews in this respect has intensified with the increasing requirement that "systematic literature reviews" be conducted using vast but discursively problematic online databases.

Whilst attempting to resist and liberate through writing, the reviews problematically reinscribed naïve medical model discourses in which individual psychopathological "conditions" such as "depression", "anxiety" and "self-esteem" were positioned as ontologically real, objectively measurable and practically amenable to individual intervention through therapy, pharmacology, etc. Whilst attempting to resist and liberate through writing, the reviews problematically reinscribed transient, continuously reconstituted (and so progressively reconstitutable), social constructs of culturally specific, sociopolitical economic-policy regimes, such as "unemployment", as real, apolitical, measurable and reducible through supply side intervention. Whilst attempting to resist and liberate through writing, the reviews also problematically reinscribed mainstream modernist social science in multifarious ways. Most importantly and problematically, they positioned the relationship between unemployment and individual psychopathological "conditions" as causal, rather than—for example—simultaneously and interconnectedly co-constituted. To summarise here, whilst attempting to resist and liberate through writing, the reviews discussed inscribed a simplistic and misguided binary contrast of ignorance with knowledge; turned a blind eye to the political nature of the warranting and deployment of knowledge claims; ignored the interconnections between knowledge and power; and confused superficial resistance *within* a frame of reference with critique of, and resistance to, a frame of reference.

As a second example of retrospectively problematic writing, the most influential theorised explanatory account of what was and is it about unemployment which is psychologically problematic was, and maybe still is, that of Austro-Marxist Marie Jahoda, who argued that, although the "manifest", that is intended function of employment is to earn a living, employment also has "latent", that is unintended functions (an imposed time structure, engagement in regular social contact, participation in a collective purpose, receipt of a social identity and required regular activity), the deprivation of which—by unemployment—is responsible for the "psychological consequences" of "unemployment" (Jahoda, 1982). Writing in 1986, Jahoda's explanation was subjected in my writing to critique. An alternative meta-explanatory approach was proposed, not in terms of the psychologically benevolent structures of employment (of which the unemployed person was deprived), but in terms of the restriction of agency by unemployment, which was socially constructed to ensure that the unemployed were relatively poverty-stricken and powerless (Fryer, 1986). This was followed up by scholarship-warranted writing emphasising the agency-inhibiting, destructive problems intrinsic to being unemployed as opposed to being not-employed, that is exploring the role of unemployed poverty (Fryer, 1990; McGhee & Fryer, 1989); lack of control over the future; and drawing attention to the glaring differences between the experiences of those made unemployed and of those laid off for an equivalent period of time but with a return to the previous employment already collectively negotiated (Fryer &

McKenna, 1987, 1988; McKenna & Fryer, 1984). Other writing drew attention to the positive experiences of some unemployed people in some ways despite deprivation of employment (Cassell, Fitter, Fryer, & Smith, 1988; Darwin, Fitter, Fryer, Smith, 1987; Fryer & Payne, 1984).

Problematically, in attempting to resist and liberate through writing, modernist notions of separate realms of individualised, agentic subjectivity and contextual social structure were reinscribed. In particular, the explanatory accounts of both Jahoda and Fryer [and of Warr (1987) who offered a hybrid] reinscribed the traditional modernist "agency–structure" binary, reproduced problematic modernist notions of the "person-in-context" and endorsed a naïve realist frame of reference in which "cause-and-effect" relations were invoked and warranted to explain the "consequences" of unemployment. In this writing, human beings were discursively positioned as unitary, rational subjects with continuity over time who were enslaved when their capacity for agentic self-determination as individual social and moral "persons-in-context" was restricted or disabled by powerful destructive social forces operating through contextual circumstances.

To turn to a third attempt to resist and liberate through writing, consider a report about the psychological effects of unemployment written by me on behalf of the British Psychological Society for the Employment Select Committee of the UK's House of Commons. It was a policy-critical report which made research-warranted knowledge claims that UK Government policies were responsible for mass unemployment which in turn caused misery, morbidity and mortality for millions of British citizens. Despite my trepidation, after it had been submitted to Members of Parliament in the Select Committee, the only feedback ever received was affirmative. The left, the right and the centre all seemed entirely comfortable with the claim that the unemployment caused by UK Government policy was very bad for the British public. Why could it be that writing positioning unemployment as "bad for people" was so very acceptable?

A clue may lie in another attempt to resist and liberate through writing. I had read Gans' classic publication, *The Positive Functions of Poverty* (Gans 1972–1973) with great interest. I decided to rehearse the arguments in relation to unemployment. I argued that unemployment provides a pool of potential workers unable to decline to do the most boring, dirty, dead end, menial, underpaid, temporary, insecure, stressful jobs; provides consumers of substandard products and services which would otherwise be economically unexploited; provides competition for jobs from unemployed people, allowing employers to drive down wages and working conditions; increases profits for employers by work being done by fewer employees so reducing wages bills; acts as an incomes policy ensuring lower wages and allowing bigger dividends and more investment; creates jobs for middle class professionals, "causes" for middle class philanthropists and rallying issues for political groups; and creates deviants which can be used to legitimate dominant norms. It was argued that unemployment—far from being a "bad thing" for rich and powerful shareholders, employers and members of other related interest groups—is actually a "good thing" for them, serving their interests in a variety of ways. However, to serve the interests of the wealthy and powerful, unemployment needs to be so undesirable that no-one wishes to become unemployed and if they do become unemployed is such that they want to cease to be unemployed as soon as possible. It was argued that this could only be achieved by unemployment being socially constructed to be inextricably linked with poverty, ill-heath, mental illness, misery, stigma, degradation and so on. Note that I was *not* claiming that unemployment is not destructive for many, but was suggesting that the destructiveness of unemployment was socially constructed in ways which served the interests of the rich and powerful in capitalist societies. The research unit at which I was working at the time was extremely keen on staff publishing so I was taken aback when my academic manager told me it would be preferred if I did not publish this paper mentioning my academic affiliation. This was my first experience of an attempt by the status quo to make my writing invisible. I published the paper in *Radical Community Medicine* omitting reference to my academic affiliation (Fryer, 1985).

In this writing, there were inter-textual traces of Marxist work on the reproduction of labour power and ideological subjection, but Marxist notions of power and of false consciousness in relation to "enslavement" and "liberation" were resisted in subsequent writing in favour of Foucauldian notions of power-knowledge and governmentality. In this later approach, enslavement is discursively positioned as having multiple loci of accomplishment, including compliance achieved through subjective reconstitution, the deployments of systems of power-knowledge practices, which take both productive and restrictive forms, and the broader project of governmentality, which in this chapter is taken to be "the techniques and procedures which are designed to govern the conduct of both individuals and populations at every level not just the administrative or political level" (http://www.michel-foucault.com/concepts/index.html).

In recent attempts to resist and liberate through writing (Fryer, 2014a; Fryer & Stambe, 2014a; Fryer & Stambe, 2014b; Fryer & Stambe, 2015), it has been necessary to engage with the huge, international, 8-decade, multi-method body of knowledge-claims about the relationship between unemployment and mental health, and to do so within a subjugated, critical, anti-psy-complex, social model frame of reference. Moreover, it has been necessary to engage with both "unemployment" and "mental health" without endorsing either as "real" in any sense other than having been constructed, legitimated and deployed to material effect through interconnected politico-economic policies, "active labour market" technologies, welfare bureaucracies and discursive systems, as well as the knowledge-work, including inscription of discourses through writing, of social and psy-complex scientists of unemployment and of mental health.

To emphasise, "unemployment" and "mental health" are positioned within this writing as "real" but only insofar as they are discursively constituted as real within problematic dominant discourses and apparatuses. Of course, because "unemployment" and "mental health" are discursively constituted does not mean they are "imaginary" in a conventional sense and does not mean they have no material effects. The oppression of people (including the auto-oppression achieved through subjective reconstitution) is not illusory or imagined (in a conventional acritical sense). Rather their existence is contingent on the persistence of the interconnected constructed and maintained social elements which produce and maintain them.

In my contemporary writing, a network of interconnected constructed and maintained social elements, including discourses of unemployment and mental health and implicated psy-complex constructions like psychological well-being, whose primary function is to control inflation, reduce wage costs, and discipline the employed work force, is positioned as simultaneously constituting as "real" a category of "the unemployed" necessary to make the neo-liberal labour market work in the interests of employers and shareholders. This category is composed of different people on the basis of varying criteria at different times and in different places. Diverse forms of social violence are visited upon and into the members of that category. The subjectivity of members of that category is reconstituted in such ways as to (re)produce the compliant human means of production required by the employers, shareholders and government within the contemporary version of the neo-liberal labour market. The apparent "relationship" between "unemployment" and "mental health" is, within this frame of reference, positioned not as to do with "natural" and inevitable psychological consequences of depriving a person of employment-related, psychologically necessary structures (Jahoda's Manifest and Latent Function Model), nor with frustrating the agency of the individual person (Fryer's Agency Restriction Model), but rather as to do with a set of interconnected manifestations of social violence necessary to make the neo-liberal labour market function optimally in the interests of neo-liberal elites. Neo-liberal labour market subjects are not, within this frame of reference, positioned as existing prior to power-knowledge but rather as being constituted by being "power-knowledged" via a range of conduits by authorities, including research-warranted writing and—crucially—by unemployed people coming to know themselves, that is power-knowledging themselves through the discourses available to them, including those discourses inscribed in writing.

Writing as an engaged method of resistance and liberation does not necessarily endorse what is positioned as "bad" (or good), even—perhaps especially—within what is widely taken to be a progressive, for example left, frame of reference. On the contrary, it resists governmentality by undermining the taken-for-grantedness of what is routinely positioned as "bad" or "good", even—perhaps especially—within a progressive (e.g. left frame) of reference. The phrase "perhaps especially" is needed because the progressive left and critical scholars are in need of critical friends, who offer critique in solidarity as allies. As Foucault put it: a critique "does not consist in saying that things aren't good the way they are. It consists in seeing what type of assumptions, of familiar notions, of established, unexamined ways of thinking the accepted practices are based" (Foucault, 1981/2001 in Faubion, 2001, p. 456). It involves "showing that things are not as obvious as people believe, making it so that what is taken for granted is no longer taken for granted. To do criticism is to make harder those acts which are now too easy" (http://www.michel-foucault.com/quote/2001q.html).

As an example of this approach to critique, Fryer (2015) engaged critically with the discourse of human rights, despite stating agreement with human rights activists' abhorrence at the abuse, injustice, oppression and social violence relentlessly directed at countless people and peoples around the world. Crucially, Fryer (2015) did not engage in critique *within* the discourse of human rights but rather engaged in critique *of* the discourse of human rights. It argued that the human rights discourse (and the apparatuses of which that discourse is but one element) actually functions to promote injustice, oppression and social violence and that what it is to be human is the result not the foundational origin of psy-complex processes.

To give another example, Fryer (2014b) critically problematised the argument that psychology cannot be Indigenous and scientific without endorsing its opposite mirror image, thus refusing both the claim that psychology cannot be Indigenous and scientific and also refusing the claim that psychology can be Indigenous and scientific. It thus rejected the binary alternatives set up both by the thesis and its opposite, and resisted the invitation to think within the frame of reference of the thesis. Linda Tuhiwai Smith refers to the way Indigenous people are repeatedly positioned as "the Indigenous problem", writing that the "indigenous problem" is a recurrent theme in all imperial and colonial attempts to deal with indigenous peoples. The question of whether psychology could or could not be Indigenous and scientific was revealed as a restatement of "the indigenous problem" in relation to scientific psychology. It was argued that the real question is not whether psychology could be Indigenous and scientific but whether out of all the indefinitely many possible, differently constructed and rhetorically legitimated Indigeneities, any are, have been or could be psychological and scientific? It was argued that it is possible, in theory, that it could one day be said, in good faith, that "psychology not only can be but is Indigenous and scientific", but that that would not happen without fundamental changes in how psychology, science and Indigeneity were constructed, legitimated and deployed. It was argued that hugely powerful vested interests are implacably opposed to, and massively deployed to prevent such fundamental change occurring so the chances of it being said are remote but that it could never be said, in good faith, that "psychology cannot be Indigenous and scientific" (as opposed to psychology will not be Indigenous and scientific because vested interests would not allow it to be so), and that whilst mainstream Western/Northern psychology continues to be colonising and oppressive (rather than decolonising and emancipatory) it will continue to be seen in circles which are critical and Indigenous as part of the problem.

Counter-Conclusions: Resisting the Terms of Engagement

The terms "resistance" and "liberation" are deployed differently within different discursive frames of reference, even within different critical discursive frames of reference. Whilst unemployment, the leitmotif of this chapter, is discursively positioned as socially constituted in destructive forms and the unemployed person is discursively positioned as destructively re-subjectified, human beings are discursively positioned as in a continuous process of social (re)constitution, their subjectivity being continually "reshaped amid economic and political reforms, violence, and social suffering" (Biehl, Good, & Kleinman, 2007) and Enlightenment "discourses rooted in the notion of a unitary, rational subject" (Henriques, Hollway, Urwin, Venn, & Walkerdine, 1998, p. ix) are explicitly resisted. Because critique is recursive, any discursive positioning of writer/author of this chapter as an individualised unitary rational subject by the reader—for example by a reviewer/referee—is also resisted. In contrast to the "individualised" "agentic" writer of Enlightenment modernism, the writer of this chapter—like all writers—is positioned as in a continuous process of social (re)constitution. The sequence of positions described as taken up in relation to writing as an engaged method of resistance and liberation in this chapter are thus not underpinned by a consistent rationale. No consistent theory and logic of writing as resistance and liberation consistently underpins the whole chapter. Nor is what is described positioned as moments on an arc of incremental linear progress over time. Nor is any model from which guidelines for imitation of how method should be extrapolated recommended. Nor is the most recent position explicated presented as unproblematic and, certainly not, as beyond critique. This chapter does not offer a "how to" cook-book approach to writing as an engaged method of resistance and liberation. Rather, it offers a "how-not-to-cook" approach.

The currently dominant metropolitan episteme of discourses, practices, authorities, technologies and so forth constitute academic writing as a site for governmentality and therefore as a site for resistance. This applies at least as much to this chapter as to any writing. Expectations of explicit conceptualisation of resistance and liberation as method; text boxes summarising key "features" of counter-inscription as "method"; and "guidelines" for those who wish to use counter-inscription as a "method" of resistance and liberation have been resisted. No domain is exempt from critique and that includes the domain within which the compliant neo-liberal academic writer is reconstituted (or not). To write in the way expected of an academic textbook writer in the neo-liberalised academy is to collude with the shutting down of possibilities for critical writing and therefore resisted. This has inevitably involved engaging with tensions and contradictions in relation to power operating not only through that which is written about (in the case of this chapter, unemployment) but also simultaneously with tensions and contradictions in relation to power operating through the commissioning, writing, policing, publishing and reading of a text, the title of which is "writing as an engaged method of resistance and liberation".

Acknowledgements I thank anonymous reviewers for feedback on a draft of this chapter.

References

Agamben, A. (2011). *Nudities*. Stanford, CA: Stanford University Press.

Aron, A., & Corne, S. (1994). *Writings for a liberation psychology*. Cambridge, MA: Harvard University Press.

Biehl, J., Good, B., & Kleinman, A. (2007). *Subjectivity: Ethnographic investigations*. Berkeley, CA: University of California Press.

Cassell, C., Fitter, M., Fryer, D., & Smith, L. (1988). The development of computer applications by unemployed people in community settings. *Journal of Occupational Psychology, 61*, 89–102.

Connell, R. (2007). *Southern theory*. Crows Nest: Allen and Unwin.

Darwin, J., Fitter, M., Fryer, D., & Smith, L. (1987). Developing information technology in the community with unwaged groups. In P. Bjerknes, P. Ehn, & M. Kyng (Eds.), *Computers and democracy* (pp. 315–334). Aldershot: Avebury Gower.

Faubion, J. D. (Ed.). (2001). *Power: The essential works of Foucault, 1954–1984* (Vol. 3). New York, NY: New Press.

Foucault, M. (1984). What is an author? In P. Rabinow (Ed.), *The Foucault reader* (pp. 101–120). London: Penguin.

Foucault, M. (1981/2001). So is it important to think? (R. Hurley, trans.) In J. Faubion (Ed.), *Power: The essential works of Foucault 1954–1984* (Vol. 3, pp. 456–457). New York, NY: New Press.

Fryer, D. (1985). The positive functions of unemployment. *Radical Community Medicine, 21*, 3–10.

Fryer, D. (1986). Employment deprivation and personal agency during unemployment. *Social Behaviour, 1*(3), 3–23.

Fryer, D. (1990). The mental health costs of unemployment: Towards a social psychological concept of poverty. *British Journal of Clinical and Social Psychiatry, 7*(4), 164–176.

Fryer, D. (2013). Book review of qualitative research methods in mental health and psychotherapy: A guide for students and practitioners by D. Harper & A. R. Thompson (2012). *Journal of Community & Applied Social Psychology, 24*, 169–171.

Fryer, D. (2014a). Unemployment. In T. Teo (Ed.), *Encyclopaedia of critical psychology* (pp. 2031–2036). New York, NY: Springer.

Fryer, D. (2014b). Psychology, indigeneity and science. In S. Cooper & K. Ratele (Eds.), *Psychology serving humanity* (pp. 91–97). East Sussex: Psychology Press.

Fryer, D. (2015). What can psychology contribute to the defence and promotion of human rights? *The Journal of Critical Psychology Counselling and Psychotherapy, 15*(4), 199–203.

Fryer, D., & Duckett, P. (2014). Publishing. In T. Teo (Ed.), *Encyclopaedia of critical psychology* (pp. 1605–1610). New York, NY: Springer.

Fryer, D., & McCormack, C. (2011). The war without bullets: Socio-structural violence from a critical standpoint. In E. Almeida (Ed.), *International community psychology: Community approaches to contemporary social problems* (pp. 213–232). Puebla: Universidad Iberoamericana.

Fryer, D., & McCormack, C. (2012). The war without bullets: Socio-structural violence from a critical standpoint. *Global Journal of Community Psychology Practice, 3*(1), 87–92.

Fryer, D., & McCormack, C. (2013). Psychology and poverty reduction. *Australian Community Psychologist, 25*(1), 7–2.

Fryer, D., & McKenna, S. (1987). The laying off of hands: Unemployment and the experience of time. In S. Fineman (Ed.), *Unemployment: Personal and social consequences* (pp. 47–73). London: Tavistock.

Fryer, D., & McKenna, S. (1988). Redundant skills: Temporary unemployment and mental health. In M. Patrickson (Ed.), *Readings in organizational behaviour* (pp. 44–70). New South Wales: Harper and Row.

Fryer, D., & Payne, R. L. (1984). Pro-activity in unemployment: Findings and implications. *Leisure Studies, 3*, 273–295.

Fryer, D., & Payne, R. L. (1986). Being unemployed: A review of the literature on the psychological experience of unemployment. In C. L. Cooper & I. Robertson (Eds.), *International review of industrial and organizational psychology* (pp. 235–278). Chichester: Wiley.

Fryer, D., & Stambe, R. (2014a). Neo-liberal austerity and unemployment: Critical psychological issues. *The Psychologist, 27*(4), 244–248.

Fryer, D., & Stambe, R. (2014b). Work and the crafting of individual identities from a critical standpoint. *Australian Community Psychologist, 26*(1), 8–17.

Fryer, D., & Stambe, R. (2015). Unemployment and mental health. In J. Wright (Ed.), *International encyclopedia of social and behavioral sciences* (2nd ed., pp. 733–737). Oxford: Elsevier.

Gans, H. J. (1972–1973). The positive functions of poverty. *American Journal of Sociology, 78*(2), 275–289.

Hansen, M. P. (2016). Non-normative critique: Foucault and pragmatic sociology as tactical re-politicization. *European Journal of Social Theory, 19*(1), 127–145.

Hartley, J. F., & Fryer, D. (1984). The psychology of unemployment: A critical appraisal. In G. M. Stephenson & J. H. Davis (Eds.), *Progress in applied social psychology* (pp. 3–30). Chichester: Wiley.

Henriques, J., Hollway, W., Urwin, C., Venn, C., & Walkerdine, V. (1998). *Changing the subject*. London: Routledge.

Jahoda, M. (1982). *Employment and unemployment: A social-psychological analysis*. Cambridge: Cambridge University Press.

McCormack, C. (2009). *The wee yellow butterfly*. Glenaruel: Argyll Publishing.

McGhee, J., & Fryer, D. (1989). Unemployment, income and the family: An action research perspective. *Social Behaviour, 4*, 237–252.

McKenna, S., & Fryer, D. (1984). Perceived health during lay-off and early unemployment. *Occupational Health, 36*(5), 201–206.

Smith, L. T. (1999). *Decolonising methodologies: Research and indigenous peoples*. London: Zed Books.

Warr, P. B. (1987). *Work, unemployment and mental health*. Oxford: Oxford University Press.

Chapter 4
Community Radio as a Vehicle for Social Change in Conflict-Affected Settings

Yeshim Iqbal and Rezarta Bilali

Community radio has played a rich role in the history of social change worldwide. An alternative to commercial and public broadcasting, community radio is a form of participatory media. Its defining characteristic is that audiences, including community members, are involved in various or all aspects of production and broadcasting (Girard, 1992), rather than being passive listeners. In the 1920s Bertolt Brecht described community radio as "... an instrument of communication in public life, in which the listener was allowed to speak" (Brecht, 1927, p. 2). Community radio is a powerful medium for those seeking political and social change due to its potential to connect to various segments of the population, including those who have low literacy skills, the marginalized, or geographically dispersed. Recently, community radio has begun to converge with the Internet to provide even greater coverage (Noronha, 2003).

There is a plethora of community radio stations around the world (Gumucio-Dagron, 2001), with no one ideal model. Community radio programs are as varied in scope as they are large in number. They vary greatly in organizational dimensions, including dimensions of financial sustainability versus dependency on external finances, local vs. global broadcasting, short-term vs. open-ended programming, and being highly planned and structured in advance vs. open to change depending on circumstances (Myers, Sebert, & Bell, 2002). Community radio stations may operate independently, or in conjunction with governments, nongovernmental organizations (NGOs), or particular constituencies such as churches, universities, trade unions, indigenous peoples movements and women's groups (Waves for Freedom, 1995). Even small radio stations have the ability to engage the community: they

Y. Iqbal (✉) • R. Bilali
Department of Applied Psychology, New York University, New York, NY, USA
e-mail: yi330@nyu.edu

M. Seedat et al. (eds.), *Emancipatory and Participatory Methodologies in Peace, Critical, and Community Psychology*, Peace Psychology Book Series,
DOI 10.1007/978-3-319-63489-0_4

often begin by playing music, which resonates with cultural identity and community pride; they then move on to announcements about local issues, and may broadcast programs on health, education, or other issues of local importance (Gumucio-Dagron, 2001).

Community radio has been used as a vehicle for supporting social change in a variety of domains. Here, we define social change as a significant alteration of patterns of behavior, norms, or attitudes in the community over time. While there are different pathways to social change (for a review see Seidman & Tseng, 2011), community radio influences social change typically through shifting social norms and encouraging critical reflection and critical action (described in detail below). For instance, community radio has been used for public health: examples include the *Taru* radio soap opera in India, whose purpose was to promote gender equality, small family size, and reproductive health (e.g., Papa & Singhal, 2009), and the *Makgabaneng* radio serial drama in Botswana to prevent mother-to-child transmission of HIV (Kuhlmann et al., 2008). Community radio has also been used to promote local, indigenous, or alternative cultures; for example, Radio Gazelle in Marseille, France was initiated by a group of youth from northwest Africa with a political desire to promote their culture and build community (Radio Gazelle, 1992). It has also been used to organize people and encourage collective action regarding grievances. Bush Radio, the oldest community radio station in South Africa, played a pivotal role in the struggle against apartheid (Bosch, 2006) by using its programming to resist apartheid racial categories; in Latin America, the El Salvadorean guerilla *Radio Venceremos* was instrumental in bringing about national liberation by broadcasting news about people's struggles and resistance (Vigil, 1992).

In this chapter, we focus on one form of community radio programming in the Great Lakes Region of Africa: education-entertainment (abbreviated as "edutainment"). We describe the principles behind edutainment, then focus on an example of an edutainment program: a community radio drama that aims to support social change by transforming conflict through reducing violence and promoting intergroup reconciliation. We also illustrate the potential and challenges inherent to community radio as an intervention that aims to promote positive social change in conflict contexts.

Edutainment Through Radio to Impact Social Change

Edutainment is defined as the "process of purposely designing and implementing a media message to both entertain and educate, in order to increase audience members' knowledge about an educational issue, create favorable attitudes, shift social norms, and change overt behavior" (Singhal, Cody, Rogers, & Sabido, 2003, p. 5). Edutainment blends educational messages about social issues into an entertaining format, such as a soap opera. Radio edutainment is commonly used to promote positive behaviors surrounding public health and social concerns such as family planning (e.g., Valente, Kim, Lettenmaier, Glass, & Dibba, 1994), and teenage sexuality which is, for instance, a focus on the radio drama *Dehleez* in India, (Pant, Singhal, & Bhasin, 2002) (for a detailed review, see Myers et al., 2002). Here, social change refers to a shift in norms surrounding the use of family planning and an increase in the number of families that use such methods. Though less prevalent, edutainment has also been used as a tool to support violence prevention. For instance, Soul City, a radio drama in South Africa that addresses domestic violence (see Usdin, Scheepers, Goldstein, & Japhet, 2005), conveys messages intended to reduce incidents of family and gender-based violence.

Edutainment programs build primarily on social learning theory (Bandura, 2004) and Freire's (1970) popular education methods, which emphasize the role of *critical reflection* for understanding and analyzing conditions underlying social issues and *critical action* to promote social change. Fictional characters in edutainment soap operas serve as role models to the audience by adopting pro-social useful attitudes and behavioral patterns to address particular challenges. Through identification with the characters, audience members can observe and vicariously experience how people similar to them can act to improve their lives. The actions taken by the positive role models provide new behavioral options, perhaps increasing the audience members' perceived efficacy to impact change in their own lives (Bandura, 2004). Similarly, negative role models exhibit detrimental behaviors and choices that the audience is meant to avoid. For example, in the popular South African series Soul City, a collective behavior like banging on pots was modeled to show how people might intervene in a domestic violence situation by alerting the abuser of the community members' disapproval of the behavior (Usdin et al., 2005).

"Radio is based on oral tradition. Every culture has traditions of story-telling, and the fascination of listening to a good tale well told has never been lost" (de Fossard, 2005, p. 30). The fictional stories in edutainment arouse strong emotional reactions through identification with characters. Edutainment that evokes emotions may encourage the audience to reconsider their behavioral choices (Papa et al., 2000). For instance, witnessing a favorite character struggle with AIDS may evoke a strong incentive among audience to adopt a prevention behavior in a way that the mere provision of information is unable to do (Airhihenbuwa, 1999). Edutainment interventions can be powerful tools for social change because they exert an influence not only at the level of individual attitudes and behaviors, but also at the community level. People often listen to the radio together, and discuss the stories with family and friends (Paluck, 2009). The edutainment shows provide a basis for starting discussions on important, and often sensitive, issues in the community. Moreover, the fictional stories introduce new social norms, which can be adopted by listeners and steer discussions in ways that further facilitate positive social change.

In the following, as an illustrative example, we review an edutainment program aimed at preventing violence and promoting reconciliation in the aftermath of mass violence in the Great Lakes Region of Africa that covers Rwanda, Burundi, and the Democratic Republic of Congo (DRC). We will describe the process of developing this mass media intervention in collaboration with local communities, and then discuss its efficacy as a tool to bring about change.

Edutainment: Preventing Violence and Promoting Reconciliation in Conflict-Affected Settings

Edutainment media has been used increasingly to reduce conflict and promote positive intergroup relations in conflict-affected countries (Paluck, 2012). One organization that produces edutainment soap operas is the Dutch NGO Radio LaBenevolencija Humanitarian Tools. The soap operas have been broadcast via radio in Rwanda since 2004 ("*Musekeweya*" or "New Dawn"), and in Burundi ("*Murikira Ukuri*" or "Shedding Light on the Truth") and the DRC ("*Kumbukha Kesho*" or "Remember Tomorrow") since 2006. Rwanda, Burundi and the DRC face immense challenges due to cyclical violence in the region for several decades. The 1994 genocide in Rwanda, a violent civil war in Burundi from 1993 to 2005, and severe ongoing violence in the Eastern DRC are only a few instances of the extreme violence in the region since decolonization. Narratives of past violence have often contributed to renewed violence, severely affecting civilians regardless of ethnicity (Lemarchand, 2009). It is in these difficult contexts that Radio LaBenevolencija initiated its edutainment campaign in order to help break cycles of violence by increasing awareness of the conditions that lead to it, and promoting behaviors that individuals and communities can endorse to prevent escalation (Staub, 2011). Social change here, then, is the reduction of violence and the promotion of peace and reconciliation between members of different groups.

The intervention consists of weekly radio soap operas aimed to bring about social change through two main mechanisms. The first is *critical reflection*. This includes promoting the understanding of collective violence and its psychological impact and providing information on trauma after violence. The educational content regarding social, cultural, and psychological factors that could contribute to collective violence is based on Ervin Staub's research on the psychology of collective violence (Staub, 1989; 2011), and Laurie Pearlman's work on trauma and healing after collective violence (Pearlman, 2013; Pearlman & Saakvitne, 1995). The assumption is that understanding the influences that lead to violence will facilitate reconciliation processes and help prevent future outbreaks of violence by equipping the audience with tools to resist manipulation by leaders (Staub, 2011). The merging of edutainment principles with psychological theory explaining the roots, evolution, and consequences of violence, as well as the effects of trauma and the process of healing, is a unique characteristic of these soap operas.

The second mechanism is *critical action*: providing the audience with practical tools to help people resist the influences that lead to violence, promote active community intervention to prevent violence and foster reconciliation, and assist with the healing process. The soap opera does this by portraying fictional conflicts that are intended to resonate with audiences' lived experiences of conflict. The characters in the soap opera are positive role models and provide audiences with new behavioral repertoires to address conflicts in their communities.

The Design, Development, and Implementation of the Radio Dramas

While Radio LaBenevolencija's edutainment interventions are not locally initiated, local stakeholders and communities have a vital role in shaping the programs and adapting the approach to the local sociopolitical and cultural contexts. Prior to the launch of Radio LaBenevolencija's programs, the needs of the population in each of the three countries are assessed through research on knowledge, attitudes and behaviors related to conflict, and these findings are then used to feed into prioritizing the educational messages to be conveyed. Workshops are conducted with representatives from national and local governments, as well as from civil society and media organizations, to introduce the edutainment approach and the educational content. These groups have substantial inclusion in deciding the content and structure of the soap operas.

In a yearly workshop, numerous stakeholders, including local scriptwriters and staff from La Benevolencija, academics, and representatives of local community organizations, government, and media decide upon the overarching storyline of the soap opera. In Rwanda for instance, representatives from grassroots organizations, the National Service of Gacaca Associations, the Ministry of Justice, and the Rwandan Bureau of Information Broadcasting are present. These inclusive workshops to develop the fictional stories are crucial to the attempt to develop context- and culturally appropriate dramas that are sensitive to the history and concerns of the local communities. This is perhaps the reason behind the soap operas' popularity: about 80–85% of the population in Rwanda tunes in, and about 65% in Burundi and the Eastern provinces of DRC (Staub, Pearlman, & Bilali, 2008).

In Rwanda, the main storyline of *Musekeweya* portrays cycles of violence between two villages, which were initially instigated in response to unfair distribution of resources by leaders and worsened due to a drought that produces food shortages. In Burundi, in order to highlight the complex power relations between ethnic groups there, *Murikira Ukuri* depicts conflict between two fictional groups that differ in education and income opportunities and representation in governance. *Kumbuka Kesho* in the DRC portrays conflict among multiple ethnic clans, and highlights corruption, problematic leaders, child labor, and poverty, all of which are issues pertinent to the DRC context (Bilali & Staub, 2016). Matching the stories to the history, culture and politics of each context makes them accessible and relevant to the local population. However, the conflicts described in the storylines are not exact replicas of reality. Given that listeners are likely to have strong opinions about the conflicts, they may use these opinions to identify which characters are members of their group and which are members of the opposing group. Such interpretations might encourage the use of a preexisting narrative, rather than learning from the story, which would not be conducive to social change. In order to avoid this, stories are written in a way that listeners are not able to identify any of the fictional groups as their own group (Bilali & Staub, 2016). In sensitive political contexts this is crucial, as it allows audiences to discuss sensitive issues in a safe space (i.e., in a fictitious context), even with members of opposing groups (Kogen, 2014). Once the yearly storyline is decided upon, local scriptwriters write the episodes, taking into account input from a team of academics who review the programs to ensure appropriate implementation of the educational material. Final edits and decisions regarding content are made by local staff, sometimes (though not always) under the supervision of the local head of the NGO. Professional local actors play the roles in the local language.

Because different stakeholders are present in the design and production phases of the soap opera, inevitably the final product is a negotiated one. Power dynamics among the stakeholders influence the process. For instance, Radio La Benevolencija is a Dutch NGO, funded by foreign governments. While most staff members are local, the heads of the NGO in each country are usually European, creating structural hierarchies within the organization. This may play out both in the day-to-day operations of the organization as well as in creating the final product. Local stakeholders who participate in the design workshops come from different segments of society, bringing different perspectives and often opposing political agendas. Bilali (2014) describes some of the delicate discussions that she heard as a member of these workshops in her capacity as an academic: "Should the fictive conflict be a victim-perpetrator story, or should it involve cycles of violence in which both groups were victims and perpetrators? What forms of justice are appropriate for perpetrators of violence? Should perpetrators be excluded from leadership positions after they serve their sentence?" (Bilali, 2014, p. 395). Workshop participants' perspectives on these important issues are informed by their backgrounds, experiences, and political orientations. An important and positive point is that while these workshops are challenging, they are also a forum for dialogue regarding these issues, which does not exist elsewhere. In Rwanda, for instance, these questions are not discussed openly: given that the conversations are about fictional characters in a soap opera, they provide an opportunity for open discussion of sensitive topics in a constructive way.

To what degree does the audience shape the programs? Listener groups representing diverse social groups are formed in different provinces to provide feedback on pilot programs, and to provide continuous feedback after the start of the broadcast (Fisher, 2004). The composition and formation of listener groups is a complex process. For instance, in Rwanda, 13 listener groups of 40 people each were created. Six of these groups included members of the general population; three groups were composed of prisoners, two with genocide survivors, and two with ethnic minorities (Fisher, 2004). These groups provided continuous feedback on the programs, including the embedded messages, the format of the show, and its entertainment value. This feedback was vital in developing the storylines, both before and after production had begun. For example, listener groups in Rwanda reported that among other things, traditional ceremonies such as a cow-giving ceremony played, an important role in reconciliation. A cow-giving ceremony was thus written into the *Musekeweya* storyline to illustrate reconciliation and, during a pretest of this episode, listeners reported appreciation of the depiction of this ceremony (Fisher, 2004).

Over the years in which the radio dramas have been broadcast, program reach and audience responsiveness have been monitored through representative audience surveys. Through text messages and letters, listeners provide feedback, describe how the show has affected them, and often advise the fictional characters on how they should behave. Some of these letters and messages are shared with the audience after the broadcast of the soap opera, and the information is considered by scriptwriters when developing subsequent episodes and storylines. However, how best to equitably incorporate diverse opinions of a diverse listenership remains an open and unresolved issue. The radio show operates under a broad national framework of unity and reconciliation, which is reflected in the drama and easily recognizable (Bilali, 2014). This may be a positive aspect of the show for some listeners, but perhaps less so for those that may be distrustful of the governments in these countries (Bilali, 2014).

The Impact of Violence Prevention and Reconciliation Radio Soap Operas on Listeners

A number of studies employing diverse methodologies, including field experiments, surveys, focus groups, and individual interviews, have examined the impact of community radio soap operas as intervention. During *Musekeweya*'s first year of broadcasting, Paluck (2009) carried out a field experiment in which she randomly assigned 14 communities in Rwanda to either listen to *Musekeweya* or to a health soap opera over the course of a year. At the end of the year, *Musekeweya* listeners (compared to the other group) revealed higher trust and less social distance toward the other ethnic group, as well as more empathy for genocide survivors, prisoners, and the poor (Paluck, 2009). *Musekeweya* listeners were also more likely to express dissent and engage in problem solving and cooperation to resolve community problems (Paluck & Green, 2009).

Bilali and Vollhardt (2013) assessed whether *Musekeweya* influenced listeners' perceptions of their own conflict, and whether it increased likelihood of taking the perspective of the out-group with regard to the history of conflict in Rwanda. They used audio priming, in which the soap opera was made salient by exposing listeners to the voice of one of the main characters. This technique allowed the researchers to assess causal impact without manipulating whether or not participants had listened to the soap opera (the soap opera was very popular and had been broadcasted for several years, making it impossible to randomly assign participants to listen to the drama or control condition (Bilali & Vollhardt, 2015)). They found that priming the soap opera led to greater out-group trust and greater openness toward engaging with the other group's narratives of conflict. In Burundi, Bilali, Vollhardt, and Rarick (2015) replicated and extended the findings from Rwanda. They found that the soap opera had a positive influence on out-group trust and social distance, and listeners were less likely to blame the out-group and more likely to admit responsibility for their in-group's violence than non-listeners. However, in contrast to Rwanda, the intervention in Burundi did not affect listeners' expression of dissent to authorities or leaders.

Bilali and Vollhardt (2015, Study 1) used the same methodology as in Rwanda (Bilali & Vollhardt, 2013) to assess the impact of the soap opera in the DRC, but found mixed results. Priming the radio drama led to more tolerance for intergroup marriage and increased acceptance of other groups' victimization. However, contrary to the goals of the intervention, priming the radio drama increased reported obedience toward leaders and the belief that a good leader should promote the ethnic in-group's success. Follow-up focus group discussions with listeners in the DRC (Bilali & Vollhardt, 2015) revealed that the stories of conflict and corruption sometimes elicited negative reactions such as hopelessness, which might result in unintended consequences. Interestingly, in one study in the DRC, encouraging group discussions of *Kumbuka Kesho* also led to reduced tolerance and less inter-group helping (Paluck, 2010). This suggests that group discussions could have counterintuitive effects under certain conditions. For instance, if listeners focus on grievances without a concrete plan for impacting change (Bilali, Vollhardt, & Rarick, 2017), it may elicit hopelessness or frustration, or polarize group discussions (Canetti, Hall, Rapaport, & Wayne, 2013).

Qualitative interviews provide a more nuanced picture of how this campaign influences communities. Focus groups with listeners of *Kumbuka Kesho* in the DRC (Bilali & Vollhardt, 2015, Study 2) showed that overall, the drama was very well received by listeners and related to their daily life concerns. One listener, for instance, said, "One day I turned on my radio and it was like it was telling my own story on this radio drama" (Bilali & Vollhardt, 2015, p. 11). Such comments speak to the extent to which listeners are able to identify with the characters and the relevance of the storyline to their lives. A few participants even reported that the drama had inspired them to start a club or association, or to work together and resolve conflicts in the community. The drama also seems to increase critical reflection on listeners' own behaviors: a focus group participant who worked as a public servant admitted that in one instance he had accepted corruption, noting that "… when I follow the show, I realize that I have done was wrong" (Bilali & Vollhardt, 2015, p. 12).

Not all reactions were positive. Some participants reported negative feelings such as sadness in response to the drama, particularly when the show reminded them of adversity in their own lives. Some participants may also draw unintended lessons from the show; for example, in reaction to a particular storyline one participant stated, "there are some people who don't want to see others get out of poverty" (Bilali & Vollhardt, 2015, p. 12), suggesting that they may be interpreting their own reality in a negative light based on characters in the show.

Radio LaBenevolencija has also carried out in-depth interviews with community leaders, including the heads of villages (Kogen, 2014). A village leader in Rwanda explained that in his community, *Musekeweya* helps them to work toward community building by emulating the example of actions portrayed in the drama. A leader in Burundi noted that in his village, conveying messages through the soap opera was more influential than providing direct messaging through news, especially among people with lower levels of education. He stated, "Villages prefer programs that are entertaining. Purely educational programs attract relatively educated people" (Kogen, 2014, p. 31).

Conclusion

Radio edutainment as a method has the potential to support positive social change due to its extensive reach. Its use of narratives and stories is appealing while simultaneously encouraging discussions of sensitive topics in local communities. As a form of public education, it encourages critical reflection about the conditions that might drive community problems, and offers options for critical action to empower people to change their situation.

However, a few cautionary notes are in order. Historically, radio, as a communication tool, has been used for both positive and negative outcomes (e.g., see Karnell, 2002). Similarly, edutainment could also be used for both purposes. Even with positive intentions, edutainment might have unintended consequences. On the one hand, the edutainment campaign that we discussed, as a method of peacebuilding, aims to increase critical consciousness and reflection; on the other hand, this approach is likely effective because it exerts its influence through masked messages, so the listeners do not feel that they are being overtly persuaded. The masking of the messages may be interpreted as being deceptive, thus raising ethical concerns for community activists. One way to address this is by ensuring ongoing community involvement and input in creating the radio shows.

Funding sources and organizational power hierarchies are important to consider when implementing edutainment programs. Radio dramas, such as those of Radio LaBenevolencija, are often initiated by international NGOs, with their own agendas and ideologies. The final soap opera is the product of a complex and challenging negotiation of goals of the NGO and numerous local stakeholders (Bilali, 2014). It is important to assess how power dynamics among the different constituencies influence the end product. Additionally, we (the authors of this chapter) are ourselves researchers, foreign to the Great Lakes Region, and at points have been members of Radio LaBenevolencija's academic team. In our capacity, we have focused primarily on providing academic input to the scriptwriters and conducting research projects on the impact of the show, and this has shaped our relationships with other members of the organization. Our high position in the power hierarchy undoubtedly influences the local staff's relationship with us. For instance, we were invited to work on this project by the Radio LaBenevolencija's central office in Amsterdam, rather than by the local staff. Therefore, we may not be privy to all of the dynamics involved in creation of the shows. As is always the case with field research, power is a factor (Merriam et al., 2001), with the research team having greater methodological knowledge and the local staff with the greater cultural and situational knowledge. As academics, we prioritized the research process, including aspects such as rigorous data collection and analysis—but this may not have been an urgent priority for the local staff.

More research is required to understand how the combination of different mechanisms of change within the same media intervention influences audiences (Bilali & Staub, 2016). We do not know which specific messages or mechanisms have the most impact, and whether some mechanisms might actually inhibit the full potential for supporting social change (Bilali, 2014). It is possible that some mechanisms might not be particularly effective, and some might work at cross-purposes, reducing the positive impact of the programs. Future research should examine these possibilities.

The variation of the evaluation findings across the different settings draws attention to the role of the characteristics of the sociopolitical context in the design, implementation, and ultimate effectiveness of the interventions. A "one size fits all" approach does not work when implementing media interventions. The nature and history of a conflict, the type of political leadership, and the cultural climate all have important consequences on people's psychologies. In order to be effective, radio interventions must carefully be tailored in accordance with these characteristics. In these cases, however, when a show aims to reach the largest number of people, inclusion of marginalized or minority groups may not be prioritized. Even when every effort is made to be inclusive, no media show can be universally popular or effective with all audiences. Different from entertainment, media edutainment has specific social change goals. It is thus important to consider how edutainment programs might influence the audience if people do not enjoy the show. Therefore, despite employing a strong theoretical background, the development of the edutainment programs in conflict contexts should not be formulaic; rather, they should be highly adaptive and sensitive to the local context and needs.

References

Airhihenbuwa, C. O. (1999). Of culture and multiverse: Renouncing "the universal truth" in health. *Journal of Health Education, 30*, 267–273.

Bandura, A. (2004). Health promotion by social cognitive means. *Health Education & Behavior, 31*, 143–164.

Bilali, R. (2014). Between fiction and reality in post-genocide Rwanda: Reflections on a social-psychological media intervention for social change. *Journal of Social and Political Psychology, 2*, 387–400.

Bilali, R., & Staub, E. (2016). Interventions in real world settings: Using media to overcome prejudice and promote intergroup reconciliation in Central Africa. In C. Sibley & F. Barlow (Eds.), *Cambridge handbook of the psychology of prejudice* (pp. 607–631). Cambridge: Cambridge University Press.

Bilali, R., & Vollhardt, J. R. (2013). Priming effects of a reconciliation radio drama on historical perspective-taking in the aftermath of mass violence in Rwanda. *Journal of Experimental Social Psychology, 49*, 144–151.

Bilali, R., & Vollhardt, J. R. (2015). Do mass media interventions effectively promote peace in contexts of ongoing violence? Evidence from eastern Democratic Republic of Congo. *Peace & Conflict: Journal of Peace Psychology, 21*, 604–620.

Bilali, R., Vollhardt, J. R., & Rarick, J. D. R. (2017). Modeling collective action through media to promote social change and positive intergroup relations in violent conflicts. *Journal of Experimental Social Psychology, 68*, 200–211.

Bilali, R., Vollhardt, J. R., & Rarick, J. R. D. (2015). Assessing the impact of a media-based intervention to prevent intergroup violence and promote positive intergroup relations in Burundi. *Journal of Community & Applied Social Psychology, 26*, 221–235.

Bosch, T. E. (2006). Radio as an instrument of protest: The history of bush radio. *Journal of Radio Studies, 13*, 249–265.
Brecht, B. (1927, December 25/2006). The radio as an apparatus of communication. In A. Gumucio-Dagron & T. Tufte (Eds.), Communication for social change anthology: Historical and contemporary readings (pp. 2–3). South Orange, NJ: CFSC Consortium (Reprinted from Der Rundfunk als Kommunikationsapparat, Berliner Börsen-Courier).
Canetti, D., Hall, B. J., Rapaport, C., & Wayne, C. (2013). Exposure to political violence and political extremism. A stress-based process. *European Psychologist, 18*, 263–272.
de Fossard, E. (2005). *Writing and producing radio dramas* (Vol. 1). Thousand Oaks, CA: Sage.
Fisher, S. (2004). Tuning into different wavelengths: Listener clubs for effective Rwandan reconciliation radio programmes. In *Fourth international conference on entertainment-education and social change* (Vol. 26, pp. 30–39), Cape Town.
Freire, P. (1970). *Pedagogy of the oppressed* (Trans. by Myra Bergman Ramos). New York: Herder and Herder.
Girard, B. (1992). *A passion for radio: Radio waves and community* (Vol. 178). Quebec: Black Rose Books Ltd..
Gumucio-Dagron, A. (2001). *Making waves: Stories of participatory communication for social change*. New York: Rockefeller Foundation.
Karnell, A. P. (2002). Counteracting 'hate radio' in Africa's Great Lakes region: Responses and lessons. *Journal of International Communication, 8*, 111–126.
Kogen, L. (2014). *Assessing impact, evaluating adaptability: A decade of radio la Benevolencija in Rwanda, Burundi and the DRC*. Philadelphia, PA: Center for Global Communication Studies.
Kuhlmann, A. K. S., Kraft, J. M., Galavotti, C., Creek, T. L., Mooki, M., & Ntumy, R. (2008). Radio role models for the prevention of mother-to-child transmission of HIV and HIV testing among pregnant women in Botswana. *Health Promotion International, 23*, 260–268.
Lemarchand, R. (2009). The 1994 Rwanda genocide. In S. Totten & W. S. Parsons (Eds.), *Century of genocide: Critical essays and eyewitness accounts* (pp. 483–504). New York: Routledge.
Merriam, S. B., Johnson-Bailey, J., Lee, M. Y., Kee, Y., Ntseane, G., & Muhamad, M. (2001). Power and positionality: Negotiating insider/outsider status within and across cultures. *International Journal of Lifelong Education, 20*, 405–416.
Myers, M., Sebert, A., & Bell, S. (2002). *Institutional review of educational radio dramas*. Atlanta, GA: CDC.
Noronha, F. (2003). Community radio: Singing new tunes in South Asia. *Economic and Political Weekly, 38*, 2168–2172.
Paluck, E. L. (2009). Reducing intergroup prejudice and conflict using the media: A field experiment in Rwanda. *Journal of Personality and Social Psychology, 96*, 574–587.
Paluck, E. L. (2010). Is it better not to talk? Group polarization, extended contact, and perspective-taking in eastern Democratic Republic of Congo. *Personality and Social Psychology Bulletin, 36*, 1170–1185.
Paluck, E. L. (2012). Interventions aimed at the reduction of prejudice and conflict. In L. Tropp (Ed.), *Oxford handbook of intergroup conflict* (pp. 179–192). New York: Oxford University Press.
Paluck, E. L., & Green, D. P. (2009). Prejudice reduction: What works? A review and assessment of research and practice. *Annual Review of Psychology, 60*, 339–367.
Pant, S., Singhal, A., & Bhasin, U. (2002). Using radio drama to entertain and educate: India's experience with the production, reception, and transcreation of Dehleez. *Journal of Development Communication, 13*, 52–66.
Papa, M. J., & Singhal, A. (2009). How entertainment-education programmes promote dialogue in support of social change. *Journal of Creative Communications, 4*, 185–208.
Papa, M. J., Singhal, A., Law, S., Pant, S., Sood, S., Rogers, E. M., & Shefner-Rogers, C. L. (2000). Entertainment-education and social change: An analysis of parasocial interaction, social learning, collective efficacy, and paradoxical communication. *Journal of Communication, 50*(4), 31–55.

Pearlman, L. A. (2013). Restoring self in community: Collective approaches to psychological trauma after genocide. *Journal of Social Issues, 69*, 111–124.

Pearlman, L. A., & Saakvitne, K. W. (1995). *Trauma and the therapist: Countertransference and vicarious traumatization in the treatment of incest survivors*. New York: W.W. Norton.

Radio Gazelle. (1992). Radio Gazelle: Multi-cultural radio in Marseille. In B. Girard (Ed.), *A passion for radio: Radio waves and community* (pp. 132–135). Quebec: Black Rose Books Ltd.

Seidman, E., & Tseng, V. (2011). Changing social settings: A framework for action. In M. Aber, K. Maton, & E. Seidman (Eds.), *Empowering settings and voices for social change* (pp. 12–37). New York: Oxford University Press.

Singhal, A., Cody, M. J., Rogers, E. M., & Sabido, M. (2003). *Entertainment-education and social change: History, research, and practice*. New York: Routledge.

Staub, E. (1989). *The roots of evil: The origins of genocide and other group violence*. Cambridge: Cambridge University Press.

Staub, E. (2011). *Overcoming evil: Genocide, violent conflict and terrorism*. New York: Oxford University Press.

Staub, E., Pearlman, L., & Bilali, R. (2008). Psychological recovery, reconciliation and the prevention of new violence: An approach and its uses in Rwanda. In B. Hart (Ed.), *Peacebuilding in traumatized societies* (pp. 131–154). New York: University Press of America.

Usdin, S., Scheepers, E., Goldstein, S., & Japhet, G. (2005). Achieving social change on gender-based violence: A report on the impact evaluation of Soul City's fourth series. *Social Science & Medicine, 61*, 2434–2445.

Valente, T. W., Kim, Y. M., Lettenmaier, C., Glass, W., & Dibba, Y. (1994). Radio promotion of family planning in the Gambia. *International Family Planning Perspectives, 20*, 96–100.

Vigil, J. I. L. (1992). The stubborn izote flower. In B. Girard (Ed.), *A passion for radio: Radio waves and community* (pp. 48–66). Quebec: Black Rose Books Ltd..

Waves for Freedom. (1995, January 23–39). *Report on the sixth world conference of community radio broadcasters*. Dakar, Senegal. Retrieved from http://www.amarc.org/?q=node/47

Chapter 5
Community Asset Mapping as a Critical Participatory Research Method

Sandy Lazarus, Naiema Taliep, and Anthony V. Naidoo

This chapter explores the use of community asset mapping, guided by the values and principles of critical forms of participatory research, as a strategy for achieving liberatory ideals. We discuss the method of community asset mapping with specific reference to a project conducted in a peri-urban Western Cape context: SCRATCHMAPS (Spiritual Capacity and Religious Assets for Transforming Community Health through Mobilizing Males for Peace and Safety). The case illustration is introduced, with its unique research design being briefly explained. This is followed by a reflection on the case, highlighting how the community asset mapping method aligned with the liberatory goals of a critical approach. The chapter concludes with a reflection on the possibilities of using community asset mapping as a practical strategy to promote liberation.

The following key characteristics of a critical approach, which have been highlighted by many (e.g., Nelson & Prilleltensky, 2010; Ratele, Suffla, Lazarus, & van Niekerk, 2010), frame and guide the reflections in the chapter: adoption of a human rights perspective; focusing on actively transforming society, with social justice as a central goal; utilising a historical and contextual approach to understand 'persons-in-context'; focusing on various issues of power and oppression; and engaging with marginalised voices.

S. Lazarus (✉) • N. Taliep
Institute for Social and Health Sciences, University of South Africa, Johannesburg, South Africa

South African Medical Research Council-University of South Africa Violence, Injury and Peace Research Unit, Cape Town, South Africa
e-mail: sandylazarus1@gmail.com

A.V. Naidoo
Department of Psychology, Stellenbosch University, Cape Town, South Africa

M. Seedat et al. (eds.), *Emancipatory and Participatory Methodologies in Peace, Critical, and Community Psychology*, Peace Psychology Book Series,
DOI 10.1007/978-3-319-63489-0_5

The asset-based trend in community research emphasises community development through the mobilisation of existing and unrecognised community resources (Kramer, Seedat, Lazarus, & Suffla, 2011). This approach represents a shift away from a deficits perspective that focuses on the amelioration of problems experienced by communities (Mathie & Cunningham, 2003), but there is recognition that a needs assessment should be part of such a process (Kramer, Amos, Lazarus, & Seedat, 2012; Kretzmann & McKnight, 1993; Lazarus et al., 2014). This kind of research is often pursued within projects aimed at conducting community assessments that aim to make contextual diagnoses and evaluations that focus on strengths and resources that already exist in a particular community, noting the identified needs, and identifying what should happen in order to promote change (Minkler & Wallerstein, 2008; Naidoo & Van Wyk, 2003).

Community asset mapping is a particular method employed to provide communities with an opportunity to identify and mobilise existing tangible and intangible resources (Cutts et al., 2016; Kramer et al., 2012; Minkler & Hancock, 2008). Characteristics of this method include: reframing communities as being resourceful and resilient; focusing on human capabilities and assets; recognising that important assets lie in networks and relationships; making community assets visible for the community as well as other relevant decision-makers; promoting leadership development and engagement; promoting agency; and facilitating group inclusivity and participation.

Asset-based approaches have produced an assortment of tools that seek to identify, recognise and utilise communities' inherent resources and resilience. Kramer et al.' (2012) literature review provides an overview of several asset mapping approaches. This includes: the Asset-Based Community Development (ABCD) approach, which was developed in the United States by Kretzman and Kretzman and has been successfully applied in South Africa (Kramer et al., 2012; Mathie & Cunningham, 2008); the Sustainable Livelihoods Approach (SLA), initially conceptualised by the Brundtland Commission and thereafter expanded by the 1992 United Nations Conference on Environment and Development (see Krantz, 2011; Serrat, 2010); Planning for Real, developed in the United Kingdom by the Neighbourhood Initiatives Foundation (2009); the Participatory Inquiry into Religious Health Assets, Networks and Agency (PIRHANA), developed by the African Religious Health Assets Programme (ARHAP, 2006; Cutts, 2011; de Gruchy, Cochrane, Olivier, & Matimelo, 2011); the Community Health Assets Mapping for Partnerships (CHAMP) method, which is an adaptation of PIRHANA, also developed by ARHAP (de Gruchy et al., 2009); the Railton Community Assessment Project (CAP), which utilised a community-based participatory research approach (CBPR) in a rural area in the Western Cape to identify community needs and assets for the purposes of prioritising actions to support community development planning and funding allocation (Lazarus et al., 2014; Railton Foundation & Stellenbosch University, 2010a, 2010b, 2010c); and finally, Geographic Information Systems (GIS) technology, which is sometimes utilised for community asset mapping and community development purposes (ESRI, 2010; Smith & Miller, 2013). Kramer et al.' (2012) analysis of the above community asset methods revealed that all of them (except the GIS method which is not always compliant with the participatory principles of community asset mapping) revealed a strong commitment to inclusion, collaboration, co-learning, capacity-building, empowerment, responding to needs, ensuring that all partners benefit, and addressing disparities and equity.

Most community asset mapping projects adopt a participatory research approach which reflects the following principles and commitments: (1) the research initiative is based on a partnership between the research institutions and community members; (2) it builds on the strengths and resources of the community; (3) there is a commitment to action, combining theory, knowledge and action to promote social change; (4) community participation in the research process is actively pursued, (5) the process promotes co-learning and co-construction of knowledge; and (6) there is a commitment to promoting community ownership and sustainability (Israel, Eng, Schultz, & Parker, 2005; Lazarus, Duran, Caldwell, & Bulbulia, 2012a; Minkler & Wallerstein, 2008; Wallerstein & Duran, 2008). These principles are usually formalised in academic-community research partnerships through memoranda of understanding or agreement which specify the ethical guidelines and accountability relationships within the partnership.

When looking at the above set of principles alongside the principles of the community asset mapping method, it is clear that community asset mapping that is located within a participatory approach can serve the interests of liberatory interests. The principles of CBPR overtly commit to furthering human rights and promoting social justice; acknowledge the need to utilise contextual analyses that critically locate the person-in-context; address issues of power and oppression; intentionally facilitate participation and capacity-building to further the goals of empowerment; and commit to processes of co-learning and co-construction of knowledge that take seriously all voices and community-embedded knowledges.

The one inherent principle in community asset mapping that is not overtly recognised as a liberatory principle is the strengths- or asset-based focus of the method. While a community asset mapping method that only looks at assets without including a needs assessment could be viewed as problematic from a critical perspective, this is seldom the case as the methods outlined earlier clearly reveal that needs assessments are included, and are linked directly to action plans that are developed to address priority social needs. We would like to emphasise that there is a danger in dichotomising 'needs' and 'assets' when reflecting on community asset mapping. Such reductionism represents a failure to recognise the dialectical linkages between the two. In practice, identifying needs alongside assets allows for existing community resources to be mobilised to address the needs and challenges highlighted. An asset-based approach is therefore central to the critical principles and processes of agency and empowerment.

Community Asset Mapping Case Illustration: SCRATCHMAPS

The case illustration described below drew on all of the above expertise in developing the overall research design and community asset mapping method used, focusing particularly on the PIRHANA and CHAMP models because of that project's particular research aims, as well as the authors' experiences in the Railton Community Assessment Project (CAP).

Project Context and Participants

The SCRATCHMAPS project focused on identifying and mobilising community assets that contribute to peace and safety, with a particular focus on spiritual capacity and religious assets, and the promotion of positive forms of masculinity. The project was a collaboration between the South African Medical Research Council-University of South Africa Violence, Injury and Peace Research Unit, the International Religious Health Assets Programme (IRHAP), hosted at the University of Cape Town, and the local community of Erijaville in the Strand, Western Cape, South Africa.

Erijaville is a peri-urban low-income community with about 164 houses and twice as many backyard dwellings. The majority of the residents are Afrikaans[1] speaking and classified as 'Coloured'[2] in terms of apartheid racial categories. The project commenced with a community stakeholders' meeting where the proposed project aims were presented by the academic partners and endorsed by community leaders and service providers. Many of these members were then actively involved in the project through an advisory committee, including approximately 30 members, who provided local oversight of the project. This was followed by the establishment of the local research team that included ten local members of the community. Beyond these two structures, members of the wider community were involved as participants through the community asset mapping method employed.

SCRATCHMAPS Community Asset Mapping Method

The principles of the CBPR approach guided the community asset mapping method used in SCRATCHMAPS. The community asset mapping workshops conducted in 2012 included three community workshops (including 74 community members across the three workshops), a service providers' workshop (including 18 service providers from various government and non-governmental organisations), and a combined community/service providers' action planning workshop (including 21 service providers and 20 community leaders) (Lazarus, Taliep & Olivier, 2014).

The asset mapping method and tools used were designed by the academic-community research team. While the academic researchers took the lead in this process, the process and tools were checked and amended by the local community

[1]An official language of South Africa.

[2]While these terms inherited from Apartheid are not accepted by the authors, researchers still use them as they represent historical and contemporary indicators of oppression and disadvantage.

Table 5.1 SCRATCHMAPS community asset mapping method

Exercise focus	Exercise details
Exercise 1: Community mapping	Participants drew community maps and identified needs and community assets
Exercise 2: Peace and safety within the community context	Participants were asked to identify the key factors that (1) contributed to and (2) undermined peace and safety in the community. These two sets of factors were then integrated to create a group-identified peace and safety index
Exercise 3: Contribution of community assets to safety and peace	This exercise combined some of the key community assets (public facilities and programmes, including religious entities) identified in the maps of Exercise 1, with key factors contributing to peace and safety from Exercise 2, to create a community-asset/peace and safety ranking matrix
Exercise 4: Religious assets and masculinity within the community context	This step focused on religious assets, with further probes on the concept of masculinity
Exercise 5: Local action	Participants identified characteristics of local examples of promoting positive forms of masculinity, and peace and safety. Opportunities for further local action and intervention were then identified

research team. The final manuals (Cutts, Olivier, Lazarus, Cochrane, & Taliep, 2012; Olivier, Cutts, Lazarus, Cochrane, & Taliep, 2012) drew extensively from the PIRHANA and CHAMP tools, with the main re-design constituting an adaptation of some of the exercises to include a focus on masculinity. These manuals were used to train the research team facilitators and then to guide the workshop processes. The asset mapping process began with a transect walk of the community, which is an information-gathering method that involves taking a pre-determined route through a community to learn about a community's social structure, and physical resources, and to identify opportunities. Following this, the five community asset mapping workshops with community members and service providers were conducted. Table 5.1 provides an overview of the logic of and steps pursued in this asset mapping process.

Workshop data were captured through the workshop exercises, and through researcher note-taking during the process. These datasets, which were presented in a separate research report (Lazarus, Taliep & Olivier, 2014), were both quantitative and qualitative in nature. These findings were shared with the broader community through a community booklet which was produced by the local research team (SCRATCHMAPS, 2014).

Reflections on Community Asset Mapping as a Critical Participatory Method

In this discussion, we share our reflections on successes and challenges experienced in the case illustration. The principles of a critical perspective frame this discussion, with the characteristics of this approach providing key themes. This includes promoting human rights and facilitating transformation towards social justice; including contextual analyses to understand 'persons-in-context'; addressing power dynamics; and engaging with marginalised voices. It should be noted that most of the reflections reveal a strong focus on power and empowerment which are central to a critical perspective.

Before proceeding with a more specific analysis of SCRATCHMAPS' community asset mapping method through the lens of a critical perspective, it is important to note that the major strength of this project was its relatively successful execution of the CBPR approach which guided the work (Cutts et al., 2016). The liberatory nature of these principles therefore facilitated an enactment of a critical approach.

Addressing Power Dynamics

Lazarus, Duran, Caldwell and Bulbulia (2012a) discuss the central importance of addressing power relations and dynamics in research, particularly in contexts where oppression has been or is institutionalised in society. They refer specifically to challenges relating to the relationship between knowledge and power, resources and power, participation and power, and power dynamics within communities and community development processes. In the analysis of power dynamics experienced in the SCRATCHMAPS community asset mapping process, this discussion will focus on the partnership framework, co-learning, reflexivity, money and power, research team group dynamics, and community dynamics.

One of the central strategies for addressing power imbalances and differentials is to work within a *partnership approach* (Springett & Wallerstein, 2008). Working together as partners was embodied in the overall partnership approach pursued in the SCRATCHMAPS project. Community engagement between the research institution and the respective community included a formalisation of the partnership through a signed ethics agreement. The partnership was also operationalised through regular meetings and events involving key stakeholders. The advisory committee structure provided a useful mechanism to facilitate this relationship. Establishing and maintaining this structure was, however, not without its challenges. An ongoing challenge was including all key stakeholders from the community (which was not possible), and retaining the same members for the full period of the research.

The principle of *learning and working together* guided practice in various ways. In particular, the project provided the research team with many opportunities for personal and professional growth and empowerment (Van Gesselleen, Taliep, Lazarus, Carelse, & Phillips, 2015). This included developing personal confidence; developing knowledge in key areas; building capacity in project management, leadership and conflict management; enhancing competencies in public speaking; conducting academic presentations and facilitating workshops; and developing a variety of research skills. It is important to note that these lessons were mutual or horizontal in nature, reflecting a model of co-learning which is central to CBPR (Lazarus, Bulbulia, Taliep, & Naidoo, 2015; Railton Foundation & Stellenbosch University,

2010a). While the imparting of research knowledge and skills was formally facilitated by the academic members of the teams, the development of the research design, and the data collection methods, instruments and analyses were strongly informed by the local knowledge of the community members of the team. Co-learning was facilitated by capacity-building that included formal workshops as well as on-the-job mentoring where academic and community researchers worked alongside one another, sharing skills and knowledge where appropriate.

Despite these gains, it is important to note that the need to address power differentials remained a challenge in the project. Academic skills and knowledge brought to the process by the university academics still dominated the teaching and learning processes. However, reflexive practice, discussed below, helped both academic and community researchers to reflect on their role in the teaching and learning process, challenging team members to 'step up' and 'step down' as appropriate. Furthermore, attempts were continuously made to draw in and on the knowledge and skills of the individual team members. This was pursued through intentional eliciting of all team members' views and strengths.

Reflexivity is a key strategy for dealing with power challenges in community asset mapping (Kramer et al., 2012; Lazarus, Taliep, Bulhulia, Phillips, & Seedat, 2012b; Lazarus et al., 2015). This refers to a process of examining one's social positionality within power relations (Seedat & Suffla, 2012). Professionals need to find ways of being constantly reflective about areas of potential dominance when developing partnerships with communities (Marais, Naidoo, Donson, & Nortje, 2007). In SCRATCHMAPS specific practices within the research team were pursued to facilitate this kind of reflection, including researcher journaling and facilitated conversations in meetings and workshops. Academic and community research team members intentionally reflected on how their social positionality in respect to race, gender, class, age, religion, language, gender identity and sexual orientation and other relevant categories affected their participation in the process. These reflections were verbalised and internalised in behaviour changes which helped to rebalance power relations in the group. In the community asset mapping workshops with community members and service providers, there was no intentional reflexive process built into the process. However, participants were alerted to instances where their positionality appeared to be influencing their contributions, or lack of contributions. This was particularly pertinent to issues of age and gender, but social class, race, religion and language dynamics were also highlighted where needed. These overt reflections in the workshops promoted participation and therefore contributed to the rebalancing of power relations in those contexts.

Power dynamics are also strongly influenced by issues relating to *money and power* which can create a great deal of conflict in community initiatives (Lazarus et al., 2012a, b). Besides the challenge of ensuring that there are sufficient resources to cover the community asset mapping processes and commitments (Railton Foundation & Stellenbosch University, 2010a; Springett & Wallerstein, 2008), the management and transparency of financial management of these funds are important areas to consider. In SCRATCHMAPS the advisory committee provided oversight of all budgeting and financial reporting processes, although the research institution held the money and ultimately had control. Within the research team and the advisory structure, the financial management process was completely transparent, and the community members were able to make key decisions regarding how the money was spent.

Importantly, the research team took over the financial management of the project in the final year of implementation; a process that included intensive capacity-building. These processes were considered to be crucial in helping to build a genuine partnership, to foster ownership and sustainability, and to rebalance power relations. Although the academics had to remain involved in the financial management because of university accountability procedures, the move to include the local community research members in all aspects of the financial management processes clearly shifted the power and responsibility in the project.

With regards to *power in the context of group dynamics in the research team* itself, the academic staff were aware that they played a major role in influencing the processes pursued, thus reflecting the typical hierarchical relationship in such ventures. While acknowledging and creatively using their power, the academic members openly recognised their limitations and used proactive inclusive methodologies aimed at actively acknowledging and valuing all contributions, which helped to make the relationship more horizontal. These strategies focused on the use of facilitation skills and personal and professional development through various capacity-building activities. Israel et al. (2005) highlight the importance of skills in managing group processes and power dynamics, including capacitation in communication, negotiation and conflict resolution skills.

Finally, challenges relating to power dynamics within the complexities of *community dynamics* are well known (Kramer et al., 2011; Lazarus et al., 2012b). Importantly, Kramer et al. (2011) focus on how the use of the term community in community asset mapping processes is simplistically applied, with community often being uncritically viewed. This includes an over-emphasis on cooperation, and assumptions that community members share the same values and norms. This simplistic view denies that the existence of conflict (particularly leadership struggles); contestation and competition are features of almost any community, but most particularly where societal inequalities are rife (Bettez, 2011; Kramer et al., 2012). In SCRATCHMAPS, this challenge was addressed through direct conflict management interventions within the research team, and the broader community, alongside an ongoing emphasis on positive and protective factors such as social cohesion at community level.

Promoting Human Rights and Transformation for Social Justice

The action-research approach, central to the CBPR approach and community asset mapping method used in SCRATCHMAPS, ensured that the research conducted informed and facilitated action in the community (Cutts et al., 2016). Although this process did not foreground human rights and social justice in its overt aims, these values and principles guided the focus on community building and addressing priority social issues identified by the community.

A key aspect of community asset mapping is *mobilising* identified community assets. Central to this challenge is recognition that personal and collective agency and empowerment strategies, central to a liberatory approach, need to be enabled and supported. Empowerment is a contested concept insofar as it tends to assume that the power to act can be transferred from the 'haves to have-nots' by way of capacity-building and advocacy exercises. However, within asset mapping, the focus is on identifying and activating the community's own self-defined capacities. This underlines the importance for external agents (e.g., academic researchers) to work alongside communities to activate agency to enable empowerment (Kramer et al., 2012).

The participatory approach adopted in SCRATCHMAPS community asset mapping process emphasised the importance of facilitating *personal agency and empowerment*. This was pursued in a number of ways, including a major emphasis on capacity-building focused on personal development and professional skills development in research, project management, and social action planning and implementation. A further strategy aimed at enabling agency was to support local initiatives in the local actions pursued by local research team and community members where their capacities were mobilised and strengthened.

The promotion of *collective agency or empowerment* includes identifying and mobilising networks and coalitions to address prioritised needs (Kramer et al., 2012). To further this aim, the service providers' workshop in SCRATCHMAPS included exercises aimed at identifying and examining networks and relationships between various organisations and groups in the community and promoting inter-organisational collaboration, especially in the identified priority areas (Cutts et al., 2016). One way in which this was done was through a 'spidergram' or network analysis exercise which provided the service providers with an opportunity to share their historical and current contributions to community building in the specific context concerned; to analyse their current relationships with other service providers; and to identify where they could develop further partnerships to address community needs.

Community members and service providers separately and together then identified key *priorities for action* in the local community. These priorities became the focus for ongoing collective action through small and larger projects, initiated and managed by community members themselves. In the final phases of the project, the local research team decided to establish a non-profit organisation to provide a structure to continue with their community building work, which included programmes aimed at addressing priority social issues such as unemployment.

In the context of community building, community research, including community asset mapping, places an emphasis on planning for and supporting *sustainability* (Cutts et al., 2016; Kramer et al., 2011; Lazarus, Taliep & Olivier, 2014). Although the concept of sustainability is often not defined in operational terms, it is assumed that this refers to building capacity and infrastructure to support ongoing community building (Lazarus, Seedat, & Naidoo, 2017). This is important if community ownership and ongoing transformation is to be pursued.

Kramer et al. (2011) argue that it is helpful if external stakeholders and representative community structures work together to develop community-specific sustainability indicators and plans. In SCRATCHMAPS this idea was activated half-way through the life of the five-year project, and intensified in the final year. A key strategy pursued to promote sustainability was the establishment of a renewed partnership between the research institution and the local community, with the community research team taking full responsibility for initiating and managing this partnership—revealing an important rebalancing of power relations.

Despite these good intentions and actions, it is important to note that the challenge of sustainability remains a central one (Cutts et al., 2016; Israel et al., 2005; Railton Foundation & Stellenbosch University, 2010a). Sustainability is dependent on ongoing capacity-building, and, in particular, on the development of leadership, networks and infrastructure to support community organising and action. The SCRATCHMAPS project focused on leadership development within the community asset mapping and general research process, but this is a long-term investment which needs long-term commitment from all partners.

Contextual Analyses of Person-in Context

Community asset mapping is a method that focuses on both individual and contextual needs and strengths. In SCRATCHMAPS, the numerous exercises that were pursued (refer Table 5.1) included discussions around key community problems and strengths, and how these factors impacted on the personal lives of the community members. The analysis of data also included an ecological categorisation of factors at the individual, relationship, community and societal levels – revealing a clear set of indicators for safety and peace at each of these levels (Isobell & Lazarus, 2014). This categorisation then informed the actions planned, including the central violence prevention intervention developed from the findings of the community asset mapping and other research methods.

Importantly, given the emphasis on strengths in the community asset mapping method, the asset-based approach also helped community members to re-conceptualise their contexts as being inherently resourceful and resilient (Kretzmann & McKnight, 1993). In the evaluation of the community asset mapping processes in SCRATCHMAPS (see Cutts et al., 2016), members of the community expressed deep appreciation for the way in which the process helped them to reframe their living contexts in a more positive way, indicating that it enabled them to develop pride in themselves, and in their communities. This is important in the context of promoting personal and collective empowerment. At the same time, throughout the life of the project, there was a tendency to revert back to both personal and collective problems experienced. This is useful in the process of identifying priority actions to address particular community needs (Railton Foundation & Stellenbosch University, 2010a). The focus on needs is particularly important from a critical perspective where the mobilisation of action is often directly spurred by identified needs. In SCRATCHMAPS, this link was pursued in a number of ways, with public community workshops being held to provide community members with opportunities to reach consensus on and plan for specific actions and projects based on priority needs identified.

Alongside the process of reconceptualising personal and contextual challenges in a positive framework, the community asset mapping workshops included discussions on the historical context, and more specifically, on apartheid and its impact on the community (Lazarus, Taliep & Olivier, 2014). This discussion constituted a major focus in the service providers' workshop, resulting in a call for community healing.

Enabling Voice: Co-learning and Co-construction of Knowledge

In this final section of the reflection, we look at the extent to which the SCRATCHMAPS' community asset mapping process facilitated co-learning and co-construction of knowledge in a way that engaged with community voices and knowledges. Although asset-based approaches often fail to reflect sufficiently on the influences of power differentials arising from the dominance of knowledge expertise, the SCRATCHMAPS research team, guided by the critical principles of CBPR, attempted to address these challenges.

The academic researchers intentionally affirmed and engaged with community voices and knowledges, using various strategies. This included foregrounding *capacity-building* relating to specific knowledge as well as research skills. As mentioned earlier, the latter was pursued within a *co-learning* environment where both academic and community researchers learnt from one another. While the academic members often dominated the training and processes relating to the research process itself, the community researchers often led on the development of quality methods and instruments, were centrally involved in the facilitation of the community asset mapping workshops, conducted the analysis of the data collected, and led on the identification and follow-up of action emerging from the process. The skills-sets amongst the academic and community researchers became progressively blurred, with co-learning occurring through the collective processes pursued.

A number of research reports on the community asset mapping process were produced and shared with key stakeholders, and practical manuals in English and Afrikaans were also produced. The local community members playing a key role in the production of these outputs, were involved as co-authors of a number of academic journal articles, and provided oral and visual feedback at community meetings and academic conferences. They have also provided training to other academics wishing to learn about community asset mapping through commissioned workshops held at a few South African universities. It is clear, therefore, that there was a real attempt to promote *co-construction of knowledge* in this project and process.

Enabling voice in SCRATCHMAPS also included addressing *language* differences and barriers. The latter is particularly important in multilingual South Africa where the majority of participants speak another language(s) yet English dominates research spaces (Kramer et al., 2012). In order to meet the needs of both English and Afrikaans speaking members in the research team and community, both languages were used continuously, and all key documents were translated into both languages.

Conclusion

Has this project, and the community asset mapping method in particular, facilitated emancipation for the individuals and the community concerned? Preliminary findings of the SCRATCHMAPS process and outcomes evaluations suggest that the project addressed various dynamics of power. This was pursued through a commitment to working within a partnership approach, learning and working together within a co-learning framework, developing reflexive practices, rebalancing power relations through the shared management of project finances, facilitation of power dynamics within the research team group, and addressing community dynamics when needed.

While the promotion of human rights and facilitation of transformation towards social justice was not an overt goal of the research, the community asset mapping method aimed to promote both personal and collective empowerment. This included the development of personal confidence and assertiveness of those involved directly in the project, and the development of personal and collective agency and responsibility enacted through various community actions and ownership of the research partnership itself.

We believe that asset mapping is a powerful method that can be used to mobilise communities by creating awareness of strengths and resourcefulness – with the asset-based approach helping to positively reframe community members' views of themselves and their community. This is an important strategy that enables people to move away from a mindset of powerlessness and learnt helplessness as well as structural impediments, towards a mindset of liberation and realisation of personal agency to effect change.

Finally, the SCRATCHMAPS community asset mapping method was guided by a commitment to enabling voice within a commitment to co-learning and co-construction of knowledge. The participatory research approach adopted, and the central commitment of the community asset mapping method to eliciting the views of the community around their needs, strengths and identified priority actions foregrounded community voices and actions to build a safe and peaceful community.

Acknowledgements We are grateful for the financial support received from the Community Engagement Programme of the National Research Foundation, and the University of South Africa's Directorate for Community Engagement. We are also grateful to our academic partners, IRHAP, and our community partners. In particular, we appreciate the invaluable contributions of the local community research team in Erijaville who were centrally involved in all the processes and outputs linked to this project.

References

African Religious Health Assets Programme (ARHAP). (2006). *Appreciating assets: The contribution of religion to universal access in Africa* (Report for the World Health Organization). Cape Town: International/African Religious Health Assets Programme, School of Public Health, University of Cape Town.

Bettez, S. C. (2011). Critical community building: Beyond belonging. *Educational Foundations, 25*(3-4), 3–19.

Cutts, T. (2011). The Memphis congregational health network model: Grounding ARHAP theory. In J. R. Cochrane, B. Schmid, & T. Cutts (Eds.), *When religion and health align: Mobilizing religious health assets for transformation* (pp. 193–209). Pietermaritzburg: Cluster Publications.

Cutts, T., Olivier, J., Lazarus, S., Cochrane, J. R., & Taliep, N. (2012). *Community asset mapping manual for community members*. Tygerberg: South African Medical Research Council-University of South Africa Violence, Injury and Peace Research Unit.

Cutts, T., Olivier, J., Lazarus, S., Taliep, N., Cochrane, J. R., Seedat, M., et al. (2016). Community asset mapping for violence prevention: A comparison of views in Western Cape, South Africa and Memphis, USA. *African Safety Promotion Journal, 14*(1), 1–14.

de Gruchy, S., Cochrane, J. R., Olivier, J., & Matimelo, S. (2011). Participatory inquiry on the interface between religion and health: What does it achieve and what not? In J. R. Cochrane, B. Schmid, & T. Cutts (Eds.), *When religion and health align: Mobilizing religious health assets for transformation* (pp. 43–61). Pietermaritzburg: Cluster Publications.

de Gruchy, S., Dooms, T., Matimelo, S., Cutts, T., Cochrane, J. R., & Olivier, J. (2009). *CHAMP/PC: Community health assets mapping for partnerships in palliative care, version 2*. Participatory inquiry workshop for health providers, Hospice Palliative Care Association of South Africa. Cape Town, South Africa: IRHAP, School of Public Health, University of Cape Town.

ESRI. (2010). *GIS for asset and facilities management: Efficient management of assets, interior space, and the building life*. Redlands, CA: ESRI.

Isobell, I., & Lazarus, S. (2014). *SCRATCHMAPS development of safety and peace indicators research report*. Tygerberg: South African Medical Research Council-University of South Africa Violence, Injury and Peace Research Unit.

Israel, B. A., Eng, E., Schultz, A. J., & Parker, E. A. (2005). *Methods in community-based participatory research for health*. San Francisco, CA: Jossey-Bass.

Kramer, S., Amos, T., Lazarus, S., & Seedat, M. (2012). The philosophical assumptions, utility and challenges of asset mapping approaches to community engagement. *Journal of Psychology in Africa, 22*, 539–546.

Kramer, S., Seedat, M., Lazarus, S., & Suffla, S. (2011). A critical review of instruments assessing characteristics of community. *South African Journal of Psychology, 41*(4), 503–516.

Krantz, L. (2011). *The sustainable livelihood approach to poverty reduction: An introduction*. Stockholm: SIDA Division for Policy and Socioeconomic Analysis.

Kretzmann, J. P., & McKnight, J. L. (1993). *Building communities from the inside out: A path toward finding and mobilizing a community's assets*. Evanston, IL: Institute for Policy Research.

Lazarus, S., Bulbulia, S., Taliep, N., & Naidoo, A. V. (2015). Community-based participatory research as a critical enactment of community psychology. *Journal of Community Psychology, 43*(1), 87–98.

Lazarus, S., Duran, B., Caldwell, L., & Bulbulia, S. (2012a). Public health research and action: Reflections on challenges and possibilities of community-based participatory research. In J. Maddock (Ed.), *Public health* (pp. 309–324). Intech (Open Access).

Lazarus, S., Taliep, N., Bulbulia, S., Phillips, S., & Seedat, M. (2012b). Community-based participatory research: An illustrative case of community engagement in one low-income community. *Journal of Psychology in Africa, 22*(4), 511–519.

Lazarus, S., Naidoo, A. V., May, B., Williams, L. L., Demas, G., & Filander, F. J. (2014). Lessons learnt from a community-based participatory research project in a South African rural context. *South African Journal of Psychology, 44*(2), 147–159.

Lazarus, S., Taliep, N., & Olivier, J. (2014). *SCRATCHMAPS community asset mapping research report*. Tygerberg: South African Medical Research Council-University of South Africa Violence, Injury and Peace Research Unit.

Lazarus, S., Seedat, M., & Naidoo, T. (2017). Community building: Challenges of constructing community. In M. Bond, I. Serrano-Garcia, & C.B. Keys (Eds.-in-Chief), M. Shinn (Assoc. Ed.). *APA handbook of community psychology: Vol. 2. Methods for community research and action for diverse groups and issues* (pp. 215–234). Washington, DC: American Psychological Association.

Marais, S., Naidoo, A. V., Donson, H., & Nortje, C. (2007). Strategic violence prevention partnerships in a peri-urban South African town: The case of the Jamestown community project. *African Safety Promotion Journal: A Journal of Injury and Violence Prevention, 5*(1), 19–30.

Mathie, A., & Cunningham, G. (2003). From clients to citizens: Asset-based community development as a strategy for community-driven development. *Development in Practice, 13*(5), 474–486.

Mathie, A., & Cunningham, G. (2008). *Mobilizing assets for community-driven development.* Participant manual. Antigonish, Nova Scotia: Coady International Institute, St Francis Xavier University.

Minkler, M., & Hancock, T. (2008). Community-driven asset identification and issue selection. In M. Minkler & N. Wallerstein (Eds.), *Community-based participatory research for health: From process to outcomes* (2nd ed., pp. 153–169). San Francisco, CA: Jossey-Bass.

Minkler, M., & Wallerstein, N. (2008). *Community-based participatory research for health: From process to outcomes* (2nd ed.). San Francisco, CA: Jossey-Bass.

Naidoo, A. V., & Van Wyk, S. B. (2003). Intervening in communities: Combining curative and preventive interventions. *Journal of Prevention and Intervention in the Community, 25*(1), 65–80.

Neighbourhood Initiatives Foundation. (2009). *What is 'Planning for Real'?* Retrieved from http://www.nif.co.uk.html

Nelson, G., & Prilleltensky, I. (2010). *Community psychology: In pursuit of liberation and well-being* (2nd ed.). London: Palgrave Macmillan.

Olivier, J., Cutts, T., Lazarus, S., Cochrane, J. R., & Taliep, N. (2012). *Community asset mapping manual for service providers*. Tygerberg: South African Medical Research Council-University of South Africa Violence, Injury and Peace Research Unit.

Railton Foundation, & Stellenbosch University. (2010a). *Railton community assessment project: Research report*. Stellenbosch: Stellenbosch University.

Railton Foundation, & Stellenbosch University. (2010b). *Railton community assessment project: Research report for the railton foundation*. Stellenbosch: Stellenbosch University.

Railton Foundation, & Stellenbosch University. (2010c). *Railton Community Assessment Project: Conducting a community assessment: A practical community handbook*. Stellenbosch: Stellenbosch University.

Ratele, K., Suffla, S., Lazarus, S., & van Niekerk, A. (2010). Towards the development of a responsive, social science-informed, critical public health framework on male interpersonal violence. *Social Change, 40*(4), 415–438.

SCRATCHMAPS. (2014). *SCRATCHMAPS community booklet on community asset mapping*. Tygerberg: South African Medical Research Council-University of South Africa Violence, Injury and Peace Research Unit.

Seedat, M., & Suffla, S. (2012). Editorial: Community engagement: Conceptualisation, methods, and illustrations. *Journal of Psychology in Africa, 22*, 483–485.

Serrat, O. (2010). *The sustainable livelihoods approach*. Washington, DC: Asian Development Bank.

Smith, R. J., & Miller, K. (2013). Eco-city mapping using GIS: Introducing a planning method for assessing and improving neighborhood vitality. *Progress in Community Health Partnerships: Research, Education, and Action*, 95–106. Retrieved from http://digitalcommons.wayne.edu/soc_work_pubs/9

Springett, J., & Wallerstein, N. (2008). Issues in participatory evaluation. In M. Minkler & N. Wallerstein (Eds.), *Community-based participatory research for health: From process to outcomes* (pp. 404–418). San Francisco, CA: Jossey-Bass.

Van Gesselleen, M., Taliep, N., Lazarus, S., Carelse, H., & Phillips, S. (2015). *Process evaluation of SCRATCHMAPS' Building Bridges Mentoring Programme research report*. Tygerberg: South African Medical Research Council-University of South Africa Violence, Injury and Peace Research Unit.

Wallerstein, N., & Duran, B. (2008). The theoretical, historical, and practice roots of CBPR. In M. Minkler & N. Wallerstein (Eds.), *Community-based participatory research for health: From process to outcomes* (pp. 25–46). San Francisco, CA: Jossey-Bass.

Chapter 6
Participatory Knowledge Co-creation: Using Digital Mapping as an Emancipatory Method

Siew Fang Law and Jose Ramos

As teachers, researchers and practitioners, we share similar aims to our students in human rights, community development, peace psychology and social change who want to make our world a better place. With our shared positive intention and aspirations, students and teachers enter the learning space together. Yet often what and how we teach immediately becomes limited once we are "inside the box". A binary relationship emerges: the teacher teaches while the students learn highly structured content according to the curriculum and "year-level" of the course and the institutional agenda. For example, the affordability of a mass-learning approach through large lecture theatres and distance learning mode may be favoured over classroom face-to-face teaching.

In the broader academic context, contemporary neo-liberal academic ideals have shaped increasingly politicised and commodified notions of "knowledge" (Dalaston-Jones, 2015; Fox, 2014). Scholars describe the ways in which academics operate in a competitive hierarchy within different paradigms and epistemologies (Guba & Lincoln, 1994; Heron & Reason, 1997). Scientific, evidenced-based, factual, objective and empirical knowing is granted the highest value and authority by influential institutions and publishers. At the other end of the spectrum, "soft knowledge" such as rituals and spiritual practices, memories, indigenous oral accounts, dreamtime

S.F. Law (✉)
College of Arts and Education, Victoria University, Melbourne, Australia

Institute for Social and Health Sciences, University of South Africa, Johannesburg, South Africa

South African Medical Research Council-University of South Africa Violence, Injury and Peace Research Unit, Johannesburg, South Africa
e-mail: siewfang.law@vu.edu.au

J. Ramos
Center for Cultural Diversity and Wellbeing, Victoria University, Melbourne, Australia

M. Seedat et al. (eds.), *Emancipatory and Participatory Methodologies in Peace, Critical, and Community Psychology*, Peace Psychology Book Series,
DOI 10.1007/978-3-319-63489-0_6

and stories are less recognised; these sources of knowledge are frequently marginalised, excluded and judged as subjective, situated, relative and "less evidenced-based" in nature. Spivak (1988) and Walker (2015) name this phenomenon epistemic violence. Even if soft knowledge is used in academia, it is more often the object rather than the means of study, and it is reframed through the researcher's voice. Connell (2007) describes how (falsely) manufacturing soft knowledge can often be exploitative to those sharing their knowledge. Soft knowledge is frequently processed through a scientific epistemology and language to gain advancement within the academic system.

Within academic systems, incentives and dis-incentives have been put in place to produce a particular type of "knowledge" (Connell, 2007; Hil, 2015). To receive internal academic recognition and promotion, academics are pressured to write and share their research findings in spaces inaccessible to the general public (Hil, 2015). Academic knowledge thus becomes a "rare resource" worth a higher price. In such systems, academic knowledge is privileged over lay knowledge. Reason (1998) contends that "the current arrangements for knowledge creation mean that the established centres of power tend to have a monopoly on the production and use of knowledge. Knowledge is produced and used in the service of dominant groups, rather than being used as a means of education toward community and agency" (p. 4). Hence, knowledge is not only divided between those who have it and those who don't; it also potentially creates segregation, disconnection and social inequality. As knowledge producers, we may inadvertently play a role in perpetuating this imbalance and inequality.

What is needed are methods that promote greater equality in knowledge creation in which the *co-creation of knowledge* and appreciation of diverse perspectives and epistemologies are possible. We need to enable people to develop critical political, ecological, epistemological and spiritual awareness through learning and sharing processes. Thus, we dismantle the hierarchical organisation of knowledge. We begin to understand that it is constructed, relative and contextual and that its misuse has the potential to marginalise communities. Teachers, students and practitioners can perceive, exchange information about, and comprehend complex issues. Such methods allow us to appreciate realities that are complex and interconnected rather than simple and disconnected (Elby & Hammer, 2001).

Elby and Hammer (2001) emphasise the importance of developing critical epistemological awareness in learning. For these scholars, such awareness allows understanding of the diverse nature of knowing reality, and appreciation of the inherent politics and hierarchy. Critical epistemological awareness is therefore crucial to teachers, students and practitioners to enable us to peel away the layers of constructs that frame our knowledge. As academics our own epistemological beliefs about the nature of knowledge influence learning and teaching research and practices, so we need to rethink what we teach, and also the ways in which people acquire knowledge, learn, research and engage with our professional practices (Bendixen & Rule, 2004). Heron and Reason (1997) articulate that "our work with co-operative inquiry, in mindfulness practices and ceremony, and our attempts at aware everyday living all convince us that experiential encounter with the presence of the world is the ground of our being and knowing" (p. 2). They argue that knowledge is embedded in everyday living and we need to participate and be present in everyday life in order to know. Their primary critique of positivist and realist paradigms is that these paradigms present truth as universal, static and unchanging fact. In order to more fully engage both ourselves and others in a deeper understanding of real-world issues, we need to reverse disengagement, disconnection, disembodiment and de-contextualisation (Reason, 1998).

Elby and Hammer (2001) contend that epistemological "sophistication consists more of having resources to sort out the complexity of knowledge in different contexts than of having a global, decontextualized opinion about this [or that] issue" (p. 566). In their study, they found that university students show progress from an absolutist to an increasingly sophisticated relativist stance toward knowledge over the period of study (Elby & Hammer, 2001).

While the politics of knowledge is a perspective less explored in psychology (Elby & Hammer, 2001), it is highly relevant, particularly in socially engaged forms of psychology. To fully understand and interpret psychological concepts and implications, learners, teachers, practitioners and researchers benefit from wider exposure through participating in processes of knowledge co-creation. The number and complexity of global–local problems in the twenty-first century means we must move beyond a narrow concept of knowledge.

Which methods will therefore enable greater opportunities for people to participate in knowledge creation or co-creation; promote more relational and equal knowledge sharing processes; and foster greater social justice, equity and collaboration in knowledge creation?

Participatory Knowledge Co-creation as Emancipation

With the above issues as the backdrop, we explore an alternative which promotes *participatory knowledge co-creation*. We argue that it promotes the idea of liberation, criticality and authentic engagement and disrupts the dominant epistemology by enabling greater engagement and participation.

Hegemonic epistemology[1] has an emphasis on disembodiment and disconnection (Murove, 2014). Reason (1998) asserts that "from an ecological perspective it is important to start from our embodied presence in the world as physical beings rather than as disembodied and deconstructed minds" (p. 11). Participatory knowledge co-creation gives value to the forms of knowledge of ordinary people: civic epistemology (Wynne, 2003), lay epistemology (Healy, 2009; Irwin & Michael, 2003) and street level epistemology (Hardin, 2002). Community development scholar, Ife (2012), asserted that the "street–level intellectual … will bring a wide range of understanding, conceptual tools, frames of reference and resources to be

[1] We acknowledge the problem of using the term "western epistemology" as it could create a binary proposition because not all work that arises from the West is hegemonic. Foucault, for example, is from the West but his work is not hegemonic. Hence, we use the term "hegemonic epistemology" to illustrate our points in this chapter.

applied in a particular and unique way" (p. 211). Participatory knowledge co-creation allows power shifting between "knowers" and "learners" and promotes a greater sense of community and environmental belonging. Participatory methods can serve as a nexus of experience and place as they offer significant potential for endeavours that educate people towards a sustainable future (Hill, 2013). We propose that *participatory knowledge co-creation* as a process can enable diverse people to contribute and create knowledge through mutual sharing, dialogue and listening. The process promotes person-to-person engagement, and also invokes both a sense of agency and critical thinking. It emancipates people and allows power shifting.

Reason's (1998) participatory theory makes links to participatory knowledge co-creation by identifying four dimensions of participation—political, ecological, epistemological and spiritual imperatives. Firstly, participatory knowledge co-creation has a *political imperative* because it allows for the amplification of ordinary people's voice in situations that affect them. Active participation enables awareness of community members' agency and ability to take private and public political actions to nurture their own development. Through such processes, traditional "experts" share a similar status with participants. Secondly, participatory knowledge co-creation has an *ecological imperative* which helps us to better understand our surroundings—our environment, our place and our cosmos (Hill, 2013). Through engaging with people of diverse socio-economic, cultural and political backgrounds, we gain first-hand understanding of the impact that people have had on our community and our environment. Through the quality of our interactions, we hear the accounts of impacts on people (as well as on animals and plants) who might be most affected by changes at global-local levels. Thirdly, participatory knowledge co-creation has an *epistemological imperative*. Our interactions with people of diverse sociocultural and religious backgrounds help us to have a much clearer understanding of the dimensions of their knowledge and worldviews. Quality relationships developed from participation open our cognitive horizons and challenge our assumptions. Fourthly, participatory knowledge co-creation can contribute to a *spiritual imperative.* Participation inspires human souls, and helps us "heal the splits" such as the disconnection from the wider natural world, division, segregation and individualism (Reason, 1998, p. 3). Participatory methods can offer more context-specific experiences that can build critical epistemological awareness. Shifting paradigms can radically "influence how evidence is interpreted—and even what counts as compelling evidence" (Elby & Hammer, 2001, p. 556).

Case Study

The following section features a case study drawing on the principles of participatory knowledge co-creation. The case study showcases a community development project, the Maribyrnong Maker Map (M3). This is a collaborative form of action inquiry using digital mapping applications to create a maker map; a map of the local productive resources in a community. The process of map-making brought together several dozen community members through active mapping, educational activities, networking and advocacy.

Reason (1998) states that "… the notion of an ecology of mind takes us toward an understanding of 'the pattern which connects'… [Mind] is immanent in the whole natural world. Mind … resides in those systemic circuits of information, the feedback loops which provide processes of balance and control, which are part of all natural ecosystems." (p. 13). The case study is a synthesis of feedback from four of the 15 participants including the second author who took part in the Maker Map Teach session.

The Maribyrnong Maker Map (M3)[2] aimed to strengthen collaboration and promote sharing among local communities. The project was initiated in early 2015 by the second author and a few community members to provide an open platform that would facilitate an inclusive method of knowledge sharing.

Maribyrnong is a residential and industrial suburb 7 km from the Melbourne Central Business District. The word Maribyrnong is an Aboriginal name for saltwater river. White settlement has introduced intensive industrial use of the river and its nearby areas. Due to industrial pollution of the river and other environmental factors, Maribyrnong has a long-standing reputation as dirty, unsafe and polluted. It has problems with crime, drugs and gangs usually associated with lower socio-economic groups. It is also home to many migrants and refugees of Italian, Vietnamese, Chinese, Indian, Middle Eastern and African backgrounds (Haffenden, 1994; Law, Grossman, & Spark, 2015).

The maker is part of an emerging subculture which consists of "a growing culture of hands-on making, creating, designing, and innovating" (Peppler & Bender, 2013, p. 23). A main characteristic of the maker movement is its:

> do-it-yourself (or do-it-with-others) mindset that brings together individuals around a range of activities, including textile craft, robotics, cooking, woodcrafts, electronics, digital fabrication, mechanical repair, or creation—in short, making nearly anything. Despite its diversity, the movement is unified by a shared commitment to open exploration, intrinsic interest, and creative ideas (Peppler & Bender, 2013, p. 23).

The maker movement is typified by citizen innovation and empowerment in both knowledge and material production. An emerging maker culture has developed where people work toward the goals of promoting *sustainability* through upcycling what already exists for zero waste. The culture promotes *openness* by creating a knowledge commons, working with others inclusively, and allowing for iterative evolution. The movement encourages *problem solving* by producing things rather than relying on existing institutions and structures. It takes the power of production back into the hands of the people.

M3 is facilitated by a cooperative enterprise called the Footscray Maker Lab. Footscray, a suburb within the city of Maribyrnong, has a rough reputation. The Footscray Maker Lab was initiated in early 2013 as a way to share space and knowledge and to collaborate on innovation projects. It sought to use advanced support

[2] http://maribyrnongmakers.com.au/about/.

Table 6.1 Background of interviewees

	Gender	Age	Profession
Interviewee 1 (I1)	Male	Mid-1930s	Anglo Australian, musician and website designer
Interviewee 2 (I2)	Female	Mid-1930s	Japanese, ceramic artist, landscape architect
Interviewee 3 (I3)	Female	1940s	Anglo Australian, artist and small business owner
Interviewee 4 (I4)	Female	1930s	Anglo New Zealander environmentalist and architect

systems to drive open innovation and adaptation to support its members and the community. In one of the initial ideation sessions, where people proposed potential projects, a small group identified an online resource maker map that could map the creative assets of the community in an open and editable way. It would catalogue the making of resources in the community, and facilitate interaction and eventually collaboration between many different types of people.

Our research is based on one-on-one conversation with participants in M3 of approximately 40 min duration. Conversation points include (1) self-description and their reasons for becoming involved in M3; (2) their involvement in and experience of M3; and (3) the degree to which they experience M3 as participatory and emancipatory. Table 6.1 outlines the background of the interviewed participants.

One limitation of this study is that the participants who agreed to be interviewed are similar in age (e.g. 1930–1940s) and as middle-class professionals do not represent the diverse demographic composition of Maribyrnong. Hence, our interviews may not capture the experiences of those who would not and did not participate in the project. We were unable to secure interviews from the other participants.

The interviewed participants talked about the "things" people wanted to make, including pre-industrial crafts, handcraft and crafted food. It also included industrial crafts such as carpentry, metalwork or welding, machine-based sewing, as well as high-tech post-industrial elements such as micro-controllers or robotics, 3D printing and laser cutting. These crafts resulted in diverse products, including props and art for festivals, refurbished items and retro fittings, experimental objects, as well as upcycled household or domestic items such as gardening boxes.

The rationale for the digital map evolved from the idea of asset mapping into a reformulated and more complex rationale (I4). All of the interviewed participants reported that there was a great deal of knowledge embedded in the community yet many people did not know each other. M3 was designed to help people to locate makers and to foster connection and collaboration among members of the local community.

M3 addressed the issues of sustainability in our contemporary consumer-driven society (I1, I3 and I4). Many people faced the problem of household, industrial and commercial waste. The waste problem was especially confronting in the western region of Melbourne. Maribyrnong was an area where light and medium industry produces a variety of waste outputs; therefore, M3 could provide a map of resources currently being wasted, such as factory or commercial waste, that could be useful for local makers as build resources, to help people transform this waste into new products or works, and enable a circular economy to emerge (I3).

All participants commented that M3 is emancipating as it could be used as a method that promotes participatory knowledge co-creation to allow a greater sense of agency, and appreciation for the region's rich qualities, locales, assets and people. It also helped the community appreciate their region in a new light. Two main factors emerged from discussions with the participants. Firstly, it is the people and the processes that define M3 as participatory knowledge co-creation. Secondly, a user-friendly and effective digital tool is crucial in facilitating and documenting people's knowledge.

People and Processes

People more and more are quite hungry to become more connected. But I think in many ways they don't really know how [to become connected]. They might see some facilities that they would be interested in finding more about. Things like the map, Facebook or Meetup … people can kind of connect from afar to begin with, and then come in when they are ready (I4).

Participants articulated various disconnections in contemporary society and their desire for greater social connection. "I don't just sit at home by myself … [I'd] much rather be engaged … I am interested in neighbor day, garage day trial or food truck. I saw the map maker as a potential tool for people like me who want to know what is going on in my area" (I4).

The operating team of the M3 project facilitated informal conversations, community meetings and mapping workshops in local cafes, university facilities, the Footscray Maker Lab, as well as in people's homes at different times to engage people with the project. Participants found out about the initiative through local newspapers, public seminars and on social media platforms such as Chuffed,[3] Meetup[4] and Facebook.[5] Crowdfunding was used not only to generate funds for the initiative, but also to create a sense of ownership around the knowledge sharing idea. The crowdfunding project itself was its own mapping journey, as the project team endeavoured to map one new maker element for each day of the campaign so that by its completion, many elements had already been mapped and new networks created. Tagged with the initiative of Footscray Maker Lab, the M3 project attracted an average of five new members a day, and now has over 800 members on Meetup and over 1000 followers on Facebook (I1). Although membership is open, M3 has largely generated interest from individuals from Maribyrnong willing to share

[3] www.chuffed.org: an online fundraising platform for non-profit initiatives and social enterprises.

[4] www.meetup.com: an online platform to bring local interest groups together to meet, interact and engage.

[5] www.facebook.com: a global social media platform which connects people through sharing updates, news and events.

knowledge and information about places and resources that could benefit their local community.

Participants commented that *people* and *processes* are critical aspects of the participatory knowledge co-creation: "The digital map doesn't create knowledge, the people do. But people need to be mobilized and organized so sharing could actually happen" (Interviewees 2 and 3). A number of community gatherings took place as part of the project. Information sessions explained the project to people while the "Meet Your Maker" event brought together local members of the community, in particular artists and other creative makers, many of whom had never met before. In Maker Map Teach sessions, people were shown how to create different maps and add new information to the M3 map. From this series of events and gatherings, the formative elements of M3 were mapped.

According to Interviewee 2, the M3 facilitator was thoughtful in the design of the community gatherings with the aim of maximising participation, exchange of ideas and collaboration. For example, in the Maker Map Teach session, 15 participants of diverse interests and backgrounds learned about the mapping method. They then formed five small groups to create different maps. Within each group, they discussed what and how the digital map could be used to address a particular problem. The composition of participants in each small group was diverse, ranging from a Japanese ceramic artist to a town planner from the local city council. Participants were able to draw on their own perspectives of a local community problem, and discuss the ways in which a digital map like M3 could connect people and map out diverse resources. Everyone in that session had the chance to create, edit and present their map on the spot. The outcome of the workshop was encouraging as the participants mapped community gardens in the neighbourhood, recycling centers and dog-friendly parks (Fig. 6.1).

Tool: Open Global Knowledge as a Foundation for Local Creativity

A digital mapping platform was used to complement participatory knowledge co-creation. The tool facilitates documentation and captures knowledge by people for people. The software technology was taken from OpenStreetMap (OSM), a global open source mapping project from France. Like Wikipedia, OSM allows people to contribute knowledge to a global map where the data is open, shared and legally open sourced, rather than proprietary. As part of the participatory processes, the project team were guided by members of the Footscray Maker Lab to explore new ideas, including using software technology to enhance the mapping processes and experiences (I1). Using another software called Umap, local specialised maps were interfaced with OSM, so that a variety of local maps could be created with different uses. One of the main other reasons for using OSM and Umap was ease of use for those with limited computer experience. With the support of OSM

Fig. 6.1 A screen print of M3 which shows different elements mapped on a Umap interface

technology, simple editing icons and buttons allow people to add elements to the maps with relative ease (I2) (Fig. 6.2).

The technology enabled participants to capture a wide range of knowledge. For example, interviewees 2 and 4 discussed how they wanted the facility to map safe cycling routes, source places that offer recycled materials, recent harvests from backyard orchards, resources for asylum seekers, as well as newly discovered hiking trails and indigenous historical sites (Fig. 6.1).

The digital map of the M3 project is open, accessible and editable so the community can augment its knowledge and awareness of local making resources. It also facilitates collaboration between local artisans, designers and other makers currently unknown to each other (I2 and I3).

Connecting M3 with Reason's Theory of Participation

Drawing on Reason's (1998) theory, knowledge in M3 is in the realm of everyday being. To a certain extent, M3 emancipates people: "It gives people an opportunity to share what is special to them. People have control to the map and can add things to it. It makes it an organic process" (I3). As a crowd-sourced map, M3 *is* the research data *by the community* and *for the community*. Knowledge captured on the

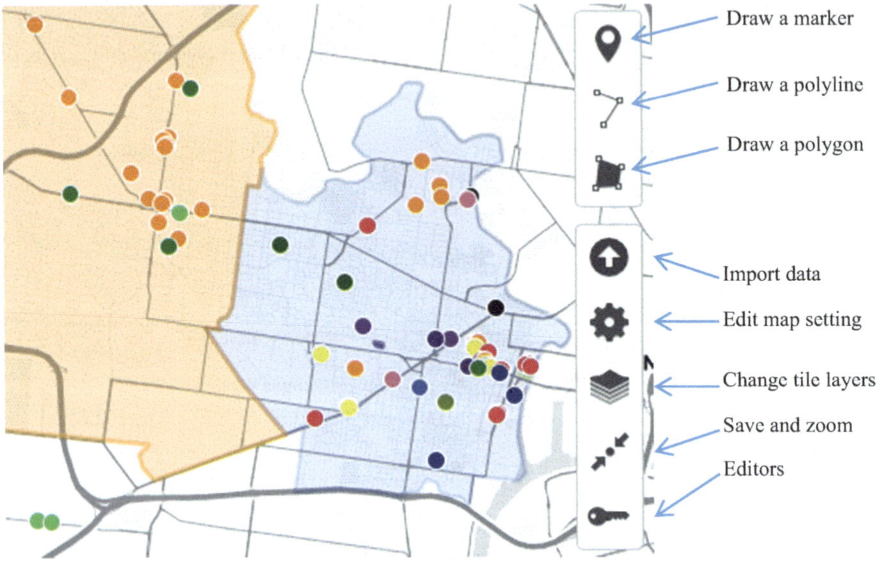

Fig. 6.2 Umap interface with icons buttons on right for adding elements

map *is* the teaching and resource material; the community members *are* the teachers; and our classrooms *can be* anywhere.

As a project which aims to promote knowledge co-creation within the community, the utility of the research data, and any analysis of the data, was best judged by its value to community members. Feedback from community consultation meetings indicated that there was strong support for the M3 project. People saw the rationale and were willing to become involved. We learned that with enough support, community members can be integral contributors.

In terms of using waste resources, a variety of opportunities emerged. Local restaurants were willing to offer organic waste for composting and worm farming. However, making the connection between waste outputs and waste inputs also requires extensive ongoing work and coordination. A project like this needs collaboration with existing programs and organisations to fulfill its promise as well as technology specifically focused on the project's explicit goals (I3).

M3 forms part of a larger social development, the maker movement (Anderson, 2012; Hatch, 2013). It brought together several dozen community members through active participation in mapping, educational activities, networking and advocacy. M3 thus provided a *political* platform for people to offer each other new ways of seeing the world, auto-productive communities, knowledge and resource sharing, as well as the potential for building circular economies (waste elimination). M3 expressed the capacity for an emergent (but still disparate) dimension within the community to recognise itself as a self-organising living system. Participant contributions of their knowledge were not just disparate, but fit into the logic of enacting a subsystem, which by virtue of its radical social and sustainability agenda is implicitly a political act. Activating and strengthening a sense of citizenship and agency for change relies on recognising one's activities in relation to an emerging ecosystem of complementary actors and elements (Ramos, 2015). M3 thus helps facilitate a network of connected community members who want to coordinate any advocacy with greater effect. The mapping process also produced data that captured the complex nature of community resources and indicates new approaches to interpretation and action (I1, I2 and I3).

M3 expressed an *ecological* imperative through its explicit intention to help create a circular economy in the community, to identify waste resources and leverage mapping capabilities to enable resource exchange. This was an ambitious goal which few modern economies have achieved. M3 was a minor step on this path to a circular economy, but still significant. The mapping process also encouraged otherwise disconnected people to step out of their everyday spaces, whether arts foundry, studio, government office, or university lecture theatre. Interviewee 1 indicated that M3 helps people to "join the dots" not only with others, but with our wider environment. By physically participating and engaging in various places and localities, the embodied experience enriches awareness of shared environmental and ecological surroundings. Interviewee 3 commented that:

> … the map has a huge potential to contribute to space design and community survey. It was very useful for me when I was doing my landscape architectural internship with a non-profit community space design organization, we were doing community engagement work like creating community gardens for primary schools. If I had known M3 at that time, the community would have been able to 'create' and communicate to us the types of garden they want; rather than the architects who create the map on paper, print it out to show the community. It could change the power dynamic between the expert and the community. (I3)

Thirdly, M3 stimulates an *epistemological* imperative. Unlike many traditional learning structures that group people of similar backgrounds in learning cohorts, M3 creates opportunities by permeating invisible structural borders and socially constructed boundaries. For example, Interviewee 1 described Abdul, an African man with a refugee background, who participated in one of the meetings. Abdul was passionate about the enabling elements of M3 to map services and resources for newly arrived migrants and refugees. Interviewee 1 reported his surprise when Abdul proposed making African jewelry using a 3D printer. Abdul considered that the bright, durable and lightweight plastic-bead necklaces had some benefits over traditional African wooden-bead necklaces. Interviewee 1 observed that the interactions and engagement facilitated through the co-mapping process revealed the worldview of this African man which positively challenged his own assumptions. Interviewee 4 shared similar sentiments and commented:

> We have different political and cultural overlays but you often don't get to find out the real nitty-gritty about what people are fascinated by and passionate about until you come together and ask people 'what would you map out in your local area?' and they come out with some of the most bizarre things that I would never have thought of mapping. Obviously this is something of interest to that person and of course to other people as well but I would have never thought of that. (I4)

Participation in M3 dialogues with members who are "different" thus challenged assumptions and stimulated knowledge exchange. As the nature of knowledge co-creation promotes collaboration rather than competition, M3 could be seen as an effective platform to instigate cooperation across levels and boundaries. Through such sharing, people reveal the nuances of their ideas and world views. Learning processes, such as those created by M3, are crucial in the twenty-first century when we need cross-disciplinary perspectives and collaboration to address complex environmental, sociocultural and political issues.

Finally, M3 promotes the types of participation that inspire human souls and consciences. M3 expresses learning distinct from traditional education with its focus on textbooks and attending lectures. Instead, M3 advocates learning through participation, embodiment and knowledge exchanges and co-creation about the things that matter to people. Engaging with this greater sense of purpose, a higher purpose, is where the *spiritual imperative* is felt. The second author acknowledged that advocating for M3 felt very different from promoting commercial and government projects as it caused him to step outside conventional frames. The risk and vulnerability was infused with a sense of undertaking a higher purpose, supporting an idea whose time had come, as well as a palpable sense of awakening. He described it as "enacting the dormant dreams of the collective spirit, of heeding that which wants to happen". This was echoed in the experiences of participants. All interviewees discussed the ways in which participating in the active mapping process strengthened their sense of belonging and connections to their local community.

Linking Participatory Knowledge Co-creation with Psychology

Research

Firstly, participatory knowledge co-creation allows researchers to hold an equivalent level of power with the researched. Numerous researchers have identified the issue of power imbalance between the roles of researchers and participants (e.g. Behar, 1996; Hegarty & Bruckmüller, 2013; Langout, 2006; Law & Bretherton, 2016). These authors address the positionality of researchers as experts and their privileged status in comparison with participants. Wessels (2015) discussed the disempowering experience of participants in research and evaluation processes. The process of knowledge co-creation addresses the issues of power imbalance as participants are positioned as having equivalent or greater expertise than researchers in the mapping process. Increasingly, more researchers have identified a participatory action research method as a more open and inclusive framework, creating spaces for an inclusive cycle of co-design, co-implementation, co-reflection and co-evaluation. We echo Reason's (1998) sentiment that:

> a variety of forms of action research have been articulated, most of which describe systematic movements between action and reflection, or varieties of research cycling between experiential, presentational, propositional and practical knowing … [A] participative epistemology

> articulates a way of knowing and acting which is both grounded in our experiential presence in the world and honours the human capacity of sense-making and intentional action. (p. 12).

Participatory knowledge co-creation considers the connections between knowledge and its political, ecological, epistemological and spiritual nature. Widening the emerging knowledge space, to include both physically situated space and online sites, offers fresh potential for contextualised problem solving and engaged participatory research.

Education

Educators in psychology can increasingly use pedagogy that draws on the principles of participatory knowledge co-creation to elicit existing knowledge from learners. Participatory knowledge co-creation emphasises the importance of power balance between those who possess knowledge. This includes critically reflecting on the practices of both teachers and learners. In classroom contexts, each learner's knowing and positionality diverges from that of their teacher. It is important to create spaces for mutual exchanges of ideas and thought processes to explore these differences. For example, traditional learning sites such as classrooms and libraries usually offer students a peaceful space to acquire knowledge. However, students can also learn by attending or participating at "real" learning sites outside classrooms to learn in spaces and places that stimulate ideas. This could involve examining the complex relationships between concepts of peace, conflict and violence with a class of students. For example, a visit to a migrant resource centre or asylum seekers resource centre offers learners a different level of theoretical understanding, such as the effects of war and civil conflicts, the global population movement, social injustice, and the challenges of language and culture in mainstreaming government services.

From a civic learning point of view, being physically present in a place creates new connections with people and situations we may have feared and helps to dissolve bias and prejudice. As part of knowledge co-creation processes, students, teachers and members of communities can share observations, experiences and reflections in well-planned sessions. Debriefing or journal writing can deepen understanding of complex thoughts and experiences.

Practice

Psychology practitioners can also apply methods of participatory knowledge co-creation in their professional work. To support safety and well-being for young people in their communities, socially engaged scholars could involve young people in co-creating knowledge by identifying and mapping safe and unsafe places and spaces, and thus provide information for policy-makers. Mapping techniques could be useful for practitioners to better understand the links between geopolitical issues and sociocultural well-being, privileges and disadvantages.

Advocacy

Considering its political, ecological, epistemological and spiritual imperatives, participatory knowledge co-creation can also be used by psychologists committed to address social injustice and advocate for social change. As illustrated in the above case study, M3 mobilised a group of people from various professions, disciplines and backgrounds. According to Interviewee 1, one of the participants aspired to map the richness of diverse cultural locales because "she does not want Footscray to change" despite rapid gentrification. She utilised the technology to collect data from local people in order to inform strategic political actions. As demonstrated in the case study of M3, participatory knowledge co-creation is transformative because the process connects people with each other, with their ecologies and environment, with processes of enacting power, and with a sense of purpose.

Conclusion

The forces of neoliberalism have contributed to the changing landscape of higher education. Hil and Lyons (2015) argued that competition and the pursuit of profits are an impediment to the use and dissemination of knowledge yet the rhetoric that "knowledge is owned" and therefore needs to be protected by institutions lingers. Various intellectual property regimes have created conceptual and practical boundaries that prohibit the free flow of knowledge and prevent sharing knowledge in open spaces. Moreover, we have witnessed increasingly depersonalised and decontextualised learning and teaching in many tertiary institutions (Hil, 2015). We have proposed methods that transcend these structural boundaries and generate and share community knowledge. Participatory knowledge co-creation has long been practiced in many communities, such as amongst indigenous and traditional peoples, as a way of mutualising well-being (Walker, 2015). Unfortunately the fundamental principles of knowledge sharing has been devalued in market-driven systems. A peaceful social movement like the maker movement "is an innovative way to reimagine education" (Peppler & Bender, 2013, p. 23). The Maribrynong Maker Map has demonstrated how participatory knowledge co-creation can be revitalised by modern technology.

It is, however, imminent to acknowledge that the application of participatory knowledge co-creation in real world settings can be messy, challenging and, at times, can contradict our initial intent. Indeed, in every step and process we encountered issues that underlay with privileges and disadvantages of participation despite careful planning and execution to ensure inclusivity. This was evidenced in our project as we discovered that the participants who are more likely to take part in the initiative are not only people who are interested in the idea of social change, they are individuals who are available. They are people who do not require to work multiple jobs in order to put food at the table, who need to care for a large family, who have dependences with disabilities. Despite efforts to disrupt existing unequal structures and systems, we discovered that some of the most active interviewees are educated, middle-class, young professionals who are fluent in English. In short, the knowledge we co-created remains *exclusive* if fairness and equal participation is assumed in an inherent uneven playing field (Law, 2016).

We believe that participative knowledge co-creation is a journey worthy of exploration and researched. We hope this chapter plants some thought seeds for the current and next generation of activists, scholars and researchers who are interested in exploring innovative approaches to engage people through learning and teaching, research, advocacy and professional practices.

References

Anderson, C. (2012). *Makers: The new industrial revolution*. New York: Crown Publishing.

Behar, R. (1996). *The vulnerable observer: An anthropology that breaks your heart*. Boston, MA: Beacon Press.

Bendixen, L. D., & Rule, D. C. (2004). An integrative approach to personal epistemology: A guiding model. *Educational Psychologist, 39*, 69–80.

Connell, R. (2007). *Southern theory: Social science and the global dynamics of knowledge*. Crows Nest, NSW: Allen & Unwin.

Dalaston-Jones, D. (2015). (De)Constructing paradigms: Creating a psychology curriculum for conscientisation education. *The Australian Community Psychologist, 27*(1), 38–48.

Fox, R. (2014). Constructing critical thinking with psychology students in higher education: Opportunities and barriers. *The Journal of Critical Psychology, Counselling and Psychotherapy, 14*(4), 238–247.

Elby, A., & Hammer, D. (2001). On the substance of a sophisticated epistemology. *Science Education, 85*, 554–567.

Guba, E. G., & Lincoln, Y. S. (1994). Competing paradigms in qualitative research. In N. K. Denzin & Y. S. Lincoln (Eds.), *Handbook of qualitative research* (pp. 105–117). Thousands Oaks, CA: Sage.

Haffenden, P. (1994). *Your history mate: The work of a community museum in Melbourne's Western Suburbs*. Maribyrnong, VIC: Melbourne's Living Museum of the West.

Hardin, R. (2002). Street level epistemology and democratic participation. *The Journal of Political Philosophy, 10*(2), 212–229.

Hatch, M. (2013). *The maker movement manifesto: Rules for innovation in the new world of crafters, hackers, and tinkerers*. New York: McGraw-Hill.

Healy, S. (2009). Toward an epistemology of public participation. *Journal of Environmental Management, 90*(4), 1644–1654.

Hegarty, P., & Bruckmüller, S. (2013). Asymmetric explanations of group differences: Experimental evidence of Foucault's disciplinary power in social psychology. *Social and Personality Psychology Compass, 7*, 176–186.

Heron, J., & Reason, P. (1997). A participatory inquiry paradigm. *Qualitative Inquiry, 3*(3), 274–294.

Hil, R. (2015). *Selling students short*. Crows Nest, NSW: Allen and Unwin.

Hil, R., & Lyons, K. (2015). A shift towards industry-relevant degrees isn't helping students get jobs. *The Conversation*. Retrieved from https://theconversation.com/a-shift-towards-industry-relevant-degrees-isnt-helping-students-get-jobs-46128

Hill, A. (2013). The place of experience and the experience of place: The intersections between sustainability education and outdoor learning. *Australian Journal of Environmental Education, 29*(1), 18–32.

Ife, J. (2012). *Human rights and social work: Toward rights-based practice*. Port Melbourne, Vic: Cambridge University Press.

Irwin, A., & Michael, M. (2003). *Science, social theory and public knowledge*. Maidenhead: Open University Press.

Langout, R. D. (2006). Where am I? Locating myself and its implications for collaborative research. *American Journal of Community Psychology, 37*, 267–274.

Law, S. F. (2016). Unknowing researcher's vulnerability: Re-searching inequality on an uneven playing field. *Journal of Social and Political Psychology, 4*(2), 521–536.

Law, S. F., & Bretherton, D. (2016). The imbalance between knowledge paradigms of North and South: Implications for peace psychology. In M. Seedat, S. Suffla, & D. J. Christie (Eds.), *Enlarging the scope of peace psychology: African and world-regional contributions* (pp. 19–38). New York: Springer.

Law, S. F., Grossman, M., & Spark, C. (2015). *River of lives: Final report*. Prepared for Maribyrnong City Council in Melbourne.

Murove, M. F. (2014). Ubuntu. *Diogenes, 59*(3–4), 36–47.

Peppler, K., & Bender, S. (2013). Maker movement spreads innovation one project at a time. *Phi Delta Kappan, 95*(3), 22–27.

Ramos, J. (2015). Liquid democracy and the futures of governance. In R. Ono & J. Winter (Eds.), *The future internet: Alternative visions* (pp. 173–191). Zurich: Springer.

Reason, P. (1998). Political, epistemological, ecological and spiritual dimensions of participation. *Studies in Cultures, Organizations and Societies, 4*, 147–167.

Spivak, G. C. (1988). Can the sulbaltern speak? In C. Nelson & L. Grossberg (Eds.), *Marxism and the interpretation of culture* (pp. 67–111). London: Macmillan Education.

Walker, P. O. (2015). Indigenous paradigm research. In D. Bretherton & S. F. Law (Eds.), *Methodologies in peace psychology: Peaceful research by peaceful means* (pp. 159–175). New York: Springer.

Wessels, M. (2015). Program evaluation: Why process matters. In D. Bretherton & S. F. Law (Eds.), *Methodologies in peace psychology: Peaceful research by peaceful means* (pp. 381–397). New York: Springer.

Wynne, B. (2003). Seasick on the third wave? Subverting the hegemony of propositionalism: Response to Collins and Evans (2002). *Social Studies of Science, 33*(3), 401–417.

Chapter 7
Harnessing the Power of Ecopsychology in Community Work

Anthony V. Naidoo, Conrad Zygmont, and Shaun Philips

The contemporary social, ecological and political challenges facing communities are so complex, interconnected and immense that this confluence requires that we re-examine our entire approach to problem solving and learn to work together in new and imaginative ways with broader frameworks (Nelson & Prilleltensky, 2010). This challenge is in alignment with the general thrust of this volume to critically engage with participatory methods that further cross-disciplinary scholarship on community, liberation, and public engagement. In this chapter, we contend that ecopsychology in concert with community psychology has a meaningful contribution to make to this discourse, offering theoretical frameworks and application possibilities at an ecological basis to facilitate engagement in liberatory community work. We explain how emancipatory community psychology and ecopsychology principles can be merged into a theoretical framework which, when implemented through wilderness programmes, fosters participation and collaboration resulting in individual and collective growth and empowerment. A community project will be used to illustrate the diverse application of wilderness based intervention activities within a CBPAR framework. We draw from research at the intersection of community

A.V. Naidoo (✉)
Department of Psychology, Stellenbosch University, Stellenbosch, South Africa
e-mail: avnaidoo@sun.ac.za

C. Zygmont
Department of Psychology, Helderberg College, Somerset West, South Africa

Department of Psychology, Stellenbosch University, Stellenbosch, South Africa
e-mail: zygmontc@hbc.ac.za

S. Philips
Building Bridges, Cape Town, South Africa
e-mail: sharp@africamail.com

M. Seedat et al. (eds.), *Emancipatory and Participatory Methodologies in Peace, Critical, and Community Psychology*, Peace Psychology Book Series,
DOI 10.1007/978-3-319-63489-0_7

psychology, wilderness experiential programming (WEP), and ecopsychology, and share critical lessons learned and challenges identified in integrating ecopsychology and community psychology praxis from our own experiences.

A Theoretical Framework for the Interface Between Ecopsychology, Critical, and Liberatory Community Psychology

We conceptualise critical community psychology as an approach to psychology that critiques traditional ways of understanding and intervening in the psychological, social, political, and economic systems that result in collective harm and oppression. Critical community psychologists seek to uncover the repressive material structures, beliefs, and practices that lead to suffering, with the goal of finding ways in which individuals and communities can achieve emancipation and thriving. South African approaches to critical community psychology developed in the 1980s as a response to the institutional and ideological racial oppression that took place under the apartheid system. In the context of an armed struggle, and mobilisation of civil society against apartheid, critical community psychologists sought to challenge mainstream psychology's apathy in addressing the needs of the oppressed. South African critical community psychology took a decidedly liberatory stance, aimed at social action to cripple the ideological and structural apparatus of the state and bring about the emancipation and healing of the oppressed and exploited majority (Pretorius-Heuchert & Ahmed, 2001). Critical community psychology engages with the effects of collective oppression as diverse as racism, sexism, homophobia, forced migration, severe economic, cultural, political, and health/well-being disparities, violence (including domestic violence, torture, war, and genocide), and assaults on human rights (Watkins & Ciofalo, 2011).

Ecopsychology, as a critical framework, suggests that collective oppression is not only directed at humans but extends to animal life, plant life, and to the very air, water, and the earth on which all humans are dependent for survival. Community psychologists must become more engaged in the global environmental crisis—a commitment to personal, collective, and relational wellness cannot be achieved or sustained without concomitant attention to the ecological wellness of our broader context (Riemer, 2010). In South Africa, the violent oppression of the black majority went hand-in-hand with devastating and widespread environmental destruction, which was "degraded far more than would have occurred if racial separatism had never been institutionalised" (Durning, 1990, p. 6). Under the post-apartheid government some progress has been made towards improving the social, economic, and political lives of disadvantaged South Africans, but the unsustainable environmental management policies of the previous regime have largely remained unchanged (Steyn, 2005). Ecopsychology, as a synthesis between ecology and psychology, is specifically concerned with the relationship between human beings and nature

(Scull, 1999). The denial or eroding of this reciprocal bond is a source of suffering for both the physical environment and for the human psyche, whereas the realisation of the connection between humans and nature holds healing potential for both (Davis, 2011; de Wet, 2007; McCallum, 2005). Ecopsychology seeks to restore this relationship and offers ways to foster healthy human-nature connections that contribute to the well-being of humanity and the planet (van Heyden, 2004). In this chapter, we suggest a theoretical framework in which globalisation, racism, industrialisation, capitalism and other oppressive systems wreak their havoc co-jointly on both the human and natural environment. In understanding these impacts, not only should nature be included in our critique, but it should form part of the methods we use for liberation and restitution.

To study community psychology and ecopsychology in the light of liberation psychology is to commit to the exploration of the profound effects of injustice, violence, and the exploitation of others and nature on psychological, communal, and ecological well-being. It is a commitment to create paths to healing, dynamic peace and reconciliation, justice, and sustainability. It is to share a disdain for industrialism (Kidner, 2012) and the gargantuan profit and power greed endemic of modern societies, producing symptoms of oppression, inequality and alienation, and to hold as a central principle that whatever contributes to small scale, sustainable, social forms and empowerment is good for our psychology and ecology (Roszak, 1992). Within this theoretical framework, empowerment and healing interventions should address the relationships between individuals their communities, society, ecological context, and transpersonal world. The context for such interventions involve self-reflection and conscientisation, dialogue and collaboration, and reorientation of our relationship to the natural world (de Wet, 2007). This ecological relationship is depicted in Fig. 7.1.

Assumptions, Conceptual Logic and Applications of Ecopsychology Through Wilderness Programmes

For ecopsychology to be of meaning to community psychology, the agenda must extend beyond a focus on nature conservation; it must be emancipatory and address social justice concerns of communities as well. This is poignantly articulated by Northcott (2005): "the divine intent to restore desert to fertile land involves also the redemption of the poor, and of other species, from the greed and corruption of the wealthy" (p. 382). The restorative, nourishing, and vitalising effects of time spent in nature are well documented (e.g. Dawson & Russell, 2012; Ryan et al., 2010). These benefits can be utilised in community building initiatives through a range of wilderness based practices and activities, generically termed Wilderness Experiential Programmes (WEPs) (Dawson & Russell, 2012; Glass & Myers, 2001). There is a myriad of terms in the literature for such programmes that share a similar base of principles and approaches (see Zygmont, 2014 for a typology). Nunez (2010) provides a

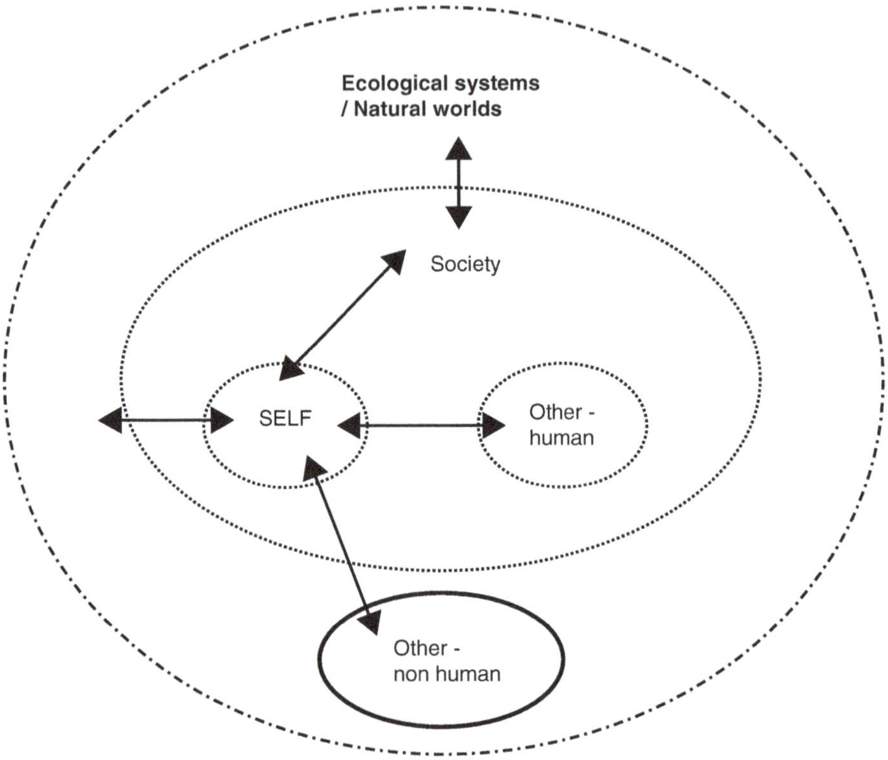

Fig. 7.1 Ecological connection between the self, society and nature (Nunez, 2010)

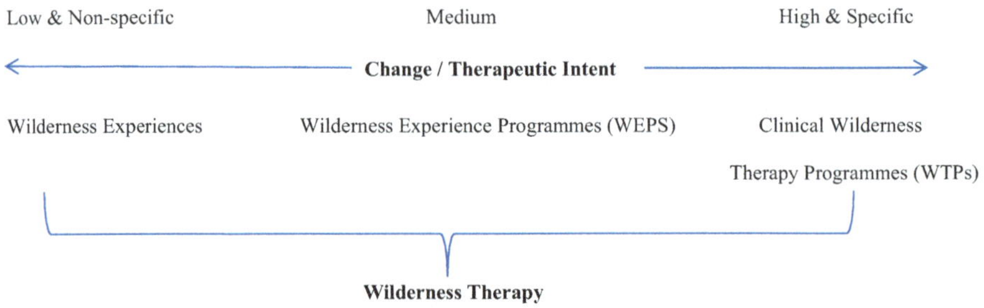

Fig. 7.2 The Wilderness Therapy spectrum (Adapted from Nunez, 2010)

helpful conceptualisation of programmes on a continuum from wilderness experiences to wilderness therapy (see Fig. 7.2 below).

Several elements are universal in all varieties of wilderness therapy:

(a) Immersion in an unfamiliar wilderness or natural environment;
(b) Group living and cooperation with peers;

(c) Individual and group therapy sessions (usually a form of eclectic therapy, i.e. family systems based, cognitive behavioural, and experiential);
(d) Educational curricula—assignment of a variety of mentally and/or physically challenging objectives (including river rafting, hiking and mastery of skills, such as fire-making, survival, and orienteering);
(e) Frequent and intense interactions that usually involve group problem solving and decision making;
(f) Stress and perceived risk;
(g) A non-intrusive, trained leader or facilitator; and
(h) Alone time (solo periods of introspective time for participants to reflect on their lives and to receive insight and inspiration; similar to rites of passage experience practised by cultures throughout the world) (Davis-Berman & Berman, 2008; Gass, 1993; Weston, Tinsley, & O'Dell, 1999).

WEPS provide a flexible methodology for the implementation of learning activities that can be tailored to address a number of values and outcomes important for community development and emancipation. Health promotion is fostered by utilising participation, collaborative problem solving, and critical refection to assist participants in identifying what they do well, applying these strengths towards fulfilling pursuits, developing values such as responsibility and service, and guiding youth to be contributing members of a social community (Benson, 1997; Weissberg & O'Brien, 2004; Zygmont, 2014). WEPs "excel at providing opportunities for youth to engage in healthy relationship building, feel acceptance, and develop socio-emotional competence—assets that are particularly powerful in promoting positive outcomes and disrupting negative outcomes" (Sibthorpe & Morgan, 2011, p. 116). Meta-analyses suggest that WEPs contribute to personal empowerment across a number of dimensions, including improved physical health and body image, academic involvement and performance, family relationships, self-concept and related constructs, social skills and psychosocial competencies, spiritual or moral development, and reductions in clinical concerns (Bowen & Neill, 2013). But their value to liberatory approaches lies in identifying, sourcing, or developing the resources, skills, and knowledge communities need in order to foster self-determination and uncover existing power relations (Speer & Christens, 2014). By building individual capacity, interpersonal commitment, self- and social-awareness, forging trust and social ties among participants, and developing conflict-resolution and other social skills that build a community's "bonding" social capital, WEPs contribute to community competence, a crucial step towards the attainment of social justice (Glass & Benshoff, 2002; Reisch & Garvin, 2016). Wilderness programmes are, however, not traditionally cognizant of how oppressive power relations may be embedded within their structure and practice, and could benefit from ensuring participants are given greater decision-making ability, be guided to select and implement principles for group collaboration, and work on an equal level with programme leaders (Evans & Prilleltensky, 2007).

In South Africa, WEPS have been used with varying success with youth with emotional and behavioural problems, militarised youth (Robertson & De Kiewit, 1998), physically and sexually abused children, children orphaned by HIV-AIDS, homeless people (Robertson, 2000), former military combatants (Schell-Faucon, 2001), and youth referred by the court system (Botha, 2007). WEPS have also been utilised in a range of positive youth development initiatives with community organisations (Benjamin, 2014; Fine & van Niekerk, 2015; Knoetze, 2003; van Heyden, 2004) and school groups (Naidoo, & van Wyk, 2003; Nunez, 2010; Zygmont, 2014).

Processes Invoked for Wilderness Programming

A useful model for understanding the processes invoked in wilderness programming is the Learning Combination Lock (Beard & Wilson, 2006). The model stresses that a number of factors need to be aligned to facilitate different learning outcomes and client or programme needs in experiential learning, including: the context in which learning should take place (including social, political, ideological, and physical), the kind of activity that would most facilitate reflection and growth, which kind of sensory experience is most powerful and memorable, the intended emotional impact of the experience, what kind of emotional processing is required, and what kind of change or transformation is required. A graphical representation of this model is presented in Fig. 7.3.

Learning experiences are sequenced to provide for different types of learning so that outcomes scaffold from awareness through reflection to change and transfer planning (Park, 2004). For example, a WEP programme may begin with a team-based adventure activity whereby each team gets to set arbitrary rules governing the other team's success, leading to emotional reactions against injustice. This could be followed by a politically oriented debrief around the evening camp fire during which power differentials and collective action are reflected on. Debriefs provide a model and valuable experience of engaged communication, self-disclosure and conflict

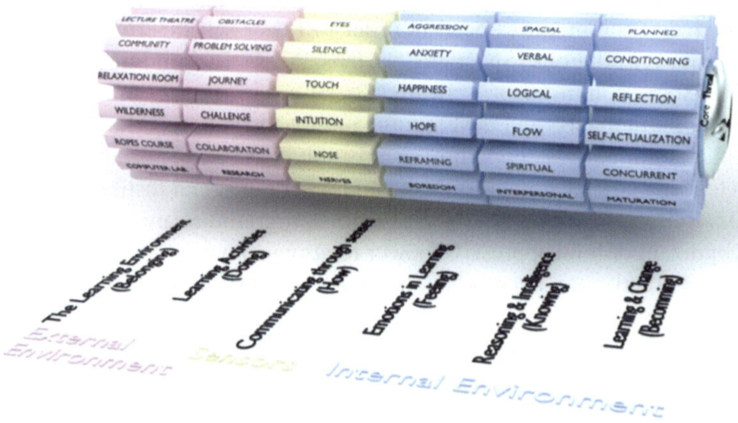

Fig. 7.3 Learning Combination Lock (Wilson & Beard, 2003)

resolution that typically progress through four stages: (a) review and description, (b) identifying patterns and making comparisons, (c) relation to life, and (d) propose solutions and examine values (Hammel, 1993). Finally, the WEP could terminate with a wilderness solo, during which learning is reflected on, consolidated, and self-motivated transfer internalised. Wilderness solos, also called vision quest, provide participants with an opportunity to spend time isolated in a pristine wilderness setting for up to 72 hours free from distractions, which are often experienced as powerful and leading to spiritual growth (Daniel, 2005; Gassner, 2008).

Recent manual publications by Fine and van Niekerk (2015) and Rousseau and Pinnock (2014) provide comprehensive information for utilising wilderness experiential programming in community settings. A community project that demonstrates the implementation of wilderness programmes integrating the above-mentioned values and outcomes for the purpose of CBPAR and development is described next.

The Usiko Project

The Usiko Project commenced as a CBPAR initiative to determine local community intervention priorities in Jamestown, a small peri-urban community in the Stellenbosch district (see Naidoo and van Wyk (2003) and van Wyk and Naidoo (2006) for an overview of this process). In responding to a request for assistance in providing psychological services at the recently opened primary health facility, a community forum meeting was convened, where university staff and students and local community leaders, service providers and staff from the clinic, schools and other non-governmental organisations were able to engage and develop a consensus for a broader engagement in the community. One of the mandates from this initial meeting was to address concerns for the youth in the community. A group of volunteers met regularly and began to evolve a youth development programme that intentionally sought to integrate wilderness based activities into an indigenous rites of passage programme based on local values and cultural considerations (Knoetze, 2003; Pinnock & Douglas-Hamilton, 1998). The development, implementation, evaluation and adaptation of what emerged as the Usiko programme has been documented and described in various studies (see Botha (2007), Fabrik (2004), Knoetze (2003), and Anthonissen (2011) for qualitative evaluations of the programme from the perspective of facilitators, mentors and youth participants; Pinnock and Rossouw (2014) provide a comprehensive manual of the components of the Usiko wilderness programme). Essentially, the Usiko project offers two youth development interventions, one for youth participants at the local high schools and the other a diversion programme for youth referred from the court system (Weston et al., 1999). Adult volunteers from the community are trained as mentors to support the staff and the youth participants in both programmes.

An integral part of the youth development work in which Usiko engages involves the guided exposure of participants to the wilderness (Anthonissen, 2011). Firstly, part of the training for the adult volunteers is conducted in wilderness settings to expose the adult participants to similar programme experiences (tasks, rituals, activities, and challenges) that the youth participants will engage with in the programme. This not only helps with developing strong team building among the adult mentor group, but also provides a connection between adult mentor and youth mentee. Both the school based programme and the diversion programme include two wilderness based activities as key components at the beginning of the programme and the other close to the end of the programme (appropriately called "crossing the threshold"). While programme activities will vary dependent on the specific goals for the programme, the number of participants and which wilderness site and type is selected, the Usiko programmes typically utilise two WEP variations: a base camp programme with all activities located at the particular site, and a hiking expedition programme. For the first wilderness activity, the youth participants are asked to prepare for a 4-day immersion into a remote wilderness setting. Information and instructions are kept deliberately vague, limited to a checklist of what kinds of clothing to bring and what not to bring (contraband, electronic devices, etc.). There is a build-up before the excursion to create a sense of expectation of the unknown. Taking the adolescent away from their everyday environment into a natural setting creates some dissonance. For some it is an escape from the routine, albeit for a short period—an opportunity to tune into a different, tranquil environment rich in metaphor. For others, it is being taken out of their comfort zone and being confronted with the unknown embodied in the wilderness (Anthonissen, 2011). There is a mixture of excitement, uncertainty, risk, and foreboding. In terms of using the wilderness as therapeutic medium, natural settings are rich in symbols and metaphors that can be used effectively in guided activities (Gass, 1993).

At the wilderness site, participants are introduced to the setting and are made aware of ecological principles and practices. They engage in a series of guided therapeutic and challenge-based experiential activities that focus on raising awareness of their environment, developing cohesive relationships amongst the participants and facilitators, and on reflective practice. A solo activity of approximately 8–10 h forms the central activity of the base camp programme. Participants are asked to note their observations of nature around them, and to reflect on some aspect of their life. They may be asked to select an object that symbolises their personal story. Participants in the diversion programme, for instance, are asked to review the circumstances that led to their referral to the diversion programme. This solo experience is thoroughly debriefed in a group session with each participant given an opportunity to reflect on their experience. Invariably, participants link aspects of their observation of nature and their symbolic object to their own narratives (Botha, 2007). For many participants, this may be a unique opportunity to relate their narrative without being judged or criticised. The first wilderness experience serves to connect the participants with nature, with one another and the facilitators, and can offer significant metaphors for the therapy process and for later discussions.

Gass (1993) suggests that the process of internal change in wilderness therapy is facilitated through the utilisation of the physical body. Wilderness therapy engages the whole body in a completely related physical and psychological experience. Ecopsychology recognises that there is an impact on cognition that results from the interaction between the body and the environment. Schell-Faucon (2001) notes that the physical route of the hike and its physical obstacles, challenges and achievements provide a rich metaphor for contemplation and processing.

When wilderness activities and their underlying goals are integrated into a broader community programme, the benefits that accrue extend beyond the individual level of change and empowerment, offering impetus to form collective engagements and actions that are reinforcing of community initiatives. For the Usiko Project, the wilderness based activities have been translated into a rites of passage practice that undergirds a strong sense of community identity and participation for all involved in the work of the project.

Critical Reflection on Wilderness Based Activities in Community Building

In evaluating the application of wilderness experiential activities in the case study, several reflections emerge from the achievements, the challenges, and the lessons learnt in the context. Central in these reflections are the following themes: the rich learning and therapeutic potential of wilderness settings and ecopsychology activities and practices as a component of community development; the CBPAR derivations and enabling practices; embedding wilderness based programmes in larger community projects; building rituals into the WEPs; raising eco-awareness in the community, and addressing gender and power.

The case study alludes to personal, social and broader programme benefits accruing from taking programme participants into wilderness settings away from the demands, distractions, comfort and constraints of their contexts (see Botha, 2007; Knoetze, 2003). The use of experiential learning activities and ecopsychology practices that directly engage the participants with the natural environment (observation exercises, hikes) and allow time for personal introspection (solos, mindfulness walks), and group processing (debriefing) appear to offer strong therapeutic opportunities for participants (Anthonissen, 2011). This allows for personal growth and a deeper level of learning and bonding among participants that impact on group cohesion and commitment to the programme (Knoetze, 2003). When the wilderness activities are linked and integrated into to a broader philosophical framework such as rites of passage or ecoliteracy education, the transfer of the experiences is enhanced. Fabrik (2004) reports that the mentors found the use of ritual to be a powerful component of social bonding and commitment in community practice. Crucial in establishing rituals in this process is the preparatory work as well as the support work after the wilderness experience for the participants. These rituals become important commitment and honouring processes for the individual and the community, representing new locally constructed rites of passage (Somes, 1998).

Significantly, while the Usiko Project utilised different variations of wilderness settings and ecopsychology practices, the actual WEPs used were embedded in a CBPAR approach. Extensive consultations with community residents, service organisations, and external role players and funders preceded the inclusion of the wilderness component as a part of a broader community development project (Lazarus, Bulbulia, Taliep, & Naidoo, 2015). The Usiko project initially used an external service provider before developing and implementing their own methodology for their wilderness processes. This shift came about when the volunteers from the community insisted on having more direct input in the content, values and desired outcomes of the wilderness processes. This helped to indigenise the wilderness intervention and use local expertise from within the community (Lazarus et al., 2015).

Participants also bring the wilderness experience back into their communities in a variety of creative ways. This may find expression in taking up gardening, wanting to set up community gardening and other greening initiatives such as recycling, restoring parks and other green spaces in the neighbourhood (Roos & Temane, 2007). There is an awareness of the link between nature and local ecology that can be taken into further action at an individual and broader level.

Notwithstanding the rich learning canvas that the wilderness and ecopsychology practices can offer, Anthonissen (2011) draws attention to the need to guard against the limiting effects of gender stereotyping in this context and for opening up opportunities for utilising wilderness as a place where gender stereotyping might be challenged. A female mentor in her study related:

> If there are men and women there is always a level of superficiality because it's like masks and certain roles which you still then carry with you. But when it is only women [on the camp] then it feels as if there's a lot more of your .. roles that you have in civilisation or so that you can shake off and can leave and actually just bring the true who you are (Anthonissen, 2011, p. 73).

Pinnock and Rossouw (2014) suggest that wilderness offers the space to be liberated from such stereotypes: "In the wilderness young participants are taken away from places where friends and family have expectations about the ways girls and boys should think of themselves and what they can do and cannot do. Wilderness reduces the hold that these stereotypes have and allows young people to explore themselves and understand how to manage situations differently" (p.11). More attention should be given to the ways in which separate camps are structured and the accompanying practices on wilderness camps that may close down possibilities for utilising wilderness experiences as a means of challenging gender stereotyping. Thus, consideration should be given to using mixed gender youth camps, exploring broader definitions of wilderness, emphasising the nurturing and emotional connectedness of wilderness experience, and using mixed gender leader teams to counter some of the previous WEP gendered practices.

Conclusion

In this chapter, we argue that using wilderness based experiential activities derived from ecopsychology in concert with a CBPAR approach can provide a common liberatory experience for youth and adult participants as an engaged method in community building. The natural wilderness provides an alternative projective space for individual reflection and social bonding that can be linked to programme objectives. These objectives may be linked to engage with participants' unique abilities, developmental challenges (difficulties at home, at school, or with peers; post-school aspirations), and programme outcomes (exposure to nature). When WEP activities are linked to the use of ritual, important elements in social bonding and community practice are reinforced. These rituals become important commitment and honouring processes for the individual and the community, embodying a community sanctioned rites of passage. We have argued that community psychology and ecopsychology have values, goals, resources, and practices that can be aligned and successfully harnessed and applied to address both social and ecological justice goals in this regard. We have presented research indicating the impact of wilderness experiential programmes and activities and how these can be intentionally selected and applied to achieve values and outcomes consonant with emancipatory community psychology. Using the Usiko case study in which ecopsychology, wilderness therapy, and CBPAR were used as frameworks, we have demonstrated how WEPs can be applied towards critical community development project outcomes aimed at fostering confidence, collaboration, and community building and restoring connection, healing, and relationships with self, others, and the natural world, for our collective well-being is inextricably intertwined to the well-being of others and our broader ecological context.

Acknowledgements The Usiko Trust, Usiko Stellenbosch and Stellenbosch University are acknowledged for their contributions to the wilderness work described in the case study. We are also express gratitude to the Jamestown community and the local school personnel who were directly involved in the development and implementation of the wilderness interventions.

References

Anthonissen, L. (2011). *Exploring the influence of gender on how female facilitators of a wilderness programme view "wilderness"*. Unpublished master's thesis, Stellenbosch University, South Africa.

Beard, C., & Wilson, J. (2006). *Experiential learning: A best practice handbook for educators and trainers* (2nd ed.). London: Kogan Page.

Benjamin, L. (2014). *Community counsellors' experiences of trauma and resilience in a low-income community*. Unpublished doctoral dissertation, Stellenbosch University, South Africa.

Benson, P. L. (1997). *All kids are our kids: What communities must do to raise caring and responsible children and adolescents*. San Francisco, CA: Jossey-Bass.

Botha, M. (2007). *Harnessing wilderness in the rehabilitation of adolescent offenders in a diversion programme*. Masters' thesis, Stellenbosch University, Stellenbosch, South Africa.

Bowen, D. J., & Neill, J. T. (2013). A meta-analysis of adventure therapy outcomes and moderators. *The Open Psychology Journal, 6*, 1–38.

Daniel, B. (2005). The significance of a wilderness solo experience. In C. E. Knapp & T. E. Smith (Eds.), *Exploring the power of solo, silence and solitude* (pp. 85–102). Boulder, CO: Association for Experiential Education.

Davis-Berman, J., & Berman, D. (2008). *The promise of wilderness therapy*. Boulder, CO: Association for Experiential Education.

Davis, J. (2011). Ecopsychology, transpersonal, and nonduality. *International Journal of Transpersonal Studies, 30*(1–2), 137–147.
Dawson, C. P., & Russell, K. C. (2012). *Wilderness experience programs: A state-of-the-knowledge summary*. Proceedings of the USDA Forest Service (RMRS-P-66). Retrieved from http://www.fs.fed.us/rm/pubs/rmrs_p066/rmrs_p066_127_133.pdf
de Wet, B. (2007). *Influence of wilderness experience on the adoption of environmentally responsible behaviour*. Unpublished master's thesis, University of Stellenbosch, South Africa.
Durning, A. B. (1990). *Apartheid's environmental toll*. Washington, DC: Worldwatch Institute.
Evans, S. D., & Prilleltensky, I. (2007). Youth and democracy: Participation for personal, relational, and collective well-being. *Journal of Community Psychology, 35*(6), 681–692.
Fabrik, C. (2004). *Reviving a forgotten custom: An evaluation of a community based mentoring intervention-The Jamestown Usiko Youth Project*. Unpublished master's thesis, Stellenbosch University, South Africa.
Fine, N., & van Niekerk, D. (2015). *In the hearts of men: Men changing lives*. Cape Town: Hearts of Men Institute.
Gass, M. A. (1993). Foundations of adventure therapy. In M. A. Gass (Ed.), *Adventure therapy: Therapeutic applications of adventure programming* (pp. 3–10). Dubuque, IO: Kendall/Hunt Publishing.
Gassner, M. (2008). A closer look at course components at Outward Bound Singapore: The solo and final expedition. In A. B. Young, S. Cortland, & J. Sibthorp (Eds.), *Abstracts from the coalition for education in the outdoors: Ninth Biennial Research Symposium* (pp. 80–82). Cortland, NY: State University of New York at Cortland.
Glass, J. S., & Benshoff, J. M. (2002). Facilitating group cohesion among adolescents through challenge course experiences. *Journal of Experiential Education, 25*(2), 268–277.
Glass, J. S., & Myers, J. E. (2001). Combining the old and the new to help adolescents: Individual psychology and adventure-based counseling. *Journal of Mental Health Counseling, 23*(2), 104–114.
Hammel, H. (1993). How to design a debriefing session. In M. A. Gass (Ed.), *Adventure therapy: Therapeutic applications of adventure programming* (pp. 231–238). Dubuque, IO: Kendall/Hunt Publishing.
Kidner, D. W. (2012). *Nature and experience in the culture of delusion*. London: Palgrave MacMillan.
Knoetze, K. (2003). *Crossing the threshold: Evaluation of a rites of passage programme in a peri-urban South African community*. Unpublished master's thesis, Stellenbosch University, South Africa.
Lazarus, S., Bulbulia, S., Taliep, N., & Naidoo, A. V. (2015). Community-based participatory research as a critical enactment of community psychology. *Journal of Community Psychology, 43*(1), 87–98.
McCallum, I. (2005). *Ecological intelligence: Rediscovering ourselves in nature*. Cape Town: Africa Geographic.
Naidoo, A. V., & Van Wyk, S. B. (2003). Intervening in communities: Combining curative and preventive interventions. *Journal of Prevention and Intervention in the Community, 25*(1), 65–80.
Nelson, G., & Prilleltensky, I. (2010). *Community psychology: In pursuit of liberation and well-being* (2nd ed.). London: Palgrave Macmillan.
Northcott, M. S. (2005). Wilderness, religion and ecological restoration in the Scottish highlands. *Ecotheology, 10*(3), 382–399.
Nunez, C. (2010). *The outcomes of a wilderness experience programme on the resilience and psychological adjustment of South African adolescents*. Unpublished master's thesis, University of KwaZulu-Natal, South Africa.
Park, N. (2004). Character strengths and positive youth development. *The Annals of the American Academy of Political and Social Science, 591*, 40–54.
Pinnock, D., & Douglas-Hamilton, M. (1998). Rites, rituals, and tradition: Rethinking youth programs in South Africa. In K. Hazlehurst & C. Hazlehurst (Eds.), *Gangs and youth subcultures: International explorations* (pp. 307–341). New Brunswick, NJ: Transaction Publishers.
Pinnock, D., & Rossouw, E. (2014). *Wild resilience*. Cape Town: African Sun Press.

Pretorius-Heuchert, J. W., & Ahmed, R. (2001). Community psychology: Past, present, and future. In M. Seedat (Ed.), *Community psychology: Theory, method and practice* (pp. 17–33). Cape Town: Oxford University Press.

Reisch, M., & Garvin, C. D. (2016). *Social work and social justice: Concepts, challenges, and strategies*. New York, NY: Oxford University Press.

Riemer, M. (2010). Community psychology, the natural environment, and global climate change. In G. Nelson & I. Prilleltensky (Eds.), *Community psychology: In pursuit of liberation and well-being* (2nd ed., pp. 498–516). London: Palgrave Macmillan.

Robertson, G. (2000). *Wilderness therapy in South Africa: The development of community-based projects*. Paper presented at the Association for Experiential Education 28th International Conference, Tucson, Arizona.

Robertson, G., & De Kiewit, S. (1998). Wilderness therapy with militarised youths in traumatised communities. *Journal of Social Development in Africa, 13*(1), 53–58.

Roos, V., & Temane, M. (2007). Community competence. In N. Duncan, B. Bowman, A. Naidoo, J. Pillay, & V. Roos (Eds.), *Community psychology: Analysis, context and action* (pp. 280–292). Cape Town: UCT Press.

Roszak, T. (1992). *The voice of the earth: An exploration of ecopsychology*. New York, NY: Simon & Schuster.

Rousseau, E., & Pinnock, D. (2014). *Wild resilience: Working with high-risk adolescents using wilderness, ritual and mentorship*. Cape Town: African Sun.

Ryan, R. M., Weinstein, N., Bernstein, J., Brown, K. W., Mistretta, L., & Gagné, M. (2010). Vitalising effects of being outdoors and in nature. *Journal of Environmental Psychology, 30*(2), 159–168.

Schell-Faucon, S. (2001). *Journey into the inner self and encounter with the other: Transformation trails with militarised youths of opposing groups*. Research report for the Centre for the Study of Violence and Reconciliation, Johannesburg, South Africa.

Scull, J. (1999). *Ecopsychology: Where does it fit in psychology*? Paper presented at the Annual Psychology Conference, Malaspina University College, USA.

Sibthorpe, J., & Morgan, C. (2011). Adventure-based programming: Exemplary youth development practice. *New Directions for Youth Development, 130*, 105–119.

Somes, M. P. (1998). *The healing wisdom of Africa: Finding life purpose through nature, ritual and community*. New York, NY: Putnam.

Speer, P. W., & Christens, B. D. (2014). Organizational and community capacity building. In V. C. Scott & S. M. Wolfe (Eds.), *Community psychology: Foundations for practice* (pp. 220–236). Thousand Oaks, CA: SAGE Publications.

Steyn, P. (2005). The lingering environmental impact of repressive governance: The environmental legacy of the apartheid era for the new South Africa. *Globalizations, 2*(3), 391–402.

van Heyden, Y. (2004). *An exploratory study of the use of metaphor in the practice of ecotherapy*. Unpublished master's thesis, Stellenbosch University, South Africa.

Van Wyk, S. B., & Naidoo, A. V. (2006). Broadening mental health services to disadvantaged communities in South Africa. *Journal of Psychology in Africa, 2*, 273–282.

Watkins, M., & Ciofalo, N. (2011). Creating and sharing critical community psychology curriculum for the 21st century: An invitation. *Global Journal of Community Psychology Practice, 2*(2), 9–18.

Weissberg, R. P., & O'Brien, M. U. (2004). What works in school-based social and emotional learning programs for positive youth development. *The Annals of the American Academy of Political and Social Science, 591*, 86–97.

Weston, R., Tinsley, H. E. A., & O'Dell, I. (1999). Wilderness adventure therapy for at-risk youth. *Parks & Recreation, 34*(7), 30–39.

Wilson, J. P., & Beard, C. (2003). The learning combination lock – An experiential approach to learning design. *Journal of European Industrial Training, 27*(2/3/4), 88–97. Doi:10.1108/03090590310468912

Zygmont, C. S. (2014). *A phenomenographical study of the qualitative variation of adventure/wilderness programme experiences among adolescents high school participants in the Western Cape*. Unpublished doctoral dissertation, Stellenbosch University, South Africa.

Chapter 8
Creative Responses to Social Suffering: Using Community Arts and Cultural Development to Foster Hope

Christopher C. Sonn, Pilar Kasat, and Amy F. Quayle

In this chapter, we draw on a collaborative community engagement and research relationship between the Community Arts Network (CAN) of Western Australia and Victoria University Melbourne that has been sustained over a period of more than 10 years. Christopher Sonn and more recently, Amy Quayle, have partnered CAN as "participant conceptualisers" (Elias, 1994) undertaking different roles, including putting in place evaluation frameworks, running workshops on intercultural work, and documenting and examining different projects. While there are different members of CAN who have been involved, Pilar Kasat (the Managing Director of CAN at the time of writing this chapter), has been a central actor in linking the University, CAN, and communities and strengthening the research outputs for CAN's work, and she was the practitioner researcher in the case study featured here. This chapter introduces Community Arts and Cultural Development[1] (CACD) and discuss this approach to working with communities, with reference to the liberation paradigm. We then describe a case study based on research undertaken by Kasat (2013), the Narrogin Stories, as an example of community engagement through the arts (see also Kasat, 2014). We also include some reflections from CAN staff member Geri

[1]Community cultural development, community arts and community-based arts are often used interchangeably in the literature. In this article, we use Community Arts and Cultural Development (CACD). The Australia Council for the Arts uses this more encompassing term.

C.C. Sonn (✉) • A.F. Quayle
College of Health and Biomedicine, Victoria University, Melbourne, VIC, Australia
e-mail: Christopher.sonn@vu.edu.au; Amy.quayle@live.vu.edu.au

P. Kasat
Sustainability Policy Institute, Curtin University, Perth, WA, Australia
e-mail: Pilar.kasat@postgrad.curtin.edu.au

M. Seedat et al. (eds.), *Emancipatory and Participatory Methodologies in Peace, Critical, and Community Psychology*, Peace Psychology Book Series,
DOI 10.1007/978-3-319-63489-0_8

about CAN's engagement with the Noongar community of Narrogin, collected more recently as part of Amy Quayle's doctoral research.[2]

The use of arts to promote social change through activist research and practice is not a new phenomenon. Finley (2005) has noted that arts-based inquiry is one approach within the broader field of qualitative inquiry that "surfaced in the context of a reflexive turn that marked the social sciences, philosophy and literary criticism, science, education, and the arts, and it is evidenced in particular by the narrative turn in sociological discourse" (p. 682). The turn to narrative, as part of the broader cultural and linguistic turn, has brought into clearer focus the need to understand human action in sociocultural and historically situated contexts (Gergen & Gergen, 2010). Within this approach there is a focus on stories as a means to understand self, others, and the social world (Bruner, 1991; Gergen & Gergen, 2010; Rappaport, 1995) because individuals evolve in "relationship with a rich local environment of discourse, culture and custom" (Watkins & Shulman, 2008, p. 233).

Arts have been used to foster social inclusion in educational contexts (e.g. Chappell & Chappell, 2016), to explore place and the sociopolitical process of place making (e.g. Schuermans, Loopmans, & Vandenabeele, 2012), to raise awareness about the effects of stigma and racism (e.g. Sonn, Quayle, Belanji, & Baker, 2015), and to improve mental health and well-being (e.g. Price, 2008; Thiele & Marsden, 2008). Bell and Desai (2011, see also Stein & Faigin, 2015) sought to connect arts with social justice pedagogy. They argued that: "The arts can help us remember, imagine, create, and transform the practices that sustain oppression as it endures across history and locality" (p. 288). We (see for example Kasat, 2013; Sonn & Baker, 2016; Sonn & Quayle, 2014; Quayle, Sonn, & Kasat, 2016) have examined CACD as a method of community engagement within a broader approach informed by community and liberation psychologies, and decolonising methodologies (Smith, 1999).

CACD and the Liberation Paradigm

CACD can be viewed as a global movement to foster pluralism, participation, and equity in cultural life (Adams & Goldbard, 2002). CACD practice is intentionally inclusive, participatory, creative and strengths-based, as it aims to draw "out taken for granted knowledge and the future aspirations of a community ... in order to express, preserve or enhance that community's culture" (Sonn, Drew, & Kasat, 2002, p. 12). The creative means can include a range of visual, theatrical, and textual arts forms. In CACD work:

> community artists ... use their artists and organizational skills to serve the emancipation and development of a community, whether defined by geography (e.g., a neighborhood), a common interest (e.g., members of a union) or identity (e.g., members of an indigenous group (Adams & Goldbard, 2002, p. 8).

---

[2]This research is focused on CAN's Bush Baby project in Narrogin.

The writing of two Brazilians, philosopher and educator Paolo Freire (1970, 1985), and theatre practitioner, Augusto Boal (1979, 1998) has played an influential role in the development of CACD worldwide (Kasat, 2013). Along with other liberation-oriented scholars (e.g. Dussell, 1985, Martín Baró, 1994), the work of Freire and Boal was explicitly concerned with liberating humanity from oppression through participatory processes and critical engagement aimed at conscientisation, that is, the process of people developing a deeper awareness of their social realities and critical capacities to transform their lifeworlds (Freire, 1970).

These ideas have also been central in writing on psychologies of liberation (Martín-Baró, 1994; Montero & Sonn, 2009; Montero, Sonn, & Burton, 2017; Watkins & Shulman, 2008). Watkins and Shulman (2008) noted that psychologies of liberation are oriented to nurturing "an imagination of alternative ways of thinking and acting together" (p. 3), to address psychological suffering, and we would add social suffering, a notion that "draws attention to the lived experience of inhabiting social structures of oppression: and the pain that arises from this" (Frost & Hoggett, 2008, p. 441). Liberation-focused approaches emphasise the standpoint of those who are excluded, oppressed, and marginalised. Critically engaging from this standpoint provides new insights into the workings of power and dynamics of oppression (Montero et al., 2017; Quayle et al., 2016).

Participation is understood as central to liberation (Freire, 1970; Montero, 2009). For Montero (2009), "Participation empowers the people and is also directed towards their conscientisation" (p. 76). The emancipative character of participation is:

> evidenced in its capacity to empower participants, strengthening their resources and developing their ability to acquire new resources and redefine themselves as able citizens with rights and duties, and the capacity to defend their achievements and demand what is due to them (Montero, 2009, p. 76).

Another central feature of liberation oriented approaches and decolonising methodologies is the importance placed on cultural practice (Montero et al., 2016; Reyes Cruz & Sonn, 2011; Smith, 1999). Anchored in a critical narrative ontology in which stories are vital to processes of deconstruction, reconstruction, and liberation (Freire, 1970), critically engaging with cultural resources and practice is conceptualised as a means of examining and challenging power and affirming devalued social identities. Therefore, as expressed by Thomas and Rappaport (1996), community arts and cultural practice "are about claiming ones right to tell existing stories about self and community and to create new ones. They are about reclaiming a history and filling in a past that helps to make a whole person" (p. 330). For Martin (2007), writing from an Indigenous[3] standpoint, "stories have power and give power" (p. 46).

[3] Following protocol, we deliberately capitalise the word "Indigenous" to refer specifically to Australian Aboriginal and Torres Strait Islander peoples; 'indigenous' refers to any 'indigenous' person from any part of the world.

> Stories are our law. Stories give identity as they connect us and fulfil our sense of belonging. Stories are grounding, defining, comforting and embracing. Stories vary in their purpose and content and so Stories can be political and yet equally healing. They can be shared verbally, physically or visually. Their meanings and messages teach, admonish, tease, celebrate, entertain, provoke and challenge (p.45).

In the next section, drawing on case study research undertaken by Kasat (2013), we describe a CACD project, to illustrate the practice, including the various processes of consultation and negotiation, the collection and re-articulation of individual and group stories through creative output, and the production and staging of a soundscape to facilitate the process of creating an alternative community narrative to foster hope.

The Narrogin Stories

The Narrogin Stories project was undertaken by CAN with Noongar[4] people in the Wheatbelt town of Narrogin in 2009–2010. At the time this project was undertaken 40% of CAN employees were Noongar.[5] We describe the process of community engagement that was aimed at establishing relationships with members of the Noongar community, and how the creative process evolved. We hope to illustrate CACD as a community-based praxis of critical engagement, focusing specifically on its application within a context marked by racialised power relations and community trauma. The Narrogin Stories project also demonstrates how arts and cultural practice can surface untold stories, which in this case, enabled the Noongar community, facilitated by CAN, to begin a process of transforming a community narrative of loss, pain, and feuding to one of hope.

The Narrogin Context

Narrogin is situated 190 km southeast of Perth. At the time of the 2011 census, Narrogin had an estimated population of 4219 (ABS, 2011). This included 394 Indigenous people with most identifying as Aboriginal; therefore 9.3% of the overall population was Indigenous (compared to 3% nationally; ABS, 2011). Tragically, in 2008 there was a spate of youth suicides with six young Noongar men from Narrogin dying by suicide. In the following year, reflective of high levels of community distress, family feuds ensued, which exacerbated an already complex and delicate community situation. Consistent with the intense media coverage that

---

[4] Noongar people are the original inhabitants of the southwest corner of Western Australia.

[5] When referring to CAN staff in the Narrogin Stories case study (which spans approximately 18 months), it refers mainly to the lead community artist Catherine Simmonds, Aboriginal personnel Frank Walsh and later Geri Hayden, and Pilar Kasat.

Aboriginal violence attracts (Cripps, 2010), the Noongar community of Narrogin featured in mainstream media, including in Australian Broadcasting Corporation primetime news bulletins in September and November 2009. This was very negative media publicity for the Narrogin Noongar community.

Since 2006, CAN had developed a presence in the Wheatbelt region, delivering a number of successful CACD projects with local Noongar people across the Wheatbelt (see Sonn & Quayle, 2014). In early 2009, in response to the suicides, CAN was approached by a local government organisation to work with the community. Before proceeding, CAN recognised the need to carefully evaluate its capacity to work with the complexities surrounding the Narrogin Noongar community and to ascertain whether CAN's presence was wanted in the town.

Laying Foundations: Forming Relationships and Generating Trust

CACD methods as practiced by CAN staff demands the investment of time and resources to learn about the dynamics of the community, form relationships, and generate trust before embarking on any project. Lewis and Weigert (1985) have argued that trust is multifaceted; it includes behavioural, cognitive, and emotional aspects that "are merged into unitary social experience" (p. 969). In their view "the bases on which trust rests are primarily social…. This raises the question of how trust in other persons and institutions is established, maintained, and when necessary, restored" (p. 969).

CAN brought to bear some existing relationships and networks in the Wheatbelt, across the Noongar community, and within relevant government organisations in Narrogin. CAN began by getting to know some of the key people, such as Elders[6] and community leaders, and cultivating relationships amongst key family groups. It was important to ensure that the information gathered came from different perspectives and included individuals from the different feuding families. The process of building relationships across the community required a sensitive and culturally appropriate approach. These informal discussions enabled CAN to develop an understanding of community dynamics, leading to more targeted contact with Elders, Noongar leaders, and other local organisations, such as the local government, the schools, and the police.

These extensive conversations took approximately eight months. During this time, CAN staff learned about the complex issues and circumstances affecting the Noongar community; issues consistent with the recognised social and economic disadvantage experienced by Aboriginal people across Australia. These issues included racism, lack of employment opportunities, poverty, low levels of formal education, poor health, substance abuse and family feuds which have been

[6]The word 'Elders' is written with a capital letter as a mark of respect.

understood through the lens of lateral violence, reflecting community trauma (Australian Human Rights Commission, 2011; Steering Committee for the Review of Government Services Provision, 2014). Given the fragility of the Noongar community at this time, CAN monitored the mood of the community very closely.

A significant moment occurred during this consultation process when representatives from the feuding families requested that CAN act as a mediator between these families. This invitation was taken as a sign that trust had been developed and, importantly, that the families were open to dialogue. CAN declined a mediating role, as this is not within the skill set of CAN staff; however, they agreed to a face-to-face meeting with representatives from the two feuding families. This meeting was considered an important opportunity and a step forward towards dialogue.

The meeting was very difficult. Representatives from both families voiced their frustration and despair with each other, but it was also clear that those present recognised that the family feuding was damaging the community. The question: "Who benefits from this family feuding?" led to a breakthrough moment. Representatives from both families stated that the feuding was negatively impacting their children and expressed a desire for it to end. This *naming* signified common ground. This meeting was significant—CAN had gained *permission* from key Noongar leaders to begin a process of consultation and engagement in Narrogin.

The Building Blocks: Engaging the Right People and Developing an Idea

Next, CAN employed a cultural worker, Geri Hayden, a Noongar woman who had lived and worked in Narrogin for over 10 years, to be based in Narrogin. This position was understood as crucial to the success or failure of CACD projects; the employee needed to demonstrate leadership, understanding, and the ability to work and communicate with and across all the families in an impartial way.

A community artist was also recruited to develop a project that would help to transform the current community narrative of pain, suicide, and violence. Catherine Simmonds, a non-indigenous theatre practitioner with extensive experience working with diverse communities, including Aboriginal communities, refugees, and trafficked women, was employed. Her task was to facilitate a creative process that would help the voicing of a new narrative from, by, and for the community.

Catherine suggested the development of a soundscape, an audio-collection of community stories. The intention was to capture many individual voices to produce a collective community narrative that could inspire a longer-term process of healing within the community. The process for producing the soundscape was very inclusive and accessible; everyone had the opportunity to participate without feeling intimidated or too self-conscious. The process did not demand specific skills, but privileged the stories of each participant.

Developing the Soundscape

The development of the soundscape began with Geri taking Catherine around town to meet, sit and talk with Noongar people. Meetings were spontaneously arranged as they saw people on the streets or visited families in their homes. Most conversations took place in people's living rooms, sitting around kitchen tables and with small groups in the bush. As discussed by Geri, "we went around to every household in Narrogin and we sat with every woman, child, young man, Elder and asked questions". People were invited to speak openly and honestly about what was happening in the community. The conflict and the family feuding had to be central to the conversation because this was the issue. These conversations happened over a period of approximately 10 days, and all conversations were recorded. The stories shared centred around experiences of discrimination, difficulty in finding work, and significantly, the desire for the family feud to end. As noted by Geri in an interview, they kept hearing the same thing, which was:

> We want to get on with life. We want our kids to be happy. We want our kids to grow up ... This needs to stop and the only way it can happen is, we gotta make these changes ourselves for our kids.

It was evident that people were yearning for opportunities to heal. As reported by Kasat (2013), one of the Elders commented:

> People need to sit down to talk about it. The womans have to sit down and get together and say how they are gonna handle anything. The mens gotta sit down and say what they gonna do. Instead of saying let's go fight one another. We gotta say 'no we don't wanna fight all our life' (p. 59).

A younger woman said:

> At the end of the day I want peace, I want it for our kids. Narrogin, everyone is a family, we all grew up together. There comes a time when you have to let it all go. If you don't forgive yourself and others you're putting yourself in a dark hole. The whole town's getting dark. If your heart forgives all the darkness goes away top to toe (p. 59).

The process of engaging the Noongar community and talking with them about their feelings and hopes helped to form relationships and build trust. The simple act of taking the time to sit down and talk, also enhanced facilitators' understanding of what was happening in the town, and provided a means to gauge community interest in participating in CACD activities. Importantly, the engagement also yielded resources from the community that would be central to developing an artistic vision for the soundscape and a community celebration.

The Creative Process: From Informal Conversations to a Community Soundscape These informal conversations with Noongar Elders, men, women, and children resulted in hours of recorded material to be used for the creation of the community soundscape. Particular attention was paid to ensure that there were even numbers recorded between the feuding families, ensuring equanimity was paramount. Similar to the initial stages of qualitative data analysis, the recorded

Table 8.1 Themes identified in the stories shared

Theme	Example
Family, culture and community	'We used to all go out together as a mob, didn't matter what family you were from we was joking and laughing'
	'People were sharing meals together, singing together laughing together'
	'Used to have that fire going, put that damper in'
Sense of loss, hurt and forgiveness	'We need time to recover and heal'
	'There is a time to let go and move on'
	'If your heart forgives the darkness goes away top to toe'
	'Walk away say I forgive you'
Hope for the future	'At the end of the day, I want peace; I want it for our kids'
	'Makes you feel good, taking little steps towards a better future for everyone in this town'
	'Nurture our land and nurture our people'
	'I want my kids to be free, play with who they want to play with'

conversations were transcribed verbatim. Following this step, the creative team, including the artists and Noongar cultural worker, selected dozens of direct quotations that could be used to form the soundscape. Geri's input and cultural guidance was crucial during this process. She knew what material could be used and what might have been damaging if shared in public. Every participant's voice had to be included in the soundscape because it needed to be a representation of the many voices of the Noongar community.

Composing the soundscape was a delicate process. It needed to acknowledge what was happening in the community, and also to emphasise possibilities for hope and healing. There were stories full of heartbreak, as well as witty and funny stories. Some stories were a declaration of remorse, some admissions of wrongdoing, and others were memories of rich and evocative descriptions of Noongar cultural life, including of laughter and connectedness. A number of themes were constructed based on the direct quotations. The themes of moort (community) and katijin (cultural knowledge) (see Collard, 2007) have been identified as two defining elements in Noongar cosmology[7] and were evident in the conversations, as captured in the first theme of *family, culture, and community*. The other themes were *sense of loss, hurt and forgiveness* and *hope for the future* (see Table 8.1), with hope often symbolised by the next generation—the children.

Based on these identified themes, the soundscape was developed to echo the community's story, and inspire a longer-term process of creating a new community narrative. All voices recorded were represented in the final product. Geri, Catherine, and Pilar developed the final composition, a musician composed original music based on the recordings, and a filmmaker supplied local footage of Narrogin and associated landscapes. Along with an editor, Catherine and Pilar worked on the visual component of the soundscape. The purpose of the visual component was to

[7] The third being boodjar (country).

Table 8.2 Creative components emerging from the stories

Creative component	Example
Playing cards	'When are you fellas gonna sit around play cards and have a yarn?'
Turning the light back on	'It's about turning the light back on in Narrogin and encouraging people to come back home'
Fire, family and food	'A paddock lit up at night with the fire of the mallee roots burning- yeah lovely'

accompany the recording to support the "listening" of the soundscape at a public launch.

A number of creative components were produced to symbolise the stories and accentuate the soundscape. These components were ultimately incorporated into the launch and are displayed in Table 8.2, with examples of what community members said.

The next part of the project was organising a public event where the community could come together to listen to their collective narrative that was embodied in the soundscape.

A Community Celebration: Turning the Light Back on in Narrogin

After many months of tension, it was considered important that the Narrogin Noongar community had an opportunity to come together to listen to their collective voice in the form of the soundscape, and to celebrate the culmination of other community arts projects that were conducted alongside the Narrogin Stories project. These projects attracted positive media coverage in print, on-line, and television. Therefore, a public launch and community celebration of Narrogin Stories was planned. The positive media reports, alongside the encouraging reaction from the Noongar community, generated high expectations for the community celebration. At the same time, CAN also recognised the potential risks involved.

Negotiating the Risk of Sharing Painful Stories CAN recognised that this event could be the beginning of a healing journey for the community, where the narrative of loss, pain, and feuding could begin to shift. At the same time, there were risks involved, as the soundscape could be a reminder of the community's grief and feuds. It could exacerbate an already volatile community situation, create a bigger rift between the feuding families, and open up wounds the agency was not capable of containing or dealing with. Further, it could destroy all the positive work done previously and risk CAN's relationships within the community and with the funding bodies.

The process of consultation and engagement that CAN had engaged in, the expressed desire of the Noongar community to move forward, and the fact that the community was coming together in celebration of other community arts projects, gave CAN some assurance about the public launch and the public airing of the soundscape. Importantly, however, CAN also had to trust the community that the night would not end in a feud. Based on this, and following advice from Noongar leaders, the decision was made to proceed and go ahead with the public gathering where the soundscape would be the central component.

The Creative Components As the symbolic and literal representation of the community's voices, the soundscape was the cornerstone of the launch. A set of *playing cards* containing some of the most poignant and hopeful quotations were designed and printed for each family to take home after the event as a reminder of the night and their own voices. The playing cards were to be enduring objects, a link for people to a good time and a reminder of the possibilities they had identified.

A second community artist was engaged to assist in decorating the venue for the launch, to symbolise *turning the light back on in Narrogin*. Together, the artists generated the idea to re-create the geographical location of Narrogin as a valley—to represent their boodjar (country), which is the third defining element of Noongar cosmology (Collard, 2007). This was achieved through cane and cloth, which was placed in the centre of a room. Tables and chairs where the audience sat were located around this centrepiece. The surrounding towns were represented by creating tissue paper lanterns in the shape of little houses positioned on plinths. Each table had a paper lantern on it. When the soundscape was played, the children were invited to light a candle located inside the paper lanterns. The fluorescent lights were turned off so that the soundscape could be heard under the soft candlelight (Narrogin Stories soundscape: https://vimeo.com/14440975) (Fig. 8.1).

The final aspect, *fire, family and food*, was embodied in the sharing of kangaroo meat the men had hunted and the women had cooked. Everyone gathered to share food around the fire, and watched two local Noongar men perform a traditional dance, that they taught the children.

To lighten up the evening, and increase the likelihood of strong Noongar attendance, CAN secured Mary G a character created by Mark Bin Bakar, an Indigenous Australian comedian and musician, to be the MC. Mary G has a big following amongst Aboriginal people in Australia. Mary G played a vital role in preparing the community to listen to the soundscape using humour.

Reflections on Narrogin Stories: "To See the Way They Were Tonight, It Blew Me Away"

Over 230 Noongar men, women, and children and a few non-indigenous people packed the John Higgins Centre in Narrogin for the launch. Kasat (2013) noted that, "The atmosphere was truly extraordinary. People laughed and people cried. I have never felt so humble and so proud of the work I do. That evening was so meaningful; I truly felt we had made a difference" (p. 68). Other comments reported by Kasat (2013), which captured the success of the evening, are provided below:

Fig. 8.1 Children and lanterns (Photographer: Bo Wong)

> This is tremendous; to see all the Noongars together like this. It just blew me away. That's why I become a bit emotional. Last time I came up here they were so split. But tonight seeing the faces of all the people who were so against each other and seeing their children all mixing up on the floor. To see the way they were tonight, it blew me away (Noongar Elder, p. 69–70).

> We have had so many issues in relation to feuding and anti-social behaviour issues in Narrogin over the past 12–18 months, it has been systemic. It's good to see that these people are coming together as a collective, and they are actually working together (Representative of Narrogin Police, p. 70).

> I know I am going to cry all the way to Perth, because just to see so many Noongars in one place, and they prove they can actually be in one place and enjoy themselves and their kids can be happy (CAN WA's Aboriginal Arts and Cultural Development Coordinator; p. 70).

> I think it's giving people a voice and empowering people, and allowing people to see that they are worth something, that they do have value and that they can contribute to other things (Mark Bin Bakar, p. 70).

Emerging Principles for Practice

The Narrogin stories project is an example of CACD practice that supported the Noongar community of Narrogin to begin a longer-term process of transforming the community narrative of loss, pain, and feuding to one of hope. There was an expressed desire from the Noongar community to start to build a better future for their children.

This project enabled CAN to build a solid foundation for future work with the Noongar community of Narrogin; a difficult context marked by social suffering.

Reflecting on the significance of the Narrogin stories project in CAN's engagement in Narrogin, Geri commented:

> I think it started from that because Noongars seen that CAN WA was for real. ..., those projects touched the ground ..., the projects were hands-on and kids were getting involved and parents were getting involved. And it's - I don't know - it's just - for the first time, I saw arts from another perspective.

Since this time, CAN has delivered a number of other projects that were specifically focused on Rekindling Stories on country—creating opportunities for cultural transmission and intergenerational dialogue, as well as sharing Noongar history, culture, and perspectives with a broader audience.

This case study illustrates some important, seldom documented, processes involved in CACD, including building understanding of the local community context, developing trust, and creating safe spaces for people to tell their own stories and be heard, as well as for cultural practice and enactment (Montero et al., 2017). Arts provided a safe vehicle to express private pain and hope. These experiences are recognised and acknowledged and shared through public expression and the opportunity for communal witnessing.

Enduring structural change to reduce oppression and the community trauma and violence it produces is not once and for all resolved. Yet it is vital to invest in building relationships within communities in contexts with colonial histories, and where there is continuing asymmetrical power relationships. Laying the foundations for action that can enable the community's stories of hope to creatively emerge requires:

- Knowledge and understanding of community histories and the dynamics of power and privilege;
- Practices for building relationships and trust, including deep listening, centering Aboriginal knowledge and perspectives, and constant questioning of one's own identities and assumptions;
- Creating settings that are safe for storytelling and witnessing, and often this involves being flexible and patient;
- Building skills and sharing resources for individual and community self-expression; and
- Adequate investment of financial resources to ensure the production of high quality arts and cultural outcomes.

Conclusion

CACD is a creative methodology that has been effectively used to foster community engagement and participation in a range of contexts. Typically, CACD focuses on bringing people together to foster connections within and between communities. Arts processes and products are central to making visible the pain produced by a history of colonialism and ongoing racism and for generating and reclaiming cultural stories that are important for restoring and fostering individual and community well-being. As noted by Montero et al. (2017), culture and cultural enactment has to be taken into account in liberation oriented work as "culture stores the past, constructs the present", (p. 27) and lays the foundation for the future.

Cultural practice is central to the process of healing, construction, and reconstruction. As praxis, CACD is not wedded to rigid procedures. Instead, it is committed to hearing, witnessing, and responding according to contextual demands and particularities (Montero, 2012). As Sarason (2004) noted about interventions (and we include CACD), they "... are messy, frustrating, patience demanding, nonlinear, and mistake-making affairs. That is the nature of the process in our very real social–interpersonal world" (p. 275). It is imperative to keep CACD's critical roots in focus, and for those who practice CACD, to remain vigilant and attend to the questions: for whom and on whose terms is the work being produced, and in whose modes of knowing and doing are the creative and cultural processes responding to oppression. Remaining faithful in this manner to the liberation paradigm, CACD can enable communities to articulate hope for the future and, in doing so, lay foundations for community building.

References

Adams, D., & Goldbard, A. (2002). *Community, culture and globalisation*. New York, NY: The Rockfeller Foundation.

Australian Bureau of Statistics. (2011). *2011 Census QuickStats: Narrogin (T)*. Retrieved from http://www.censusdata.abs.gov.au/census_services/getproduct/census/2011/quickstat/LGA56520?opendocument&navpos=220

Australian Human Rights Commission. (2011). *Social justice report 2011: Aboriginal and Torres Strait Islander Social Justice Commissioner*. Retrieved from www.humanrights.gov.au/social_justice/sj_report/sjreport11/index.html

Bell, L. A., & Desai, D. (2011). Imagining otherwise: Connecting the arts and social justice to envision and act for change: Special issue introduction. *Equity & Excellence in Education, 44*(3), 287–295.

Boal, A. (1979). *Theatre of the oppressed* (C.A. McBride & M. Leal Mc Bride, Trans.). New York, NY: Theatre Communications Group. (Original work published 1974).

Boal, A. (1998). *Legislative theatre: Using performance to make politics* (A. Jackson, Trans.). New York, NY: Routledge.

Bruner, J. (1991). The narrative construction of reality. *Critical Inquiry, 18*(1), 1–21.

Chappell, S. V., & Chappell, D. (2016). Building social inclusion through critical arts-based pedagogies in university classroom communities. *International Journal of Inclusive Education, 20*(3), 292–308.

Collard, L. (2007). Wangkiny Ngulluck Nyungar Nyittiny, Boodjar, Moort and Katitjin: Talking about creation, country, family and knowledge of the Nyungar of south-western Australia. In S. Morgan, T. Mia, & B. Kwaylullina (Eds.), *Speaking from the heart: Stories of life, family and country* (pp. 279–297). Fremantle, WA: Fremantle Arts Centre Press.

Cripps, K. (2010). Indigenous family violence: Pathways forward. In N. Purdie, P. Dudgeon, & R. Walker (Eds.), *Working together: Aboriginal and Torres Strait Islander mental health and wellbeing: Principles and practice* (pp. 145–154). Barton, ACT: Commonwealth of Australia.

Dussell, E. (1985). *Philosophy of liberation* (A. Martinez & C. Morkovsky Trans.). Eugene, OR: Wipf and Stock.

Elias, M. J. (1994). Capturing excellence in applied settings: A participant conceptualizer and praxis explicator role for community psychologists. *American Journal of Community Psychology, 22*, 293–318.

Finley, S. (2005). Arts-based inquiry: Performing revolutionary pedagogy. In N. K. Denzin & Y. S. Lincoln (Eds.), *The Sage handbook of qualitative research* (pp. 681–695). Thousand Oaks, CA: Sage.

Freire, P. (1970). *Pedagogy of the oppressed* (M. Bergman Ramos, Trans.). New York, NY: Continuum.

Freire, P. (1985). *The politics of education*. (D. Macedo, Trans.). Westport, CT: Bergin & Garvey.

Frost, L., & Hoggett, P. (2008). Human agency and social suffering. *Critical Social Policy, 28*(4), 438–460.

Gergen, K. J., & Gergen, M. M. (2010). Scanning the landscape of narrative inquiry. *Social and Personality Psychology Compass, 4*(9), 728–735.

Kasat, P. (2013). *Community arts and cultural development: A powerful tool for social transformation*. Unpublished Master of Sustainability and Social Change Dissertation, Murdoch University, Perth, Australia.

Kasat, P. (2014). Tools for social transformation: Making the personal creative and political. *Griffith Review, 44*, 7-17. Retrieved from https://griffithreview.com/wp-content/uploads/Notes_from_the_Front.pdf

Lewis, J. D., & Weigert, A. (1985). Trust as a social reality. *Social Forces, 63*(4), 967–885.

Martin, K. (2007). *Aboriginal people, aboriginal lands and indigenist research: A discussion or re-search pasts and neo-colonial research futures*. Unpublished dissertation, James Cook University, Cairns, Queensland, Australia.

Martín-Baró, I. (1994). Toward a liberation psychology. In A. Aron & S. Corne (Eds.), & A. Aron (Trans.), *Writings for a liberation psychology* (pp. 17–32). Cambridge, MA: Harvard University Press.

Montero, M. (2009). Methods for liberation: Critical consciousness in action. In M. Montero & C. C. Sonn (Eds.), *Psychology of liberation: Theory and applications* (pp. 73–92). New York, NY: Springer.

Montero, M. (2012). From complexity and social justice to consciousness: Ideas that have built a community psychology. *Global Journal of Community Psychology Practice, 3*(1), 1–13.

Montero, M., & Sonn, C. C. (Eds.). (2009). *Psychology of liberation: Theory and applications*. New York, NY: Springer.

Montero, M., Sonn, C. C., & Burton, M. (2017). Community psychology and liberation psychology: A creative synergy for an ethical and transformative praxis. In M. A. Bond, I. Serrano-Garcia, & C. B. Key (Eds.), *APA handbook of community psychology: Theoretical foundations, core concepts, and emerging challenges* (Vol. 1, pp. 149–167). Washington, DC: American Psychological Society.

Price, N. (2008). Without the labels: Narratives of a diagnosed culture. In A. Lewis & D. Doyle (Eds.), *Proving the practice: Evidencing the effects of community arts programs on mental health* (pp. 46–59). Perth, WA: DADAA.

Quayle, A., Sonn, C., & Kasat, P. (2016). Community arts as public pedagogy: Disruptions into public memory through aboriginal counter-storytelling. *International Journal of Inclusive Education, 20*(3), 261–277.

Rappaport, J. (1995). Empowerment meets narrative: Listening to stories and creating settings. *American Journal of Community Psychology, 23*(5), 795–807.

Reyes Cruz, M., & Sonn, C. C. (2011). (De)colonizing culture in community psychology: Reflections from critical social science. *American Journal of Community Psychology, 47*(1-2), 203–214.

Sarason, S. B. (2004). What we need to know about intervention and interventionists. *American Journal of Community Psychology, 33*(3), 275–277.

Schuermans, N., Loopmans, M. P., & Vandenabeele, J. (2012). Public space, public art and public pedagogy. *Social & Cultural Geography, 13*(7), 675–682.
Smith, L. T. (1999). *Decolonizing methodologies: Research and indigenous peoples*. London: Zed.
Sonn, C., Drew, N., & Kasat, P. (2002). *Conceptualising community cultural development*. Perth, WA: Community Arts Network.
Sonn, C. C., & Baker, A. M. (2016). Creating inclusive knowledges: Exploring the transformative potential of arts and cultural practice. *International Journal of Inclusive Education, 20*(3), 215–228.
Sonn, C. C., & Quayle, A. F. (2014). Community cultural development for social change: Developing critical praxis. *Journal for Social Action in Counseling and Psychology, 6*(1), 16–35.
Sonn, C. C., Quayle, A. F., Belanji, B., & Baker, A. M. (2015). Responding to racialization through arts practice: The case of participatory theatre. *Journal of Community Psychology, 43*(2), 244–259.
Steering Committee for the Review of Government Services Provision. (2014). *Overcoming indigenous disadvantage: Key indicators*. Canberra, ACT: Productivity Commission.
Stein, C. H., & Faigin, D. A. (2015). Community-based arts initiatives: Exploring science of the arts. *American Journal of Community Psychology, 55*(1-2), 70–73.
Thiele, M., & Marsden, S. (2008). P(ART)icipation: Art, dual diagnosis and the Artful Dodgers Studio. In A. Lewis & D. Doyle (Eds.), *Proving the practice: Evidencing the effects of community arts programs on mental health* (pp. 60–73). Perth, WA: DADAA.
Thomas, R. E., & Rappaport, J. (1996). Art as community narrative: A resource for social change. In M. B. Lykes, R. Liem, A. Banauzizi, & M. Morris (Eds.), *Myths about the powerless: Contesting social inequities* (pp. 317–336). Philadelphia, PA: Temple University Press.
Watkins, M., & Shulman, H. (2008). *Toward psychologies of liberation*. Basingstoke: Palgrave MacMillan.

Chapter 9
Threading Life Stories: Embroidery as an Engaged Method

Puleng Segalo and Michelle Fine

> Mere exposure to a work of art is not sufficient to occasion an aesthetic experience. There must be conscious participation in a work, a going out of energy, an ability to notice what is there to be noticed in the play, the poem, the quartet, "Knowing about," even in the most formal academic manner, is entirely different from creating an unreal world imaginatively and entering it perceptually, affectively, and cognitively (Greene, 1995, pp. 379–380).

The social sciences has long relied on spoken language as a way of according meaning to people's lived realities. In many ways the assumption that one has to verbally express thoughts and feelings to make meaning is problematic. Given the limitations of the spoken language, it becomes necessary to think of the role that art as creative resources to storytelling and knowledge production might offer, and the power of embodied sharing through embroideries as a form of artistic expression. We are interested in art as a space where theory is provoked, analysed, performed and circulated. John Dewey distinguished aesthetic and anesthetic experiences: the former provocative and the latter numbing (McDermott, 1981). We are interested in the epistemological possibilities that unfold when aesthetics are the medium through which stories are constructed. In this chapter, we focus on a particular form of aesthetic production, the stitching of a life onto a blank, black screen: embroideries as an engaged method that privileges creativity and subjectivity.

Embroideries allow a space for celebration, resistance, affect, anger, questioning, and healing all weaved together in an art-form that refuses to be bound by

---

P. Segalo (✉)
Department of Psychology, University of South Africa, Pretoria, South Africa
e-mail: segalpj@unisa.ac.za

M. Fine
The Graduate Center, City University of New York, New York, NY, USA
e-mail: mfine@gc.cuny.edu

M. Seedat et al. (eds.), *Emancipatory and Participatory Methodologies in Peace, Critical, and Community Psychology*, Peace Psychology Book Series,
DOI 10.1007/978-3-319-63489-0_9

methodological restrictions and 'clear cut' approaches. Embroidery as a form of narrative allows for messiness and multiple meaning-making that show the complexities of the so often assumed clear-cut ways of understanding the world and lived experiences. Like other aesthetic forms, embroideries offer a particularly powerful medium for cultivating and circulating images of pain, trauma and possibility; affect and politics; intimacy, history and structure. This chapter looks at embroidery as a liberatory and engaged method that acknowledges various ways in which stories can be told over time, drawing from history into the present. We intend to look at the ways in which embroideries allow and offer space for the embodied to be externalised, felt and released onto a canvas that shows the contours, straight lines, holes, as well as the spaces in between. We intend to also speak to some of the challenges that might be experienced when engaging in visual methods such as embroideries.

We will be drawing from an embroidery research project that Puleng, the first author, engaged in to demonstrate how embroidery allows space for speaking back to dominant narratives—in this case, narratives of Black women in South Africa. We will be hearing from/with/witnessing the lives of Black women in South Africa, reflecting back and forward, in the shadows of the "official" channels for speaking of apartheid—the Truth and Reconciliation Commission (TRC), and the unofficial channels of talk within community life. Puleng created a space where everyday women could display for global audiences how they stitched a life, speaking of the journey through the spectacular prism of apartheid as violence, through the 21 years that are anything but "post" conflict, especially for Black African women.

Brief History on the Making of Embroideries

In some parts of the world, such as the USA and South Africa, the making of embroidery, quilting, and sewing have for a long time been reserved for and perceived as women's duties. Sewing has historically been perceived as a symbol of childhood and female bondage. It was intended to "inculcate in little girls their class or gender virtues of neatness, submissiveness, docility and patience" (Hedges, 2014, p. 14). Sewing was therefore intended to prepare girls for conventional notions of womanhood. Needlework was similarly reserved for women; used to keep them from active political participation. However, many women in various parts of the world used their needlework skill for making political statements and expressing their life circumstances through images as early as the mid nineteenth century (Schwartz & Przyblyski, 2004). In this way, there was a redefinition of the role that needlework played in women's lives especially. Needlework has also contributed in providing an opportunity for women to be economically self-sustained (Segalo, 2011).

Embroidery as a form of needlework allows those participating in its space to construct narratives. As researchers we work with "the assumption that increased participant control of data generation through production of visual images will help to illuminate important aspects of lived experience that might otherwise have been overlooked or ignored by researchers—perhaps even been invisible" (Guillemin &

Drew, 2010, p. 176). Unlike many other data generating and gathering strategies, such as conducting interviews or facilitating a focus groups, the making of embroidery requires an extended period of time and is an exercise that cannot be completed within a limited period. In addition, making embroideries provides time and space to reflect, and remember, at one's own pace and in one's own space. It allows people to express the unsayable.

Embroidery as a Visual Method

According to Luttrell and Chalfen, (2010, p. 197) "images often represent a mid-point rather than an end-point in knowledge production, interventions and social action". Visual methodologies act as enablers and empowering tools that allow the creators the freedom to carve narratives that speak to multiple audiences and lend themselves to the possibility of multiple interpretations. This is a point also noted by Guillemin and Drew (2010) in their assertion that visual methodologies benefit both the researcher and the participants. They further note that both are actively involved in the research process as the generating of the data and the analysis thereof is not the responsibility of the researcher alone. Visual methodologies allow for multiple knowings, wherein participants are perceived as knowledge producers who play a critical role in the research process (Guillemin & Drew, 2010).

The decision to use embroidery as a visual method should be guided by the research question(s) posed. It is also crucial to note that participants require the skill of sewing/needle work to be able to weave their stories onto cloth in the form of embroidery. There are various ways in which images can be analysed and this involves the possibility of participants being actively involved in the data generating and the analysis processes themselves, as highlighted earlier. Images lend themselves to multiple interpretations; for example, we can look for the content and meaning thereof, and/or look for patterns in how narratives are told through images and how these flow in the threading of the story. Luttrell and Chalfen (2010, p. 198) argue that "contexts within which photographs (embroideries) are displayed—these all interact with viewers' social and cultural backgrounds to influence responses and meanings attributed to an image". Some argue that to see sketch after sketch of women embroidering their suffering is "to become aware of a tragic deficiency in the fabric of life" (Greene, 1995, p. 379). Embroideries place the spotlight on the complexities of everyday life experiences. They assist in highlighting how one can be both an outsider and an insider at the same time. Greene (1995, p. 379) observes that "encounters with them (the arts) frequently do move us to want to restore some kind of order, to repair, and to heal". Embroidery allows us to move away from what Greene (1995) refers to as the "freezing of the imagination" (p. 379) where the everyday is frozen in time and viewed via a single lens.

Embroideries therefore allow people to document their stories, pains, voices, struggles, subjectivities and dreams as they perceive them; they refuse linearity, transcendance or single-voicedness and enable narratives typically silenced. Embroidery further allows space for the interweaving of people's life stories with history and structure. It highlights the importance of acknowledging the interconnections between the individual's narratives, and how their experiences cannot be separated from those of their families and communities. Embroidery forces researchers to analyse the complexities, contradictions and multidimensional understandings of life experiences. As Maxine Greene has articulated (1993, p. 214) "...encounters with the arts can awaken us to alternative possibilities of existing, of being human, of relating to others, of *being* other...". Accordingly, we need to look for ways that enable people to be able to name the world for themselves. Greene (1993, p. 219) suggests that "it is only when persons are enabled to shape their own experiences in their own fashion, when they become critical of the mystifications that falsify so much, that they become able to name their worlds".

According to Lykes (2010), using visual images such as embroideries to tell stories "enables women who survived horrific assaults against material, social and cultural bodies to reclaim them and reconstitute discontinuous subjectivities, and reposition themselves ..." (p. 251). Lykes et al. (1999) contend that "the power of the visual image is unlike other forms of communication as it is universally comprehensible and accessible, and can be used to facilitate discussion, document experience, and facilitate critical analysis of social reality and problem solving" (p. 217). Elsewhere, Segalo (2011) argues that:

> the use of the visual image is a useful tool that can be used to tell people's stories of oppression, liberation and survival. Visual images can be used purposefully to mediate reality in a 'performative' way, and furthermore, they allow for collective emotional response. (p. 230)

Segalo (2016, p. 14) further argues that:

> art can be used as a form of social transformation. The art is a great contributor that creates (a collective) space for self-representation and multiple interpretations of lived realities. It is, therefore, critical to pay attention to the role that individual and collective artistic expression can play towards the attainment of a just society.

Embroidery is therefore a visual method that offers space and voice to the unspeakable. As a method, embroidery refuses to be categorised and boxed into predetermined and structured ways of knowledge production. It offers space for contextual understanding and an evolving meaning that is not time specific. For a long time, the Eurocentric mode of knowledge production has assumed a hegemonic standpoint in how the world in general, and people's experiences of it in particular, can be understood. Alternative ways of knowing continue to be on the margins and often assumed as anecdotal and "unscientific".

Embroideries allow for an epistemic disobedience, a way of knowing that refuses to be restricted and guided by existing and accepted forms of knowing. It is through looking on the outside of what is already taken for granted and assumed to be the norm that alternative forms of understanding the world can be uncovered. Greene's (1995) contributions are useful at this point as she draws us to the anaesthetic, that which numbs and leaves a person watching helplessly, and the aesthetic, that which allows for creativity, involvement and multiple perspectives. The anaesthetic does not allow space for voice; instead the individual becomes the spectator of what is happening around him/her. The aesthetic on the other hand allows for the chorus of voices to be heard—it is an awakening that brings to the fore that which might have been hidden for a long time. Greene (1995) explains that "encounters with the arts nurture and sometimes provoke the growth of individuals who reach out to one another as they seek clearings in their experience and try to live more ardently in the world" (p. 382). The chorus of emotions, experiences, meaning-making, and wrestling with pain, anger and love, and the combination of these can be seen in how a work of art such as embroidery becomes assembled.

On Making an Embroidery

Conducting research offers us an opportunity to obtain some understanding of our social world, and also a platform to critique the injustices, oppression and inequalities that plague our societies. It provides a space to explore and look for alternatives as we strive for a just world. It is important to think about the reasons that lead researchers to conduct the kind of research that they do, and to acknowledge their position as scholars representing academia, and more specifically the universities that they are a part of. We have multiple locations and represent multiple systems which influence how we may be perceived by our participants when conducting research. As a Black South African woman, Puleng felt that it was somewhat easier for the participants to relate to her and some even considering her as their daughter. The affectionate term most of them used, *ngwanaka* (my child) pointed to the closeness they felt towards her. She acknowledges the possible power imbalance that might have played a role in how they responded to her due to the fact that they also saw her as someone from the university who is therefore "knowledgeable"; she kept this in mind during her interaction with them. Puleng also grew up in a township during apartheid South Africa, albeit she was still young when the country attained democracy. Even though she has not been residing in a township for years now, her childhood experiences assisted in how she engaged with the participants as she could in some ways relate to some of their experiences. One of the factors that facilitated a connection between Puleng and the participants was the fact that she could speak the local languages that the women spoke (Sesotho and isiZulu). This enabled communication to be easier and made the participants comfortable in the way they expressed themselves.

The research participants, more specifically marginalised communities, and women may see researchers as people who have the potential to bring about positive change into their lives. Because of this "trust", they *allow* researchers to speak for them. It is therefore crucial for the researcher to be constantly aware of self, the researched, context, and the process; researchers should also be aware about the shaping influences of their theories. Researchers should acknowledge their indebtedness and accountability to their participants. Because of the power that researchers carry when entering other people's worlds, it is crucial for them to always look for ways to contribute to positive change in the lives of those they encounter in their research endeavours.

The Process

As a way to create a space for the aesthetics, Puleng initiated a community engagement project that sought to utilise artistic expression in the form of embroideries to enable Black women to produce visual counter narratives about growing up during apartheid and their lived experiences thereafter. The project enlisted ten women who are part of an existing embroidery collective called Intuthuko, based in the Gauteng Province of South Africa. The women who formed part of the project were between the ages of 45 and 75 years of age as the focus was on women who grew up during the apartheid era. Most of the women had minimal formal education, with only two having completed high school. The women already had some background and experience in embroidery making and this contributed towards them being able to carve their personal narratives visually somewhat easier. The embroideries project was meant to enable participating women to narrate stories about their experiences of growing up in South Africa, things they did to survive during the apartheid period, their schooling experiences, and the changes that have occurred since the country's inception of political democracy. They also had the space to articulate thoughts about the future of the country and generations to come.

Ten pieces of materials were cut and put aside. After consultation with the women, they suggested sketching/writing their stories on pieces of paper before sketching on the actual material. This process took two weeks, and in the meantime Puleng provided the women with various colored threads to use for their embroideries. Throughout this process the women sought direction from Puleng and kept asking what type of stories would Puleng like to hear. Puleng did not want to lead them hence the above *script* became useful in guiding them on ways they could shape their narratives. They took 3 months to complete their embroideries and this length of time allowed them to work at their own pace, and time. This extended engagement with their artworks allowed the women to reflect, remember and work in their own safe and comfortable spaces. They opened up their lives and allowed themselves to be vulnerable, and expressed their emotions onto the cloth on which they were threading their life experiences. As the researcher engaging with the participants, Puleng had to respect their vulnerability and find ways to create a safe space for them to freely share and express their emotions. Most of the participants drew Puleng in and reflected on the past in a way that included her as part of that past.

For the purpose of this chapter, a single embroidery is used as an illustration of how this form of visual method can be employed and analysed. What follows is the image of the embroidery and the interpretation thereof. Puleng analysed and made interpretations of the embroidery. Additionally, the participants also

Fig. 9.1 Illustration of embroidery: A story within a story

had the opportunity to reflect and offer a narration of the embroideries they produced.

The embroidery was sketched by Nosipho (pseudonym) and it illustrates her experiences of growing up during apartheid in South Africa (see Fig. 9.1). We are using it as an example here to illustrate the ways in which embroidery can be used as a method to "tell a story" and also to show how numerous stories can emanate from one story. In this particular embroidery, multiple aspects, such as the historical, economic, political, social and geographical, are seen to merge and complex life experiences can be observed in how the narrative is threaded together. The embroidery offers us an explicit representation of Nosipho's perception of the country as divided, a place with clear borders. The rigid weaved in line that separates Natal (now called Kwazulu-Natal, one of the nine provinces of South Africa) and Town may be perceived as highlighting the notion of inclusion and exclusion. The passes and permits that were constantly required by the police during the apartheid regime was a constant reminder of black people's precarious citizenship. In this embroidery, Nosipho shows the complex ways in which the notion of home was defined. The permits that people had to carry determined where they could live, thereby what or where people could call home was pre-determined. This process was further complicated by the migrant labour system which forced many people to leave their homes in search for employment in other parts of the country. By pointing Nosipho towards the direction of Natal (as depicted in the embroidery), the police officer may be perceived to have been giving her the message that *the Town is not her home*, and therefore she does not belong there. She did not have permission to be in Town and therefore she did not belong there and had to leave or face possible arrest. Her embroidery is "a graphic depiction and dramatization of, and ingenious response to, historical and political event and change" (Hedges, 2014, p. 13).

The above embroidery speaks to the politics of knowledge production and challenges knowledge that speaks of victimhood and sense of helplessness; this can be seen in Nosipho's visual representation of women working the land. With embroidery, there is space to look beyond the perceived hopelessness— to resistance, courage and determination. Furthermore, embroidery offers the opportunity to highlight structural violence and inequalities that have direct impact on people's everyday encounters. Embroidery enables what Weis and Fine (2012) call "critical bifocality" which compel us as scholars and researchers to stand back and notice through the artwork, the interweaving of history, politics, and the role of various institutions in the making and unmaking of lives and communities.

Embroidery offers space to those who embody the injustices to create knowledge, produce and lay out their experiences onto the cloth that then becomes multilayered with stories of pain, anger, resilience, resistance, hope, love and desire. Nosipho's embroidery offers a historical lesson wherein one gets an understanding of the way in which apartheid South Africa functioned. She visually narrates how a piece of paper served as a form of exclusion or inclusion. She focuses on the notion of resilience by sharing her story of how even though she knew the risks of "crossing the border", she took the chance of crossing in search for a better life. This resilience is linked with resistance as she also reflected on how the artificial borders were not seen as permanent deterrents. Her hope and desire for a better life and opportunity to access resources that could positively change her circumstances, propelled her to risk arrest. Nosipho's embroidery further highlights sense of agency and provides a fuller understanding of how the past affected her life in particular, and black South African women in general. By being in control and using personal artistic expression, participants teach and offer us a renewed understanding of how conflict and oppressive structures affect lives; a point also made by Luttrell (2010, p. 225) in her assertion that "visual research and analysis is dynamic, relational, and offers space for individual subjectivities and exercise of multiple voices". We need to seek ways and methodologies that can create safe spaces for creativity, various ways of self-expression and ones that acknowledge and treat participants with dignity. Embroidery has the potential to lead us towards that direction.

Embroidery forces a rupture in the persistent miscarriage of justice, refusing to naturalise inequalities. By making embroideries, participants move beyond and challenge the often imposed categories and labels of "being vulnerable" and/or being perceived as "marginalised". With the above embroidery, Nosipho visually highlights how she (and many others in similar positions during apartheid) did not sit back and accept being vulnerable to possible arrest, and thereby be compliant with the prescribed zones of movement. Instead, she challenged authority by moving between zones without prior permission and stamp from the farm owner on whose property she and her family lived. Through the making of embroideries, the participants bring to the fore "an absence we know to be present" (McClelland & Fine, 2008, p. 233), that of survival, resistance, hope, tenacity, and love; what indigenous theorist Gerald Vizenor calls "survivance"—the sweet and sour blend of survival and resistance.

Some Points to Consider When Using Visual Methods

When looking at the meaning of voice in visual images, it is important to acknowledge the co-construction of voice. Luttrell and Chalfen (2010) raise issues pertaining to complexities of images, the types of images presented, and whether images are meant to illustrate or complement the text produced within the research process. They further highlight the ethical implications with regard to the circulation of images. This is a crucial issue that needs to be discussed and negotiated with the participants. These negotiated terrains should be acknowledged in our analysis and theorising. When conducting research, a collaborative decision needs to be made, and conversations need to be had about who will have ownership of the visual images, such as embroideries. Furthermore, it is critical to ascertain whether the participants are willing to have their artwork exhibited as a way of sharing their expression of history and personal experiences.

It is also critical to interrogate and understand how we continuously produce inquiry that reproduces silences, covers up ruptures, and re-tells the dominant story because those are the only discourses available. It is at this point where engaged methods such as embroidery open up opportunities to pierce the "cellophane" (McClelland & Fine, 2008), that cushion dominant discourses, and contest epistemologies of ignorance that saturate popular culture and the discipline of psychology. Beyond the TRC's call for events of spectacular testifying, and the everyday violence of living in townships, these narrative fabrics offer an opportunity to speak beyond the local, about the banal, with one's own signature.

In their attempt to engage with how images are constructed and the implications thereof, Luttrell and Chalfen (2010, p. 199) contend that:

> it may not always be clear for whom the pictures and embroideries have been created; imagined audience(s) can change and play important roles in what is "said" or left unsaid; and interpretation is highly dependent on contextual features of the viewing situation.

This may be perceived as a weakness or strength of visual methods depending on the intention of the researcher. Because embroideries lend themselves to possible multiple interpretations, it remains the viewer's choice on how the interpretation will be made. This flexibility in interpretations allows for complexity and highlights the complicated nature of people's lived experiences.

The embroidery forces the viewer to ask questions about why certain colours were used, or why this particular story was told. Can the audience see their story within this (embroidered) story? Another challenging question is posed by McClelland and Fine (2008, p. 242) when they ask: "how do we both respect the positions that participants take when making embroideries and still analyse critically the ideologies and discourses through which the participants make embroideries?" It is critical to find a space where faith and suspicion can co-habit, where the multiple layers of truths can be acknowledged. Visual methods offer us a compass towards this direction.

This multiplicity of truths and understandings of the world may be uncomfortable for those who are normally comforted by a single truth, a reliable and valid analysis, and a trustworthy and measurable story. Moving out of this comfort zone requires us to shift from the single vision/lens that we so often use when conducting research. We need to allow ourselves to learn from the bottom up and to acknowledge contradicting, and sometimes diverging views of understanding the world. It is at these intersections that knowledge takes place.

Conclusion

> The work is never limited to the painted, sculpted or narrated object. Just as one perceives things only against the background of the world, so the objects represented by art appear against the background of the universe … [T]he creative act aims at a total renewal of the world. Each painting, each book, is a recovery of the totality of being. Each of them presents this totality to the freedom of the spectator. For this is quite the final goal of art: to recover this world by giving it to be seen as it is, but as if it had its source in human freedom. (Jean-Paul Sartre, 1964)

Visual methodologies have slowly made their way into the academic space and are used as methods that assist in speaking back to master narratives, and also stitched in complex knots with grand narratives about race, gender, family, government and violence that so often leave many voices in the margins. Such methods contest the hegemonic singularity of dominant narratives and allow for the co-creation of meaning, theories of violence and demands for social change.

References

Greene, M. (1993). Diversity and inclusion: Toward a curriculum for human beings. *Teachers College Record, 9*(2), 211–221.

Greene, M. (1995). Art and imagination: Reclaiming the sense of possibility. *The Phi Delta Kappan, 76*(5), 378–382.

Guillemin, M., & Drew, S. (2010). Questions of process in participant-generated visual methodologies. *Visual Studies*, 25(2), 175–188.

Hedges, E. (2014). Quilts and women's culture. *Radical Teacher, 100*, 10–14.

Luttrell, W. (2010). 'A camera is a big responsibility': A lens for analyzing children's visual voices. *Visual Studies, 25*(3), 224–237.

Luttrell, W., & Chalfen, R. (2010). Lifting up voices of participatory visual research. *Visual Studies, 25*(3), 197–200.

Lykes, M. B. (2010). Silence(ing), voice(s) and gross violations of human rights: Constituting and performing subjectivities through PhotoPAR. *Visual Studies, 25*(3), 238–254.

Lykes, M. B., Mateo, A. C., Anay, J. C., Caba, A. L., Ruiz, U., & Williams, J. W. (1999). Telling stories-rethreading lives: Community education, women's development and social change among the Maya Ixil. *International Journal of Leadership in Education, 2*(3), 207–227.

McClelland, S. I., & Fine, M. (2008). Writing on cellophane: Studying teen women's sexual desires, inventing methodological release points. In K. Gallagher (Ed.), *The methodological dilemma: Creative, critical and collaborative approaches to qualitative research* (pp. 232–260). Abingdon: Routledge.

McDermott, J. J. (Ed.). (1981). *The philosophy of John Dewey: Volume 1. The structure of experience. Volume 2: The lived experience*. Chicago, IL: Chicago University Press.
Sartre, J. (1964). *Situations, IV*. Paris: Gallimard Publishers.
Schwartz, V. R., & Przyblyski, J. M. (2004). *The nineteenth-century visual culture reader*. New York, NY: Routledge Taylor and Francis Group.
Segalo, P. (2011). Our lives through embroidery: Narrative accounts of the women's embroidery project in post-apartheid South Africa. *Journal of Psychology in Africa, 21*(2), 229–238.
Segalo, P. (2016). Using cotton, needles and threads to break the women's silence: Embroideries as a decolonising framework. *International Journal of Inclusive Education, 20*(3), 246–260.
Weis, L., & Fine, M. (2012). Critical bifocality and circuits of privilege: Expanding critical ethnographic theory and design. *Harvard Educational Review, 82*(2), 173–201.

Chapter 10
Community Psychology's Gaze

Deanne Bell

iv.
The rastaman thinks, draw me a map of what you see
then I will draw a map of what you never see
and guess me whose map will be bigger than whose?
Guess me whose map will tell the larger truth
Kei Miller, 2014, p. 19

Since its inception as a method to "see people—their feelings, thoughts, and actions—within a social context" (Orford, 2008, p. xi), community psychology has attended to the social world in which people's lives are constituted. Drawing from theories such as Lewin's (1951) action research, Freire's (1970) conscientization, Fals Borda's (2001) participatory research, and Martín-Baró's (1996) attention to unjust social conditions that oppress poor people, this subdiscipline of psychology has turned its attention away from the main discipline's focal point of the individual toward visible relationships between small groups of people and social determinants of their misery. This outward facing focus has led to an examination of, among other things, the effects of violence, economic hardship, and discriminatory socio-political institutions on community life.

The domain of community psychology has been cast as the intersection of social and cognitive behavioral aspects of group life. From here the field has analyzed the impact of antisocial ideologies on the life of communities, which has positively impacted social policy and buttressed civil society. It can be argued, as have Martín-Baró (1996) and Nelson and Prilleltensky (2005), that community psychology has been successful in producing first order, ameliorative change, that is, change *within* systems. Critiques along these lines observe that prevailing community psychology

D. Bell (✉)
School of Psychology, University of East London, London, UK
e-mail: D.Bell@uel.ac.uk

M. Seedat et al. (eds.), *Emancipatory and Participatory Methodologies in Peace, Critical, and Community Psychology*, Peace Psychology Book Series,
DOI 10.1007/978-3-319-63489-0_10

has also incorporated the biomedical model's approach of prevention and behavioral control as key indices of desirable change. Social transformation, however, that second-order process that "strives to change the system and its assumption" (Nelson and Prilleltensky, 2005, p. 144) has, except in small measure, eluded the field. Nelson and Prilleltensky suggest that the failure of community psychology and other social sciences to consistently contribute to structural metamorphosis is based on their adherence to "rational-empirical problem-solving" (p. 144). This orientation, emanating from mainstream psychology's social-cognitive theory, targets social change as a series of logical intergroup behavior change projects. Missing from its consideration is the subjectivity (the sense of selfhood) of the oppressed-psychological experiences (both conscious and unconscious) negated by the hegemonic presence of the neocolonial order that, were they to be granted expression in social space, hold the potential of illuminating and transforming people's lifeworlds.

Reducing community psychology to psychology's research standards of quantitative measurability of human behavior narrows our view of the psychic life of communities, diminishes our understanding of the effects of power on the psyche, and eliminates the possibility of developing theory that can explain the psychodynamics of domination leading to their transformation. Omitting unconscious determinants of social relations produces superficial analyses of social problems and constraints. But other kinds of awareness, articulated in feminist theory and Rastafarian philosophy from the Global South, including Chela Sandoval's (2000) oppositional consciousness, Gloria Anzaldúa's (1987) *mestiza* consciousness, Rosi Braidotti's (1994) nomadic consciousness and Kei Miller's (2014) Rastafari reasoning, take us beyond the thin logic of rational knowledge to reveal psychic realities capable of informing understandings that can contribute to reconstructing people's psychosocial worlds.

In this chapter, I critique community psychology, arguing that the field is blind to much of psychological life that is affected by and affects forces of oppression that could be transformed. In the section titled Constructing the Gaze, I outline the conceptualization of a participatory research project undertaken in an inner city community in Kingston, Jamaica. I include extracts of a letter I wrote to human rights organizations which describe my social location and some of the ideas that informed my approach to this project. In the section titled The Rational Empirical Problem Solving Gaze, I reflect on how the project unfolded and review why oral history was chosen as the primary method through which narratives were collected. In Animating the Gaze, I describe concrete steps we took to engage with members of the Tivoli Gardens community. In the section, The Turn Toward Sociogeny, I argue that the field is oriented toward what is external to the psyche as opposed to both psychic interiority and exteriority and that this is to both our and participants' peril. Finally, in the section Multiple Modes of Consciousness, I point to knowledge being generated as a result of taking a depth psychological approach to analysis and engagement with community participants. This approach leads to actionable ideas that may eventually contribute to social transformation. I also discuss what we fail to perceive, even though it is readily available to be seen, and how an altered gaze, one that simultaneously looks within and without, would bring it to awareness. I propose that we reimagine conscientization (Freire, 1970), with the aim of enlarging its parameters to include mobilizing unconscious and semi-conscious thought and affect, experienced by both community members and the researchers who accompany them, arguing that this could increase the transformative potential of participatory research methods.

Constructing the Gaze

Violence, observes Deborah Thomas (2011), is foundational to the formation of Jamaica. Structural violence, a modality of colonialism, legitimates physical violence and together these produce sociocultural fragmentation, peril, and fear. Relations of power between Kingston's urban poor and the (post)colonial state have been mediated by the state's vicious use of law enforcement that leaves inner city survivors unprotected and vulnerable (Harriott, 2003). Accompanied by social alienation, a product of race/class dynamics, violence has made these communities insecure and defenseless.

Against the backdrop of marginalization by the broader society, inner city communities have turned to criminal gang activity and participation in the transnational drug and arms trade in order to support themselves financially. No longer dependent on the political apparatus for financial support, now able to wield military power, garrison communities, that is, politically polarized inner city communities, are reshaping their relationship to sociopolitical life (Gray, 2003, 2004). In contrast to how subaltern groups elsewhere have used their social power to overthrow the state, Kingston's combatants have channeled their potency into the creation of a culture of insubordination, one in which violence and an anti-society identity are valorized. Here, social prestige, known as "badness-honour," a mixture of "personal freedom and racial group honour" (Gray, 2003, p. 17) may compensate for feelings of inadequacy, the loss of self-esteem and other forms of psychological suffering experienced by the oppressed.

Against this backdrop in February 2012, I began constructing a truth and memory project based on the loss of at least 76 civilian lives that took place during a state of emergency imposed on some sections of Kingston in May 2010. The police and army occupied Tivoli Gardens and Denham Town, two adjacent inner city communities in Kingston, as the government attempted to capture and extradite a known drug lord, Christopher "Dudus" Coke, who was wanted on drug and arms trafficking charges in the USA. What drove me to conceive of the project was knowing that a hotline, created for children who had endured the invasion, was flooded by calls from adults. In addition to the hotline, the government provided excursions to the beach for community residents and brief counselling for survivors who were experiencing traumatic distress. Based on community members' responses it was evident that the hotline, short-term therapy, and fun days proved inadequate for their healing.

In September 2012 I wrote to the International Center for Transitional Justice (ICTJ), Center for Constitutional Rights, Physicians for Human Rights and Human

Rights Watch in an effort to engage international human rights actors in several layers of community healing work. I sent a letter, similar to the one below, to all four human rights organizations. I include a copy here to describe my understanding of the psychosocial conditions that community members faced at that time and to outline some of the features of a process that the community and others could engage in.

September 17, 2012
Mr. Eduardo Gonzalez
Director, Truth and Memory Program
ICTJ
5 Hanover Square. Floor 24
New York, NY 10004

Dear Mr. Gonzalez,

Re: *The Labour Day War* Project

I am writing as someone who has deep regard for how ICTJ's Truth and Memory Program helps societies reveal truth and aid understanding of human rights atrocities. I am particularly inspired by your collaborative approach where you share your expertise with local justice seeking actors giving them the benefit of your global knowledge. It is this expertise that I wish to ask you to consider applying to a human rights abuse in Jamaica, which has come to be known as *The Labour Day War*.

In May 2010, the government of Jamaica acquiesced to the US government's demand for the extradition of a known drug lord, Christopher "Dudus" Coke. Coke was the leader of Tivoli Gardens, a politically polarized inner city community in Kingston. Tivoli Gardens forms part of the constituency of the then Prime Minister, Bruce Golding. After declaring a state of emergency the police and army were sent in to Tivoli Gardens, surrounding and attacking residents for several days, in what became known as *The Labour Day War*. The police report that during that week they killed 73 people in a 4000+-member community. Unofficially, the death toll is reported to be between 125 and 140 people (Please see Mattathias Schwartz's article in The New Yorker entitled *A Massacre in Jamaica* for excellent background information http://www.newyorker.com/reporting/2011/12/12/111212fa_fact_schwartz).

Earl Witter, Jamaica's public defender, completed an investigation into deaths caused by the militia's operation and the alleged use of extra-judicial force. Two plus years later his report has yet to be made public. In 2011, a public enquiry was held into the government's handling of Coke's extradition request. This enquiry reviewed the hiring of Mannatt Phelps, a US legal firm, to lobby and stall the US government in their extradition request. Civil society groups in Jamaica characterize these investigations as having failed the public. Neither probe is determined to have revealed the truth nor held anyone accountable for their acts.

I am a middle class, mixed race Jamaican, now living in the US. I am also a founding member of the civil rights action group Jamaicans for Justice (http://www.jamaicansforjustice.org). I completed my dissertation in liberation psychology where I explored how Jamaican middle class bystanders to human rights atrocities turn away from others' suffering. I found that racism, classism, and denial dominate the way in which we relate to the oppressed thus permitting atrocities such as *The*

Labour Day War. According to UNDP, Jamaica has one of the highest per capita homicide rates, 39.3 per 100,000 in 2012. Jamaicans for Justice & the International Human Rights Clinic of George Washington University Law School report that the police murdered almost one out of every five persons killed in 2007, yet there is little public outrage.

I am concerned about the chronic and acute human rights abuses poor black people in Jamaica endure. The bodies of the 73 murdered residents of Tivoli Gardens have not all been identified. They have not all been properly laid to rest. Their families and community have not been granted full knowledge of the circumstances of their deaths. Recently, in response to signs of Post Traumatic Stress Disorder (PTSD) symptoms, the Ministry of Education opened a hotline for school-aged children of Tivoli Gardens. The hotline was flooded by calls from the adults. The people of Tivoli Gardens continue to suffer from the trauma of the events of *The Labour Day War*. As a psychologist, I do not believe the diagnosis of PTSD applies to their experience. For the people of Tivoli Gardens, indeed for Jamaica's poor, there is no "post" to their trauma.

It is my hope that under the Truth and Memory Program ICTJ will participate in working to help Jamaica transition to a humane society. I see this as a process that could potentially include some of the following ideas:

1. Produce a historical record of the victims of *The Labour Day War*, through a civic investigation.
2. Provide an opportunity for families to honor their dead, with dignity, potentially contributing to personal, community and national healing.
3. Document testimonies of family and community members of Tivoli Gardens.
4. Create a memorial for victims of *The Labour Day War*.
5. Promote civic dialogues about racism, classism and denial that permit these atrocities to take place.

I believe there is an urgency to begin this work because memories fade and witnesses are not always available. It is my hope that ICTJ will be willing to collaborate on this project by bringing ideas and practices that you have found to be beneficial elsewhere to this particular situation. I would also welcome your ideas about other groups and people with expertise who might be able to help with such a project, including the financing of it.

The Rational Empirical Problem Solving Gaze

In November 2012 I met with officers of ICTJ who endorsed *The Labour Day War* project and supported efforts to engage with the community by sharing strategies used in memory initiatives elsewhere. At the end of 2012 I met Deborah Thomas, an anthropologist at the University of Pennsylvania, and Junior "Gabu" Wedderburn, a Rastafari, musician and cultural worker who along with John L. Jackson, Dean of Social Policy and Practice at the University of Pennsylvania, produced the documentary *Bad Friday: Rastafari After Coral Gardens*. *Bad Friday* chronicles the experience of a community of Rastafarians living in the hills overlooking Montego Bay who experienced deadly state violence in 1963. The documentary highlights the role the imagination plays as community members conceptualize a new future, one that they believe could be aided by reparations. In *Bad Friday*, community members' voices are foregrounded so that it is they who narrate their experience of oppression. The creation of an aesthetic social space for people to speak for themselves led me to invite Gabu and Deborah to collaborate on *The Labour Day War* project. The three of us agreed that we would create a platform for community members to memorialize loved ones lost and break historical silences. Deborah framed the interviews as an oral history project, naming it *Tivoli Stories* as by then it appeared that residents of Tivoli Gardens wanted to have their story heard by a public other than subscribers to mainstream media. Deborah also conceptualized the aesthetic product of our work as a multimedia artwork for installation in museums.

Oral history as a form of qualitative interviewing for research purposes seeks to retrieve knowledge and perspectives from which historic events are documented (Leavy, 2011). Okihiro (1996) observes that "oral history is not only a tool or method for recovering history; it also is a theory of history which maintains that the common folks and the dispossessed have a history and that this history must be written" (p. 209). It shares the goal, with second-wave feminism, of revealing subjugated knowledge held by historically marginalized people in order for research to include voices of the oppressed. The meaning of oral history participants' speech is sought and utilized to empower communities interested in social change. When shared aurally, social acts of recollecting history and reminiscing may aid in building group identity, intergroup relations, community cohesion and vitality. When retained in oral form but moved out of the archive into public presentation, oral history narratives are capable of impacting the present and the public sphere. Shopes (2015) explains that oral history:

> Matters as a way of opening up public understanding of often misrepresented, ignored, or suppressed elements of the past, and because of the particular authority of the first-person voice, it matters in ways the public can often "get" better than work that tells rather than shows (p. 301).

As a subversive mode of inquiry and representation, documentary evidence of narratives can help to reconstruct dominant narratives, inaugurate respect for subjects, and contribute to efforts to resist social injustice and inequalities (Shopes, 2015). When used within a participatory research framework, oral history generates community history and creates participants' authority over their narratives by distinguishing their voices from the researcher's interpretations.

As an "audience-centered model of representing history" (Dunaway, 1996, p. 7), oral history promotes a turn toward understanding the past, cultural norms for articulating memory, and subjectivity that produces this knowledge. It also engages narrators, researchers, and audiences in this process together and publicly. It furthermore calls into question hegemonic accounts of histories. As a meaning-making process, oral history can illuminate relationships between how events are experienced and the conditions of psychic life—that is, we may come to know more about the collective psyche through expressions of and reactions to the telling of stories and subsequent interpretations of events. Additionally, historical soundscapes, the sounds of memory which comprise the social world, hold the potential of registering affectively within the researcher/interpreter and the audience.

Oral history making takes places within specific sociopolitical and historic circumstances. Patterson (2013) observes that in the context of the apartheid regime in South Africa, testimony projects such as the South African Truth and Reconciliation Commission created expressive social spaces through which people previously denied voice could actively resist silencing. But, she warns, oral history research that fails to analyze the political economy in which brutality exists falls short of transformative praxis. The full potential of oral history narratives is realized through a decoding process that occurs through shared social understanding (Tonkin, 1986). Additionally, Seedat (2015) shows that orality is a mode of performance that holds the potential to instigate reflection, interpretation, and interrogation when utilized as a strategy to resist oppressive social systems.

Animating the Gaze

At the end of 2012 I relocated to Kingston and began developing relationships with members of the Tivoli Gardens community, including gatekeepers. The gatekeepers I met had a relationship with Coke but spoke sparingly about their relationship with him and his organization, the Shower Posse, which is still in existence.

Through Deborah's access to resources at the University of Pennsylvania and the Penn Museum and my limited financial resources, we began videotaping interviews with community members in February 2013. Later, when I joined the psychology faculty of Antioch College, the Antioch College Faculty Fund made a financial contribution to this project.

Over the period of 3 years we recorded 26 interviews. Initially, gatekeepers identified community members who wished to tell their story and brought them to the recording studio. Over time word spread about the project and people unaffiliated with the gatekeepers volunteered to tell their story. Participants included males and females spanning an age range from teenagers through early sixties. Most of the people who came forward to tell us their stories continue to live in Tivoli Gardens. Many of them were born in Tivoli or have lived there most of their lives. Some participants enjoy home ownership in Tivoli Gardens while others rent or benefit from housing given the mores of garrison community living arrangements.

Many participants told us stories about what took place leading up to, during and in the aftermath of the state of the emergency. What mark their narratives are memories of their experiences during the incursion and loved ones they were with. There is, however, an absence of how participants understand the psychosocial trauma they experienced within the larger context of Jamaica's (post)colonial history and race/class dynamics, despite our efforts to explore these issues with community members. The fact that violence is ongoing in their community and that critiques of the garrison and national political systems bear life-threatening risk explains some self-silencing.

One woman who expressed a desire to tell us her story has been unable to do so on camera because recounting the memory of what took place is destabilizing for her. Since the state of emergency she rarely leaves her apartment on the third floor of a four-story apartment block, an apartment that continues to bear visible signs of the violence she witnessed. One man who came into the recording studio and who started to tell his story was unable to continue, so painful is the suffering that persists. We chose to end an interview with a woman who became mentally confused once she began recalling her experience of *The Labour Day War*. Follow-up checks with her confirmed that remembering the events while experiencing the anxiety of being taped proved too much to bear. Another man who willingly told us a version of his story in the recording studio met with us afterward, off camera, to say more. The oral history method thus allowed us to document some portion of each participant's subjectivity, but not all.

Recognizing the limits of oral history as a method through which participants' subjectivity may be engaged resulted in an expansion of ways we sought to facilitate memorialization and rupturing of silence. In the summer of 2014, undergraduate students from the University of Pennsylvania conducted a photography workshop for youths in the community. The youths' photos were presented at a showing attended by members of the board and senior staff of Jamaica's National Gallery. In January 2015, Antonio Rossi, an Emmy award winning filmmaker, joined us pro bono in Kingston to film a walking tour of the community. The tour was guided by community leaders since it is uncommon for outsiders of the community to enter and take photographs or record video while there.

In May 2013 and 2014, we marked the anniversary of the loss of people's lives by hosting sacred drum healing circles. Rastafari drummers from across the island travelled to Kingston to, along with local dancers, commemorate and celebrate the lives of the deceased and invoke an indigenous African healing process. Although some members of the community expressed appreciation for the healing circles, others experienced them as salt in a wound they were trying to forget. Some of the drummers were concerned about violence in the community and refused to perform if circles were held in Tivoli Gardens or if the events were held downtown after dark. We held the first healing circle at Roktowa, a community art school, and the second at Liberty Hall, a cultural and educational institution centred on Marcus Garvey's heritage. Both institutions are supportive of the work that we are doing and are in walking distance from Tivoli Gardens. Both events were held on Sunday afternoons to enable maximum participation since Sundays continue to be a day of rest in Jamaica. Given participants' concerns about safety, we have not hosted a healing circle since May 2014.

In 2014, the government of Jamaica, under pressure from local and international human rights actors, created the West Kingston Commission of Enquiry (WKCOE) with a remit to, amongst other things, investigate the circumstances that led up to and operationalized the invasion of the community (Ministry of Justice, 2016). The WKCOE also attempted to investigate charges of extra judicial killings by the state. *Tivoli Stories* oral history interviewing and the inquiry occurred in parallel. As a result of residents' experience of giving testimony to the commission and based on their lack of faith that the findings of the WKCOE will yield justice, they asked us to create a film to be shown to the international human rights community whom they believe to be the only actors who can compel the government to deliver justice. At the time of this writing, Deborah, Gabu, and I are finalizing a filmic representation of community members' experiences titled *Four Days in May*.

The Turn to Sociogeny

When I began to analyse Tivoli Gardens participants' narratives I discovered a gap in scholarship in the field of community psychology. Meanings of the psychic interiority of the oppressed are significantly undertheorized in the literature, as is collective trauma. What then do the dominant approaches in community psychology see when they work to understand a community such as Tivoli Gardens and its dynamics? And what do these approaches lead researchers not to see?

Community psychologists who engage in research with historically marginalized participants often draw from both critical pedagogy and critical theories that seek to deconstruct ideologies and constitute theories and praxes that reflect the lived experience of the oppressed. These efforts reflect a desire to collaborate with communities who seek liberation from oppressive social structures that undermine people's well-being. This orientation has evolved into critical community psychology—a form of psychology concerned with doing research and taking social action with community participants in order to transform the causes and effects of assaults on their lives and create conditions in which they may experience well-being (Watkins & Ciofalo, 2011). Kagan, Burton, Duckett, Lawthom, and Siddiquee (2011, p. 35) argue that "it is fundamentally an ethical project" (utilizing interdisciplinary resources in order to cocreate a socially just world in which interdependence and interconnection are valued and realized).

Critical community psychologists, particularly those who work in the Global South, also employ postcolonial theory in an effort to analyze the effects of coloniality (the conditions the subjugated endure as a result of the legacies of colonialism) and neocapitalism as forms of destructive social power that disproportionately impact the lives of the black poor. This turn, toward psychic exteriority, contextualizes the ways in which subjective experience can be more meaningfully understood and theorized. But focusing only on the external world bears the risk of removing researchers and participants from knowledge and understanding of psychic interiority, that is, latent structures and content of psychic life that animate people and their social relations.

In arguing for the creation of a mode of psychological analysis that incorporates the social in situations of oppression, Fanon (1967) writes:

> The analysis we are undertaking is psychological. It remains, nevertheless, evident that for us the true disalienation of the black man [person] implies a brutal awareness of the social and economic realities ....Reacting against the constitutionalizing trend at the end of the nineteenth century, Freud demanded that the individual factor be taken into account in psychoanalysis. He replaced the phylogenetic theory by an ontogenetic approach. We shall see that the alienation of the black man [person] is not an individual question. Alongside phylogeny and ontogeny, there is also sociogeny (Fanon, 1967, pp. xiv – xv).

In his critique of psychoanalysis, whose conceptualization of suffering is the development of pathology within the individual, Fanon (1967) imagines a way forward toward the development of an integrated psychosocial analysis. Were critical community psychologists to seize his vision we would not, as some have done, abandon analysis of the psyche in favor of producing community-based sociocognitive theory, but, rather, analyze psychic *and* social life together, thus utilizing the force of this amalgamation in the struggle for profound structural change.

Sloan (2003), reflecting on the contribution a psychoanalytically infused critical community psychology could make, argues that unless we understand the power of the intrapsychic *and* the ideological we fall into observing what is happening on the surface of social interaction. He traces this form of engagement (or rather disengagement) to community psychology's allegiance to levels of analysis associated with social psychology (surface interactions and small groups), analyses that overlook unconscious and ideological processes that arise out of structures of domination, such as, colonialism and capitalism. Sloan (2003) observes that were we to produce more thorough analyses of how communities are structured in relation to the larger socioeconomic order, fundamental social transformation would become a possibility. But because our intelligence is only surface deep, the effectiveness of interventions is severely limited. He states:

> We turned to community psychology for answers about mediating levels between social order and subjectivity but found a flattened zone of concepts and practices of a non-dialectical sort. This flattening happens, I believe, because of the oft-criticized allegiance of psychology in general to natural-scientific, objectivistic, and reifying epistemologies and related instrumental and mechanistic models of intervention" (Sloan, 2003, p. 58).

Turning away from community psyche is understood as a form of collusion with the neoliberal academy and is seen as symptomatic of academic imperialism. Sloan (2003) furthermore notes:

> Mainstream community psychology is actually itself a fine example of the effects of the colonization of the lifeworld ... the colonization of the lifeworld occurs when the requirements of economic and bureaucratic systems take precedence over the processes that maintain and reproduce meaning, culture, solidarity and identity. In the case of mainstream community psychology, social spaces in which citizens, villages, friends or neighbors might reflect and act to solve shared problems in living in creative, generous, and courageous ways are supplanted by extensions of the system's interests in social control and the maximization of profits (Sloan, 2003, p. 58).

Community psychology, a project whose raison d'être is to cocreate emancipatory possibilities with communities, perpetrates psychic colonization through adherence to methodological artifacts of mainstream psychology. It has failed to invent methods capable of engaging with communities at the level of their deep meanings.

Multiple Modes of Consciousness

If I were to analyze Tivoli Gardens community members' experiences through a mainstream community psychology lens, the insights would be superficial. Gone would be the ideas developed out of engagement with their psychic life that I have written about elsewhere (Bell, 2017) and theorized utilizing concepts such as depth psychology's collective trauma and diacritical hermeneutics, including:

- The meanings of their plain and metaphoric speech within a culture of silence
- The possible meanings of their silences
- The effects of coloniality, the way it erases being and erodes subjectivity, weakening the ability to self articulate
- The critical examination of the invisible social forces that foreclose on people's lives
- The knowledge that "dominative silence produces a loss in self-awareness and self-understanding impairing the ability to mobilize consciousness about traumatic experience, reducing conscientization possibilities community psychologists rely on to co-produce meaningful social action" (Bell, 2016, p. 125).

In its place would be analyses of cognitive behavioral acts. Without really entering into dialogue during interviews and while analyzing narratives it is possible to take what participants say and do at face value. Such analysis produces flat interpretations of the meanings of their lives, justifiable by allegiance to conscientization (Freire, 1970). Maritza Montero (2014) defines conscientization as a dynamic process that "uncovers the effects of oppression and exclusion, and increases awareness of unjust circumstances, events, and relations that have been ignored and normalized or considered part of daily life" (p. 1). She emphasizes that this mode of consciousness "is not raised," i.e., it does not arise from the depths of being. From this perspective, awareness is ready-to-hand, available through engagement in dialogic praxes that include problematization, deideologization, and disalienation.

We come to a critical question: In the (post)colonial situation, where traumatization produces not only social alienation but alienation from the self, in which what is known is not acknowledged but, rather, is both suppressed and repressed, how can critical consciousness (the outgrowth of conscientization) emerge without a working out, a working from what has been concealed?

Kei Miller's (2014) Rastaman does not succumb to the narrow logic and perception of colonized consciousness. Rather, he sees beyond its hyperlogical confines. Chela Sandoval's (2000) oppositional consciousness, a method through which the oppressed come to know, to increase their knowledge of the social determinants of their suffering, including what opposes its expression, achieves its aims through a depth approach, a "hermeneutics of love." Rosi Braidotti's (1994) nomadic consciousness liberates the impulse to roam, to discover obscured parts of the self nestled in the depths of soul. The nomadic psyche, she observes, fuels our living and knowledge generating capacities and thus points us toward our liberation.

Gloria Anzaldúa (1987) advocates for:

> A deeper sensing … that breaks into one's everyday mode of perception, that causes a break into one's defenses and resistance, anything that takes one from one's habitual grounding, causes the depths to open up, causes a shift in perception. This shift in perception deepens the way we see concrete objects and people; the senses become so acute and piercing that we can see through things, view events in depth, a piercing that reaches the underworld (the realm of the soul) (p. 61)

Deeper modes of awareness take us "down," into psyche—"As we plunge vertically, the break, with its accompanying new seeing, makes us pay attention to the soul, and we are thus carried into awareness—an experience of soul (Self)" (Anzaldúa, 1987, p. 61).

A revised definition of conscientization would therefore include an awakening to multiple modes of consciousness capable of sensitizing us to the fullness of people's psychological life. An understanding of psyche, as the deep site of people's experience of the social order, is a fund of subjective knowledge about the effects of social injustice. Perceiving, representing and deploying community psyche in service of social transformation could increase our vision and, I would argue, the efficacy of our work. Altering the gaze of community psychology to include participatory research, oral history, and psychosocial analyses of voice and silence may together produce modes of consciousness that meaningfully contribute to efforts to transform the social world.

Final Thoughts

In this project, oral history, as a method of recovering subjugated knowledge held by members of the Tivoli Garden's community facilitated some expression of participants' subjectivity, but not all. It did not catalyze a deideolization process with community members capable of "linking current conditions to socioeconomic legacies" (Seedat, 2015, p. 32). Participants have therefore not directly contributed to analysis produced about the effects of direct or structural violence on their lives or possibilities for social transformation.

It can be argued that because community psychology turns away from the dynamics of psychic interiority that structure psychosocial space, it fails to grapple with community psyche and has yet to develop methods for engaging with community soul. But from the depths of the community's soul could emerge new consciousness capable of illuminating the meanings of people's experiences and possibilities for how different social conditions can be created; conditions in which psychosocial well being can exist. The question becomes: How then can community psychology engage with communities' psychic interiority and exteriority so that second-order processes of social transformation become fruits of our work?

Acknowledgments I wish to thank Catherine Peyroux, Christopher Sonn, Deborah Thomas and Tod Sloan for invaluable feedback they gave me on an earlier version of this chapter.

References

Anzaldúa, G. (1987/1999). *Borderlands/La frontera: The new mestiza* (2nd ed.). San Francisco, CA: Aunt Lute.

Bell, D. (2016). Retrieving psychosocial signs of structural violence in (post)colonial Jamaica. *Community Psychology in Global Perspective, 1*(2), 114–126.

Bell, D. (2017). Researching to transgress and transform. In A. Melling & R. Pilkington (Eds.), *Paulo Freire and transformative education: Changing lives and transforming communities*. London: Palgrave Macmillan.

Braidotti, R. (1994). *Nomadic subjects: Embodiment and sexual difference in contemporary feminist theory*. New York, NY: Columbia University Press.

Dunaway, D. K. (1996). Introduction: The interdisciplinarity of oral history. In D. K. Dunaway & W. K. Baum (Eds.), *Oral history: An interdisciplinary anthology* (pp. 7–22). Walnut Creek, CA: AltaMira.

Fals Borda, O. (2001). Participatory (action) research in social theory: Origins and challenges. In P. Reason & H. Bradbury (Eds.), *Handbook of action research: Participative inquiry and practice* (pp. 27–37). London: Sage.

Fanon, F. (1967). *Black skins, white masks* (R. Philcox, Trans.). New York, NY: Grove.

Freire, P. (1970). *Pedagogy of the oppressed*. New York, NY: Continuum International.

Gray, O. (2003). Badness-honour. In A. Harriott (Ed.), *Understanding crime in Jamaica: New challenges for public policy* (pp. 13–47). Kingston, Jamaica: UWI.

Gray, O. (2004). *Demeaned but empowered: The social power of the urban poor in Jamaica*. Kingston, Jamaica: UWI.

Harriott, A. (2003). Social identities and the escalation of homicidal violence in Jamaica. In A. Harriott (Ed.), *Understanding crime in Jamaica: New challenges for public policy* (pp. 89–112). Kingston, Jamaica: UWI.

Kagan, C., Burton, M., Duckett, P., Lawthom, R., & Siddiquee, A. (2011). *Critical community psychology*. West Sussex: Wiley.

Leavy, P. (2011). *Oral history: Understanding qualitative research*. New York, NY: Oxford University Press.

Lewin, K. (1951). *Field theory in social science*. New York, NY: Harper.

Martín-Baró, I. (1996). *Writings for a liberation psychology*. Boston, MA: Harvard University Press.

Miller, K. (2014). *The cartographer tries to map a way to Zion*. Manchester: Carcanet.

Ministry of Justice. (2016). *Report Western Kingston Commission of Enquiry 2016*. Retrieved from http://moj.gov.jm/content/report-western-kingston-commission-enquiry-2016

Montero, M. (2014). Conscientization. In D. Christie (Ed.), *The encyclopedia of peace psychology* (pp. 1–3). Hoboken, NJ: Blackwell.

Nelson, G., & Prilleltensky, I. (Eds.). (2005). *Community psychology: In pursuit of liberation and well-being*. Basingstoke: Palgrave-Macmillan.

Okihiro, G. Y. (1996). Oral history and the writing of ethnic history. In D. K. Dunaway (Ed.), *Oral history: An Interdisciplinary anthology* (pp. 199–214). Walnut Creek, CA: AltaMira.

Orford, J. (2008). *Community psychology: Challenges, controversies and emerging consensus*. West Sussex: Wiley.

Patterson, M. E. (2013). The ethical murk of using testimony in oral historical research in South Africa. In A. Sheftel & S. Zembrzycki (Eds.), *Oral history off the record: Toward an ethnography of practice* (pp. 201–218). London: Palgrave Macmillan.

Sandoval, C. (2000). *The methodology of the oppressed.* Minneapolis, MN: University of Minneapolis Press.

Seedat, M. (2015). Oral history as an enactment of critical community psychology. *Journal of Community Psychology, 43*(1), 22–35.

Shopes, L. (2015). After the interview ends: Moving oral history out of the archives and into publication. *The Oral History Review, 42*(2), 300–310.

Sloan, T. (2003). Community psychology and/or critical social theory? A personal and reflective perspective. *Network, 14*(1), 57–59.

Thomas, D. (2011). *Exceptional violence: Embodied citizenship in transnational Jamaica.* Durham, NC: Duke University Press.

Tonkin, E. (1986). Investigating oral tradition. *Journal of African History, 27*, 203–213.

Watkins, M., & Ciofalo, N. (2011). Creating and sharing community psychology curriculum for the 21st century: An invitation. *Global Journal of Community Psychology Practice, 2*(2), 9–18.

Chapter 11
Exploring Participant-Led Film-Making as a Community-Engaged Method

Nick Malherbe and Brittany Everitt-Penhale

The primary values and ideals of critical scholarship, including critical community psychology, as a movement and a practice, comprise self-determination; respect for diversity; participation and collaboration; as well as social justice and accountability (Dant, 2003). Considering its apparent potential to advance these values, as well as the ubiquity of film as a medium of expression in many contemporary societies, participant-led film-making appears to be an underused methodological resource. This is reflected in the dearth of literature exploring the theoretical underpinnings of the method and its accompanying analyses. Indeed, liberatory community-engagement projects appear to interact with visual methodologies somewhat uncomfortably, and oftentimes multimodal languages and visual meaning-making are displaced for more traditional linguistic-based methods (Kress & Van Leeuwen, 2006). Further, there is almost no exploration into the social learning processes, or even the enjoyment, in which participants partake whilst producing films (Milne, Mitchell, & de Lange, 2012). Film-making as a participatory method lacks standardisation, and is understood predominantly as a kind of 'alternative', theoretically wanting, method.

Boog (2003) defines emancipatory, or liberatory, processes as those that are developed as a means of freeing the self from the restraint, control, and/or power of others. In order to utilise community-engaged meaning-making processes in liberatory ways that critique structures of power, Kagan and Burton (2001) posit that participants and facilitators must develop a reflexive working relationship that strives to

N. Malherbe (✉) • B. Everitt-Penhale
Institute for Social and Health Sciences, University of South Africa, Johannesburg, South Africa

South African Medical Research Council-University of South Africa Violence, Injury and Peace Research Unit, Cape Town, South Africa
e-mail: nicholas.malherbe@mrc.ac.za

M. Seedat et al. (eds.), *Emancipatory and Participatory Methodologies in Peace, Critical, and Community Psychology*, Peace Psychology Book Series, DOI 10.1007/978-3-319-63489-0_11

make accessible different concepts and practices. Both parties may then collaboratively act towards a free, equal, and just society. By exploring both the liberatory character and enactment of the participatory film production process, this chapter argues for the immensely rich community-engagement potential inherent to participant-led film-making, as well as to visual methodologies more broadly. Indeed, the process of producing and screening films allows for a critical reflection among researchers as well as participants, audience members, and community leaders.

The multimodal nature of film, which includes locating meaning at the intersection of sound, moving image, and speech, is able to represent viscerally various cultural and historical moments and meanings (Olivier, de Lange, Creswell, & Wood, 2012). If multimodal languages are to emerge from the peripheries of community-based work, more theoretical attention must be extended towards visual methodologies. Participant-led film may be an especially effective means of tapping into the multimodal voice, with its production and screening processes forming key liberatory sites for participants and their communities.

Participant-Led Film-Making

Visual methods such as Photovoice, collaging, and film-making are inscribed with a visual language. It is not the visual itself that communicates meaning; rather, meaning is constructed within a discursive space that lies between producers, subjects, community, and authority (Corneil, 2012).

Film-making as a community-engaged liberatory method has, at different times, been referred to as collaborative video, community video, or participatory video (Mitchell & de Lange, 2011). In this chapter, we understand this to mean the involvement of participants (also referred to as "producers") in constructing films as a way of exploring their interactions with their social environment, and how the video text can be used to stimulate post-screening dialogue, social action, and reflection among audiences, facilitators, and participants. Film's multimodal language has the potential to be less susceptible to mistranslation than exclusively visual or verbal communication, and may afford participants the confidence to express themselves and to tell their stories (Kress & Van Leeuwen, 2006).

It would appear that within the broader social sciences, there is a general discomfort when drawing on visuals. Aside from visual sociology and some anthropological studies, participant-led film-making has arguably been under-examined within community-engaged work, with most projects using visual images as a subsidiary accompaniment to linguistic text (Banks, 2001). However, it is crucial that film—like all visual text—is considered independently from written or verbal text, and that it emerges as its own mode of meaning-making, as visual language is able to tap into that which cannot always be expressed with written or spoken language. The verbal and written texts which pervade much community work have limited access to the emotional and symbolic facets of experience that are mediated by video. Tensions tied up with differences in linguistic and cultural expression may also, to an extent, dissolve when drawing on film's multimodal language (Niesyto, Buckingham, & Fisherkeller, 2003). Indeed, film does not convey more or less knowledge than lingustic-based expression. Rather, it is able to convey *different* knowledge (MacDougall, 2011).

Participant-led film-making has seen only minimal methodological standardisation. As a result, projects that make use of the method are furnished with a radical kind of openness, becoming exposed to that which cannot be epistemologically anticipated. For example, Mitchell and de Lange (2011) recount a number of challenges related to the unexpected group dynamics that were encountered within their project's cinematic training. They also caution against addressing sensitive topics without having a history of sustained community-engagement as some films may deal with particular topics in an unintentionally insensitive or problematic manner. Nonetheless, the method's inherent openness enables participants to exercise a greater kind of ownership over meaning-making processes; such ownership which is usually alluded to, but rarely embodied within much community-engaged work (Sanon, Evans-Agnew, & Boutain, 2014).

As a means of demonstrating critically the liberatory potential of participant-led film-making, we explore some of the literature surrounding the method and describe a South African case example. We argue that despite, and in some ways because of, the open-ended nature of participant-led film-making, it is both a fruitful and adaptable community-engaged liberatory method within the intervention sciences. However, in order to allow for the theoretical development that is required to shift film-making towards the centre of community-engaged intervention as well as liberatory meaning-making, aspects of the method will have to undergo a degree of standardisation.

Youth and Film-Making

Within community-engaged work as well as broader society, young people's voices are continually marginalised. The issue of diminished, or structural, weakening of youths' voices is compounded when living in conditions of poverty. Reduced familial and financial support may also limit young people's ability to engage meaningfully with issues in their lives. Film-making has been noted as especially useful in exploring the social performances and experiences of youth (MacDougall, 2011). It is, however, crucial that film producers select which issues are addressed in their films. Therefore, film topics can be loosely guided, but never fully predetermined, by particular project agendas (Mitchell & de Lange, 2011).

Participant-led film-making has been shown to ignite a sense of purpose, self-awareness, and reflection among young people, thereby furnishing the method with immense liberatory potential (Rich & Chalfen, 1999). Working together to make a film, as well as engaging with community members about the film, allows youth to feel heard and respected, and it is hoped that feelings of empowerment encourage community members to act towards sustainable community change. Empowerment within participant-led film-making projects is understood as a contextually-bound negotiation between various agendas, and an open-ended, emergent process of social learning. Yet empowerment is not guaranteed within all participant-led film-making endeavours (Mak, 2012). It furthermore cannot be assumed that all participants do not have a voice, or that the method is always able to facilitate the effective use of participant voice. However, if participants engage critically and reflexively with the production of the film, they may begin to feel that they have genuinely participated in working towards destabilising oppressive power structures (Corneil, 2012).

Perhaps the dearth of projects that rely on participant-led film-making is so jarring because of the ubiquity of film in so many societies. Technological advancements in video-recording equipment, as well as the availability of relatively cheap camera equipment, allow for simple and rapid film production. Wide-scale exposure to the iconic and indexical qualities of film and cinematic convention has endued the genre with a particular kind of recognisable communicative effectiveness (Pauwels, 2011). With this mind, Zaslow and Butler (2002) highlight that youth do not come to video projects as blank slates. They are experienced readers of video language as well as contemporary visual cultural codes, and thus are able to render the unfamiliar as familiar when using film to draw on common cultural symbols. Indeed, complex issues are presented as more lucid and accessible to audiences when they adhere to the filmic convention in which people are socially saturated. One may readily concur with Niesyto's (2000) thesis, which postulates that considering young people's self-made media products allows us to explore their largely media-driven, lived experiences in an especially meaningful manner.

Film-Making and the Community

Community-engaged methods aim to promote participants' ownership and control over knowledge and meaning-making processes. They can be used within community engaged-work as a way of sanctioning various liberatory outcomes, such as a collaborative and reflexive critique of power structures (Kagan & Burton, 2001). Young people engaged in participant-led film-making become both collaborators and potential agents of social change through a critical reflexive engagement with themselves as well as their communities.

In situating participant-led film-making as an enactment of community-engagement, participants work together to develop a film's concepts, its storyboarding, the planning shots, and later take the lead in the shooting, screening and dialogue processes. A community-engagement framework also ensures that participants' voices are centralised throughout the project, and that the concerns of the community are prioritised.

Case Example: The Engaging Youth Project

Early projects that made use of participant-led film-making restricted their foci to material culture, technology and physiology. Today, work of this kind explores a number of social issues, typically related to intersectional experience, meaning-making, and participant expression (MacDougall, 2011). The unstandardised nature of participant-led film-making is apparent in the various projects that refer to the method by different names, and sometimes use it in diverse, even conflicting, ways (Mitchell & de Lange, 2011; Niesyto et al., 2003). In this regard, the method becomes moulded by the context in which it is used, and specific characteristics of a project—such as funding, ethical procedure, focus, and participants—dictate the manner in which it is employed. This malleability is one of participant-led film-making's greatest strengths as a tool of liberatory community-engagement, notwithstanding that methodological standardisation is required if sufficient theory is to be developed. What follows is a critical account of a case example that utilises this malleable method as a means of enacting community-engagement.

Project Background

The Engaging Youth Project was undertaken in 2014 at a high school in a peri-urban community near Cape Town, South Africa, and was facilitated primarily by the second author. The project was undertaken by the Masculinity, Tradition and Social Change Programme, which is housed in the Institute for Social and Health Sciences at the University of South Africa. When employing participant-led film-making within community-engaged work, it is crucial that facilitators have a sound understanding of the community in which the project takes place. Laying the foundation for this project were several other community-engaged projects. In 2011 and 2012, programme staff - in collaboration with several schools - organised a number of Youth Day campaigns that were held in the specified area. These one-day events focused on issues chosen by school learners within the community. Reflecting on these campaigns, learners confirmed that a single-day event was inadequate to address community concerns. Accordingly, in 2013 sixteen learners participated in a Photovoice project that sought to examine youth representations of fatherhood (see Malherbe, 2015). During each of these projects, rapport, trust, and cooperation was developed between the learners and programme staff.

The Engaging Youth Project served as an extension of these earlier projects, and therefore used as its base the relationships formed with the school's staff and students as well as the insights and learnings garnered from the preceding engagements. The vice-principal of the school at which the project was conducted served as the gatekeeper. We offered the learners who participated in the 2013 Photovoice project the opportunity to enlist in the Engaging Youth Project, with most accepting this offer. Additionally, through word-of-mouth other students became interested, with the final group consisting of 15 participants, aged 14–17. As Rich and Chalfen (1999) note, from mid-to-late teens, youth tend to be more enthusiastic about producing films, and generally this cohort is able to engage creatively with instructions, whilst taking the project seriously. The group comprised of eight girls and seven boys, each of whom identified as black and as South African. It was agreed that the film would be produced in isiXhosa, the home language of almost all of the participants.

With regards to our status as facilitators, we respectively identify as male and female South Africans. We are white, university-educated social scientists from middle-class backgrounds who, at the time of this project, were in our mid-20s. We acknowledge that each of us came to this project with our own set of left-leaning politics that are informed largely by feminist, constructivist world views.

Aims

This project aims to address the relative dearth of critical work around visual methodologies by showcasing the manner in which film is able to afford participants a legitimate, accessible and liberatory multimodal language. By exploring the process of participant-led film-making, the Engaging Youth Project served to develop the method theoretically, thereby facilitating the elevation of the status of visual methods more broadly within participatory community-engaged interventions.

Ethical Issues

Being a relatively new method within the social sciences, participant-led film-making sometimes finds itself within complicated ethical straits, and it can be difficult to obtain clearance from ethics committees as it is not always possible to know exactly to what participants are consenting. For example, the ways that the film will be used or the roles that each participant will play in its production are not always clear at a project's early stages. Further, gaining informed consent from youth, their guardians, as well as film subjects can be challenging as many people find the notion of informed consent difficult to understand, may not feel comfortable signing the consent forms, may be formally illiterate, and/or might not trust the project co-ordinators. Added to this, some participants may later decide that they do not want their work to be screened at all (Gubrium, Hill, & Flicker, 2014).

For this project, we informed participants verbally about the nature of the project and the issue of intrusion that accompanies film as a mode of seeing. Later, we obtained written informed consent from the participants and their parents. We assured participants that they were able to withdraw at any time without negative consequence, and at each stage they were offered the opportunity to indicate the aspects of production in which they wanted to participate. Ethics approval was provided by a relevant ethics board.

It was important for the participants and their parents to be aware of the limitations of confidentiality. Given the visual nature of film and the goal of screening the film at the school, full confidentiality was neither possible nor viewed as desirable in this project. However, the participants agreed to respect and keep confidential any personal information that may be offered by other participants during the production process.

Procedure

For several weeks focus groups were conducted on issues that participants felt were pertinent to their lives. These were generally mixed-gender groups. In order to facilitate comfort in discussing any gendered concerns, during one session the group was sub-divided into a "boys' group" and a "girls' group". Thereafter, both groups reported back to the larger group as a means of intergrating their discussion material into the overall process. As project facilitators, we then shared with the participants examples of social change projects that have been conducted by school learners around the world. The participants decided unanimously to use film as a medium through which to tell their story.

Although early stages of community projects are often marked with the kinds of inter-group challenges that typically accompany facilitation (Mitchell & de Lange, 2011), this process was made somewhat manageable because the participants had developed rapport with one another, and us, in the preceding Photovoice project. As those who did not want to participate or did not work well within the group had dropped out of the previous project, the current group of participants worked quickly and well together. The relative facilitative ease that we experienced throughout this project highlights the importance of prolonged community-engagement when undertaking work of this nature. Participant-led film-making requires that participants are comfortable working with one another as well as with facilitators, and it is important that such projects allocate sufficient time to the development of sustained community-engagement and relationships.

We provided the participants with cinematic training that covered storyboarding, script-writing, camera angles and shot framing. With little methodological standardisation, participant-led film-making training may be somewhat challenging to implement effectively, especially where—as was the case with this project—there is insufficient budget set aside for professional cinematic teaching. However, if professional training is inaccessible there is a wealth of free online resources that can be used to assist facilitators in this task [see Lunch and Lunch's (2006) *Insights into Participatory Video*].

The participants decided collectively that they would produce a single film based on a preliminary storyboard (which focused on teenage pregnancy) that was created during the film training. After extensive group discussions on the film content, and remoulding the original storyboard, the group was divided into smaller subgroups who were respectively assigned the task of writing the basic dialogue for each scene. However, this dialogue was improvised significantly by the actors during filming.

Many of participant-led film-making's primary aims—such as amplifying voice, liberatory enactment, critical reflection, and social action—are premised on storytelling (Olivier et al., 2012). Particular focus should thus fall on storyboarding training, especially if participants are unfamiliar with narrative construction. Such training should emphasise the importance of this stage in the production process, equipping participants to challenge dominant scripts within and beyond their film. In the Engaging Youth Project, whilst storyboarding training could have been more extensive, participants engaged in numerous critical discussions around the film's narrative, and whether the discourses represented aligned with their intended message.

de Lange and Mitchell (2012) argue that it can be very difficult to challenge problematic discourses that are re-presented within participants' scripts without obscuring a project's participatory enactment.[1] Relinquishing representational control to participants can therefore locate facilitators on somewhat difficult ethical grounds as any kind of facilitator intervention—with respect to that which participants wish to voice or how they wish to voice it— may subsequently obscure a project's participatory process. Throughout the scriptwriting procedure, we attempted to encourage an open discussion that privileged participants' voices. In an effort not to impose our own politics and perspectives on the group, thus compromising the level of community engagement, we reminded participants of their own challenges to particular discourses that they had asserted in previous discussions. This facilitated their interrogation of the contradictions inherent to their own belief systems. Having had a long-term engagement with participants thus equipped us to challenge particular representations in a manner that upheld liberatory principles. Significantly, however, our beliefs and values unavoidably impacted the direction, organisation as well as the shape of the narrative during this process.

In collaboration with an independent film-maker who was hired by the project team, participants shot the film in a single afternoon at their school. Despite the filmmaker undoubtedly improving the film's aesthetic quality (and therefore enhancing the level of audience engagement), the extent of the project's overall participatory engagement was compromised in this regard. As a means of partially addressing this participatory shortcoming, the participants decided upon the location and format of each scene prior to the filmmaker's involvement. They also rehearsed the entirety of the film in accordance to their own creative decisions. On the day of filming, participants were furthermore heavily involved in the shooting and shot-selection procedures, with the filmmaker providing gentle advice rather than explicit instruction.

[1] This was found in their work, where an all-male group who produced a film entitled *Rape* was said to reproduce some of the hegemonic discourses around sexual violence that it aimed to challenge. Although we concede that films such as these can be useful both in exploring how certain young people think about particular issues and as an historical document of such thought, the reproduction of problematic discourses in participant-led film production cannot be received uncritically.

Training sessions within participant-led film-making projects should stress that each person is crucial to the production process. In the case of this project, those who expressed interest in filming were given basic instructions regarding how to use and look after the video camera. With respect to set design, the participants brought props from their homes. Each member of the production team had an acting role, with many also assisting with technical issues, such as stabilising the microphone. Throughout the participatory production procedure, we were challenged with conveying that each role within the shooting process is important as there is often an underlying implication that those who are given the most dialogue, or have more on-screen time, contribute more valuably to a film's production than those whose production roles are off-camera. As Mak (2012) notes, participatory film production does not necessarily empower everyone involved. Yet inclusive participation should be the aim, and should be facilitated by both participants and facilitators. In the Engaging Youth Project, mitigating this issue somewhat, each participant was involved with directing the actors throughout the process of shooting. The relatively small group also meant that during the overall production process, each participant took on a number of functional roles, each of which was determined somewhat by self-identified interests and strengths. These factors assisted in providing participants with a sense of ownership over this process.

Another challenge that we experienced during shooting relates to interplays of power between those in front of and behind the camera. As a film's subject is placed within a particular cinematic narrative, he or she often becomes a stereotype (such as that of a hero or victim) who is robbed of agency. One way of addressing this concern is to enact what is known as an "ethics of access"; that is, improving the access to the means of film production for both subjects (or actors) and filmmakers (Corneil, 2012). By ensuring that each participant was both filmmaker and subject, they produced a film in which representational power dynamics were addressed as much as is feasible (as every participant performed both on- and off-screen production roles), thus acting towards an ethics of access.

The open nature of this project's production allowed the actors an interpretative freedom of their characters. Such freedom was evident during the written dialogue's transformation from simple, concrete English, to the rich and lengthy speech - spoken in isiXhosa - expressed by the performers during the shooting. Rather than the script being static and prescriptive, the actors continually morphed their screenplay beyond its original parameters. This was crucial in conceptualising the fluid nature of participant voice, whereby dialogue that was altered or changed was not understood as a failure to plan accordingly, but rather as signifying the exploratory, developmental process by which participant-led film-making allows for collaborative meaning-making.

Involving participants in editing their films promotes a greater sense of ownership, and provides an opportunity for learners to acquire a new skill-set. However, even learning how to use simple editing programmes like Adobe® Premier® takes considerable time, and requires access to expensive equipment. It also becomes difficult for a film to meaningfully engage with or capture the attention of an audience if it is edited poorly. For these reasons the participants involved with this project agreed that all editing would be outsourced. Future projects may consider running workshops that provide training in the use of film editing software so that participants are able to exert maximum control over the storytelling process (MacDougall, 2011). Yet it must be kept in mind that the feasibility of this option is contingent on available resources, and it is important that the film remains engaging and accessible. An unintended benefit of this project's outsourced editor not understanding isiXhosa was that no dialogue was cut (lest any crucial narrative was omitted), and the final product adhered entirely to the participants' complete performances. Participants later provided relevant English subtitles to their film so that it was able to reach a wider audience. Lastly, several of the participants performed and recorded music which served as the film's score.

Dissemination

Once the film - which participants titled *My Teenage Years* - was completed, we worked extensively with the participants to plan and promote a screening event at their school. This was attended by over 100 learners—the maximum capacity of the available venue. Although we were able to provide a projector and screen, we acknowledge that access to such equipment is often difficult in under-resourced communities. However, with that being said, the screening event is an essential element of the participant-led film-making process, both as a means by which to ignite critical community dialogue and as a way of promoting participants' ownership of their work. The event was chaired by one participant, and several others performed songs and poetry. A representative of Free Gender, a human rights organisation, was invited to speak about discrimination and violence against queer people in the community—a concern highlighted by the group in earlier discussions as a significant problem.

At the film's conclusion, attendees engaged in a discussion around various interpretations of the film and its import within the community, as well as that which can be done to address teenage pregnancy and related concerns. Although there was some contestation during this discussion—particularly with regard to the privileging of either secular or religious values—there was little antagonism between audience members. Participants later suggested that for a more robust discussion to have occurred, policy-makers, teachers, activists, and leaders within the community would need to be present at the screening. Future projects should note the importance of careful planning with regard to inviting a rich variety of critical community voices to public screenings of the film.

The film produced within the Engaging Youth Project was not given an online platform. Although publishing a film online may increase exponentially its reach, participants unavoidably lose control over their work in various ways, raising both practical and ethical concerns. Many popular video-sharing websites, including YouTube, own certain rights to each video uploaded. Participants are also unable to interact directly with an online audience, and problems linked to appropriation and redistribution may arise. Further, placing a participant-led film text online increases the risk of harm for participants as it is difficult to prepare them adequately for potential mass exposure and recognition. Additionally, online videos are often subject to trolling or deliberately inflammatory and abusive user-comments (Teitelbaum, 2012).

The accent of this project fell on the process of film-making, rather than the film text's ability to engage a diverse audience. This was most apparent in that storyboarding and group discussions took place over several months, whilst filming, editing, and screening were completed in just over two weeks. This imbalance was primarily due to unanticipated delays (for example, multiple sessions were postponed due to communication challenges with the gatekeeper) which were compounded by the time-constraints, such as study leave, that one faces when working with school learners. Our experiences in this regard can be seen as indicative of the challenge of ensuring that each stage of participant-led film projects—and their accompanying liberatory enactment—is fully realised and accommodated.

Reflexivity

Among its participants, the Engaging Youth Project aimed to ignite critical reflexive processes at three central levels: *the primary text* (that is the film, whereby participants engaged with issues related to social identity as well as broader community concerns, while reflecting on their respective subjectivities); *the production text* (the making of the film where participants worked towards constructing a message whilst engaging in the team-building and compromise processes that typically accompany collaborative work); and *the secondary text* (the audience's engagement, which gave way to a reflexive dialogical space) (Fisk, 1987, as cited in Olivier et al., 2012).

It was crucial that we as project facilitators engaged in an ongoing reflexive process (Milne et al., 2012). Willig (2001) posits that such reflexivity requires researchers to deliberate critically upon how the work that we do is affected and shaped by, "our own values, experiences, interests, beliefs, political commitments, wider aims in life and social identities" (p. 10). Significantly, our subjective roles and identities relative to that of the learners placed us in a position of authority throughout the project. Whilst positioning participants as experts of their communities assisted in mitigating this somewhat, our relative position of power is important to acknowledge. Although we attempted to avoid imposing our perspectives, as facilitators we unavoidably and indelibly shape facilitation in significant (and often damaging and unpredictable) ways. Furthermore, the meanings attributed to our various identity markers—such as age, 'race', and socioeconomic status—would have facilitated the emergence of particular narratives, whilst limiting others. Therefore, although the central aim of the project was to promote the expression of participants' voice, the facilitators' identities, values, and perspectives, as well as the explicit feminist lens that undergirded the project, undoubtedly influenced the film that was produced by the participants.

Conclusion

By drawing on familiar cultural symbols, participant-led film-making allows participants to communicate complex issues in an accessible manner. In this chapter, we have argued that participant-led film-making, like other visual methods, enables a visceral means of promoting reflective community-engagement among participants and their broader communities. The method is able to provide youth—who frequently have less social power and agency, especially in impoverished contexts—with a space in which they can work together in harnessing a multimodal language that addresses various community issues and concerns. In understanding participant-led film-making as a community-engaged method, community voices—both those outside of and directly involved with the film's production—are galvanised and conscientised towards critical reflection and social change.

The case example examined in this chapter presents a number of considerations for future community-engagement projects that utilise participant-led film-making. Firstly, standardising participants' cinematic training may enable the method to take on a recognisable form that can be developed and critiqued. However, such a standardised training should not encompass a set of rigid and chronological stages. It should be marked by an adaptability so that it can be moulded to the requirements, constraints, and available resources of a particular project. For example, if especially high-quality video recording equipment is available, project facilitators may wish to concentrate training on the shooting process. Employing a training procedure of this kind thereby attempts to address the paradox of standardising participant-led film-making whilst maintaining its flexibility.

Training participants in and familiarising them with participant-led film-making should emphasise, and allow for an interrogation into, the social and inter-group power dynamics that the film could address, whilst highlighting the importance of each participant's role throughout the production process. Storyboarding workshops are also integral to this approach, as narrative construction is paramount to the method's liberatory aims of empowerment, inclusivity, and enhancing participant voice.

The case example examined in this chapter demonstrates the importance of long-term engagement with a community. Certainly, this kind of engagement is able to streamline the film-making process, allow participants a sense of comfort within the group, and equip facilitators to challenge various discourses without compromising the method's participatory character.

Finally, given the nature of community-engaged work, it is advisable to take into account the likelihood of unanticipated setbacks or delays. Unexpected postponements in our project meant that relatively little time was available for organising the film's dissemination—a result of which was that post-screening dialogue was less robust than it might have been had more diverse community voices been present. Whether the focus of such a project falls on its production or screening, it is crucial that each phase is attended to adequately.

Participant-led film-making presents an exciting, visceral and largely underutilised means of engaging participants and broader community audiences in a liberatory, multimodal language. We wish to encourage those involved in community-engaged work to grapple with the ambiguities of the method which, if implemented successfully, is marked by a capacity to support critical reflection and social action.

References

Banks, M. (2001). *Visual methods in social research*. London: SAGE.

Boog, B. W. M. (2003). The emancipatory character of action research, its history and present state of the art. *Journal of Community and Applied Social Psychology, 13*, 426–438.

Corneil, M. K. (2012). Citizenship and participatory video. In E. J. Milne, C. Mitchell, & N. de Lange (Eds.), *Handbook of participatory video* (pp. 19–34). Plymouth: AltaMira Press.

Dant, T. (2003). *Critical social theory: Culture, society and critique*. London: SAGE.

de Lange, N., & Mitchell, C. (2012). Building sustainability into work with participatory video. In E. J. Milne, C. Mitchell, & N. de Lange (Eds.), *Handbook of participatory video* (pp. 318–330). Plymouth: AltaMira Press.

Gubrium, A. C., Hill, A., & Flicker, S. (2014). A situated practice of ethics for participatory visual and digital methods in public health research and practice: A focus on digital storytelling. *American Journal of Public Health, 104*, 1606–1614.

Kagan, C., & Burton, M. (2001, March). *Critical community psychology praxis for the 21st century*. Paper presented at British Psychological Society Conference, Glasgow. Retrieved from http://www.compsy.org.uk/GLASGOX5.pdf

Kress, G., & Van Leeuwen, T. (2006). *Reading images: The grammar of visual design*. London: Routledge.

Lunch, N., & Lunch, C. (2006). *Insights into participatory video: A handbook for the field*. Oxford: Insight. Teitelbaum, 2010.

MacDougall, D. (2011). Anthropological filmmaking: An empirical art. In E. Margolis & L. Pauwels (Eds.), *The SAGE handbook of visual research methods* (pp. 99–113). London: SAGE.

Mak, M. (2012). Visual postproduction in participatory video-making processes. In E. J. Milne, C. Mitchell, & N. de Lange (Eds.), *Handbook of participatory video* (pp. 194–207). Plymouth: AltaMira Press.

Malherbe, N. (2015). *Interrogating the 'crisis of fatherhood': Discursive constructions of fathers amongst peri-urban Xhosa-speaking adolescents*. Unpublished master's thesis, University of Cape Town, Cape Town.

Milne, E. J., Mitchell, C., & de Lange, N. (2012). Introduction. In E. J. Milne, C. Mitchell, & N. de Lange (Eds.), *Handbook of participatory video* (pp. 1–18). Plymouth: AltaMira Press.

Mitchell, C., & de Lange, M. (2011). Community-based participatory video and social action in rural South Africa. In E. Margolis & L. Pauwels (Eds.), *The SAGE handbook of visual research methods* (pp. 171–185). London: SAGE.

Niesyto, H. (2000). Youth research on video self-productions: Reflections on a social—Aesthetic approach. *Visual Sociology, 15*, 135–153.

Niesyto, H., Buckingham, D., & Fisherkeller, J. (2003). VideoCulture: Crossing borders with young people's video productions. *Television & New Media, 4*, 461–482.

Olivier, T., de Lange, N., Creswell, J. W., & Wood, L. (2012). Mixed methods research in participatory video. In E. J. Milne, C. Mitchell, & N. de Lange (Eds.), *Handbook of participatory video* (pp. 131–148). Plymouth: AltaMira Press.

Pauwels, L. (2011). An integrated conceptual framework for visual social research. In E. Margolis & L. Pauwels (Eds.), *The SAGE handbook of visual research methods* (pp. 3–23). London: SAGE.

Rich, M., & Chalfen, R. (1999). Showing and telling asthma: Children teaching physicians with visual narrative. *Visual Sociology, 14*, 51–71.

Sanon, M., Evans-Agnew, R. A., & Boutain, D. M. (2014). An exploration of social justice intent in photovoice research studies from 2008 to 2013. *Nursing Inquiry, 21*, 212–226.

Teitelbaum, P. (2012). Online participatory communication: Re-seeing participatory video practices and research. In E. J. Milne, C. Mitchell, & N. de Lange (Eds.), *Handbook of participatory video* (pp. 412–425). Plymouth: AltaMira Press.

Willig, C. (2001). *Introducing qualitative research in psychology* (1st ed.). Philadelphia, PA: Open University Press.

Zaslow, E., & Butler, A. (2002). "That it was made by people our age is better": Exploring the role of media literacy in transcultural communication. *Journal of Popular Film and Television, 30*, 31–40.

Chapter 12
Catalysing Transformation Through Stories: Building Peace in Recognition, Struggle and Dialogue

Ursula Lau, Shahnaaz Suffla, and Lesego Bertha Kgatitswe

Our everyday lives are saturated with stories. We tell stories about events that occur in our lives, stories about ourselves, and stories about the world around us. One way or another, we tell stories to entertain, to transmit information, values, morals and culture or to make sense of situations and events that make up the often bewildering world in which we live. Simply defined, storytelling is telling another that something has happened (Smith, 1981), but beyond this simple definition, storytelling and its purposes have been illustrated in various contexts. In narrative therapy, Epston and White (1990) have documented the therapeutic power of stories. Narrative therapy operates from the assumption that people experience problems when the stories that have been written for them fail to represent their lived

U. Lau (✉)
Institute for Social and Health Sciences, University of South Africa, Johannesburg, South Africa

South African Medical Research Council-University of South Africa Violence, Injury and Peace Research Unit, Cape Town, South Africa

Institute for Dispute Resolution in Africa, University of South Africa, Pretoria, South Africa
e-mail: ursula.lau@gmail.com

S. Suffla
Institute for Social and Health Sciences, University of South Africa, Johannesburg, South Africa

South African Medical Research Council-University of South Africa Violence, Injury and Peace Research Unit, Cape Town, South Africa

L.B. Kgatitswe
Sociology Department, University of the Witwatersrand, Johannesburg, South Africa

M. Seedat et al. (eds.), *Emancipatory and Participatory Methodologies in Peace, Critical, and Community Psychology*, Peace Psychology Book Series,
DOI 10.1007/978-3-319-63489-0_12

experiences. In this respect, re-storying lives to incorporate subjugated knowledges holds therapeutic value. The healing power, however, lies in the rewriting inasmuch as it is in the "provision of the space for the performance of these knowledges" (Epston & White, 1990, p. 31). Within the context of post-trauma healing, the act of retelling the traumatic story with its attendant horrors and emotions within a safe space is an important aspect in the transformation process (Bussey & Wise, 2007).

Beyond these clinical settings, the transformative potential of stories has also been illustrated in the broader social contexts. In peacebuilding, storytelling has been utilised to foster mutual recognition between opposing sides, acting as a catalyst for humanisation and empathy for the suffering of the Other (Senehi, 2009). Rappaport (1995) suggests that for communities who lack social, political or economic voice, the available cultural narratives written for them are often narrow or stigmatising. By creating a new communal narrative, a community is empowered to seek opportunities for new selves, identities and role opportunities. When personal stories are sustained and find the support of a collectivity, empowerment is enhanced through processes of discovery, creation, amplifying voice and witnessing of others' stories. Moreover, in speaking out against oppression and injustice, the speaker is viewed as a person of authority, as one who "knows in her own experience" (Zingaro, 2009, p. 148). The act of identifying or disclosing oneself to others becomes the conduit and process through which an experience shared amongst fellow members of a marginalised group is validated, along with the possibilities of voice, power and resistance (Zingaro, 2009).

As Brodkin (2007) explains, the ability to narrate one's own life story is an essential part of becoming what she calls a political actor. Being the narrator/interpreter of events, we exercise personal agency and act upon society. What these examples highlight is that in the processes of storytelling and story listening, meaning is made out of the seemingly inexplicable and bewildering life struggles (Zingaro, 2009). However, meanings are also being reproduced, negotiated, resisted or changed (Senehi, 2009). Therefore, storytelling is not simply telling what we already know; stories also hold persuasive power that forms the basis for action. How we interpret our experiences opens up possibilities for stories to be constructive, transformative and liberatory, or alternatively, destructive, divisive and regressive. Jackson (2002), for instance, refers to the "dual potentiality of stories to either reinforce or degrade the boundaries that normally divide seemingly finite social worlds from the infinite variety of possible human experience" (p. 25).

Storytelling as a Social Interaction

What then makes a story and by extension the processes of storytelling healing, empowering or liberatory? Meichenbaum (2006) proposes that aside from the pre-trauma, trauma and post-trauma factors, the types of stories that people tell themselves after a traumatic event, whether as individuals and groups, has bearing on the "final common pathway" that influences the level of stress versus degree of resilience (p. 356). In other words, the self or group narrative, when dominated by characteristically negative features (e.g. self and other blaming, self-focused thinking, rumination on the past, focused on helplessness and victimisation) are associated with persistent and higher post-trauma distress levels in survivors of trauma. Alternatively, thinking patterns oriented towards growth are those that are benefit-seeking for self and others (e.g. "This has brought us together"), have a future orientation (e.g. "I see new possibilities") and have a resolved meaning (e.g. "I survived for a purpose") (Meichenbaum, 2006, p. 363). Within the broader context of peace work, Senehi (2002, 2009) distinguishes between constructive versus destructive storytelling. Whereas constructive storytelling fosters the cornerstones of peace— power balance, mutual recognition, critical awareness and even acts of resistance—destructive storytelling, to the contrary, displays coercive power, exclusionary practices and a lack of awareness and mutual recognition (Senehi, 2002). In peacebuilding, stories therefore potentially play an instrumental role in fostering understanding and mutual recognition. Yet mutual recognition encompasses more than passive listening; it necessitates that parties engage in dialogue and struggle through differences (Deutsch, as cited in Senehi, 2009).

The view adopted by us is that whilst stories may in themselves be growth-promoting or growth-limiting, constructive or destructive (Senehi, 2002), it is also the social context of the telling that contributes to their narrative potency for either constructive or destructive ways (Raheja & Gold, as cited in Senehi, 2002). The story itself cannot be isolated from the context in which it is told, whether that be a two-person encounter, group or mass audience. When enacted within a safe space, the setting affords the avenue for catharsis for both the storyteller and the listeners who identify with a common struggle (Senehi, 2009). This shared and interactive safe space therefore also enables a co-construction of healing (Lieblich, McAdams, & Josselson, 2004).

Digital Storytelling

The act of storytelling accords the narrator the power to influence the processes of social construction and interpretation. In this chapter, we highlight storytelling as an interaction that takes place between the storytellers and the listeners. We focus on storytelling as an interactive and intersubjective process to identify two process dimensions that emerged between and within a group six community leaders of Thembelihle, a peri-urban township community in the south-east of Johannesburg, South Africa and the facilitators of the story circle in the context of a digital storytelling workshop.

Digital storytelling is the practice of merging stories in the form of short vignettes with multimedia content (images, sound and video) to create a short movie (Rossiter & Garcia, 2010). With its roots in the oral tradition of storytelling, digital storytelling in community contexts has been used to share knowledge, ideas and culture, and has increasingly been used as a vehicle to explore, understand and intervene in the everyday lives of ordinary people to improve their material conditions and promote social recognition (Gubrium & Turner (2009)). Through the platform of encouraging voice—voice as talk, voice as identity and voice as power—digital storytelling is a powerful modality to support the empowerment of individuals in marginalised contexts. What distinguishes the digital story from a professionally made short film or documentary is its handmade quality and feel, which contributes to its poignancy and effectiveness as a social justice tool that fosters agency and voice.

Though the process of digital story creation is documented in a step procedure (see Lambert, 2013), in the community context in which we worked, the unfolding of the story as content was typically unstructured. In particular, the process dimensions of group work were salient and molded the shape of the stories told. By illustrating these process dimensions, we elucidate how storytelling, story listening and scripting involved a co-construction of meanings between our participants and between facilitators and participants. We illustrate how, through oscillations between dialogue, struggle and recognition (Senehi, 2009), the community leaders and facilitators collaboratively unite common elements of their individual stories to achieve a group story. Through this process, they *perform* peace and initiate healing in an individual and collective way. We further illustrate how, through active facilitation, the initial stories of struggle and hardship were merged with a counter-narrative of resilience, hope and change, in order to foster a constructive (as opposed to) destructive story outcome. Before we illuminate these process dimensions, we outline the *Community Storylines* project as a backdrop to our work with the community of Thembelihle and the six leaders who volunteered as participants in the workshop.

Community Storylines

Situated on the peri-urban fringes of the greater Johannesburg metropolitan, Thembelihle is a sprawling township settlement. The settlement has been a physically, legally and publicly contested space resting on dolomite land that is vulnerable to sinkhole collapse. Whilst some residents have resisted relocation to neighbouring townships, citing insufficient geological evidence to warrant eviction, others have willingly relocated (Modingoane, 2010). These concerns, along with long-standing development concerns, such as water, electricity and housing needs that residents have embattled on a daily basis, have fueled recurring spirals of protest violence over the years. Echoing these fault lines in the community, its leaders and residents alike have been torn by mistrust and divided by staunchly opposing political agendas. The six men who are the storytellers and participants in our workshop share the leadership platform on these issues relating to the community but are also, as we had come to learn in our earlier engagements (see Lau & Seedat, 2015), strongly divided as political rivals, each holding to an alternative vision for moving the community out of the current impasse.

Inserted in the midst of these contesting domains of representation is *Community Storylines*, a collaborative project between the University of South Africa Institute for Social and Health Sciences, the South African Medical Research Council-University of South Africa Violence, Injury and Peace Research Unit, and the Institute for Dispute Resolution in Africa. Situated within a larger violence prevention and peace-building initiative that speaks to issues of structural, episodic and epistemic violence, the project is focused on eliciting community narratives of peace and violence, and local knowledge in dispute resolution through various modalities of storytelling. The project seeks to privilege local voices to mobilise community meanings to create community-generated solutions to challenges, as well as advocate possibilities for social justice actions. It draws upon three interrelated conceptual elements, which we refer to as *the community story*, *relationality* and *process* to bridge indigenous and Western epistemologies as a means to elicit community-centred meanings (see Lau & Seedat, 2015). In sum, these elements are envisioned as avenues to elicit bottom-up, subjective worldviews of participants as active meaning-makers, which are privileged alongside processual insights to reveal relational, interactive and community-specific ways of knowing. We do not prescribe specific forms of knowledge but allow these to emerge in the spaces of interaction between individuals and within the community itself. To date, the project has resulted in an evolving nexus of data collection and intervention modalities, such as group oral storytelling, forum theatre and digital storytelling.

Storytelling as Methodology

This chapter focuses on not so much on digital storytelling per se, but rather the stories that were shared and created in the intimate space of the story circle and scripting phases of the workshop respectively (Lambert, 2013). From a digital storytelling framework, the story circle is a group process led by a facilitator who invites participants in the circle to share a personal story that could be created into digital format. Within this context, the purpose is to elicit meanings, feelings and axis points that signal moments of change in the story. At the same time, participants are coached around the aesthetic elements of their stories, which may include visualising their stories in the form of images and sounds (Lambert, 2013). Here, we focus less on these design choices, but rather on the interpersonal processes that emerged in telling and listening, as well as in the scripting of a group story.

We locate our group storytelling method, having emerged and evolved as a method of collecting stories in a group setting very much akin to the story circle of digital storytelling. More accurately, however, our approach is a hybrid method in which we draw on elements of narrative research (Lieblich, Tuval-Mashiach, & Zilber, 1998), indigenous storytelling (Lavallée, 2009) and narrative therapy (Epston & White, 1990). In our recent work, we attempted to implement a group storytelling approach in our efforts to collect oral stories from our participants (see Lau & Seedat, 2015). Drawing on the logic derived from the narrative research tradition, the method was intended to elicit participants' everyday meanings of peace and violence as they emerge naturally in the processes of storytelling, as opposed to eliciting more socially contrived responses through direct questioning. The approach we adopted, however, departed somewhat from a one-on-one approach to gathering stories typically seen in traditional narrative research. In our efforts to bridge a Western framework with an indigenous one, we drew on elements that reflected indigenous modes of knowledge-sharing and creation, specifically the oral tradition of telling and listening to stories in groups. A similar method is termed shared circle by Lavallée (2009) in her work with Aboriginals in Australia. This method of collecting data in a group setting may be likened to a focus group discussion, but with distinct differences. Rather than interrupting with prompts and questions, group storytelling is about being with each person's unfolding story in an empathically attuned manner, in a sense, drawing on an indigenous view of knowledge as fluid, relational and non-linear (Lavallée, 2009).

In the story circle of digital storytelling, our approach was to listen to each story without interruption and then actively provide feedback. In hindsight, our orientation to facilitation in this context was reminiscent of the strategies of narrative therapy, the underlying premise being that as people separate themselves from their stories, they experience themselves as having active and transformative influence in their lives (Epston & White, 1990). These strategies were, however, by no means an attempt to smooth over the realities of structural violence and oppression that make up the everyday reality for Thembelihle residents. Consistent with the application of narrative approaches within a critical framework, this orientation supported the emergence of "critical tales" (Van Maanen, 1988, p. 27) to illuminate the social, political, symbolic or economic issues that mark the lived realities of the oppressed. In this sense, critical tales represent a critique of the unequal social conditions that constitute structural violence. At the outset, participant storytellers were briefed about our intentions to rescript a story that, in line with the objectives of the Community Storylines project, was intended to be a powerful tool to advocate for social change, and one that required the voice of activism, purposeful meaning making and visionary leadership. To the contrary, as the next section reveals, the participant storytellers were very much facilitated (through the storytelling processes) to act as their own agents of change.

Located within a critical narrative approach, our process of analysis therefore drew from the theoretical assumption that personal narratives are constructed and situated in socio-structural spheres, which obliges scrutiny of issues of power and/or macro social discourses in the examination of the complex ways in which language and the social world are entwined (see Souto-Manning, 2014). Specifically, our analysis was guided by the broad epistemic principles outlined by Emerson and Frosh (2004), which argue for a constructionist approach to understanding language, and ways of hearing and interpreting narrative material that reveal both canonical as well as counter-hegemonic narratives. A key claim underlying this analytic standpoint is that engaging participants in ways that privilege and create space for their personal narratives, as was done through the our storytelling method, avails the kind of texts that can deepen understanding of how participants situate themselves and engage with wider social discourses through talk, as well as the discursive mechanisms by which marginalised subject positions are interrogated and/or sustained, and/or themselves interrogate dominant discourses and practices. In this way, critical narrative analysis draws attention to existing and potential resources for change and equally the possibilities for change, both in reference to personal responsibility as well as through foregrounding and challenging social accountabilities for change. Consistent with the approach offered by Emerson and Frosh (2004), our analysis therefore probed the emerging narrative material for articulations of constructive storytelling, further elaborated below.

Illustration: A Constructive Story

In this section, we draw from audio recordings of our interactions with the community leaders in the story circle and scripting phases of the workshop to highlight two process dimensions that emerged. We refer to the first as *facilitating a story of hope and change* and the second as *navigating crises of meaning*, both of which, we argue, precipitated the co-construction of the group story towards a constructive (as opposed to a destructive) end. Across the two process dimensions was an interplay and oscillation between dialogue, struggle and recognition. Both dialogue and the struggle to voice and work through differences are key to achieving mutual recognition and form the basis of storytelling for constructive conflict resolution (Senehi, 2009). Within this framework, we attempt to illustrate the two process dimensions.

Facilitating a Story of Hope and Change

Within the story circle, each of the six community leaders shared individual stories. Although the emphasis was placed on the personal story ("your story"), each story shared was also a community story about life in Thembelihle. Common to all stories were themes, words and phrases that denoted movements, signaled by distinct emotional tones that started with hope (beginning a new life in Thembelihle) to loss of hope (unfulfilled promises of development), to struggle, hardship and suffering (experiencing the poverty, violence and neglect), and finally a rise to actions towards community liberation (resistance, agency, community building). The emotional resonances of the stories, however, were initially not that of triumph over struggle. To the contrary, the stories at the onset took on a characteristically defeated tone, wherein community leaders constructed themselves as helpless agents overpowered by a structurally oppressive system.

P_1 volunteered his story first and in opening, he highlighted the day-to-day hardships emanating from persistent failures by the State to recognise Thembelihle as a formal township. Against the continuing community struggles and lack of services, P_1 reiterated: "Nothing. Nothing. NOTHING, although we have tried as human beings to put our own water system." His emphasis here was on the extent of community neglect by State and municipal authorities and sheer desperation of "human beings" to meet their basic needs, even resorting to illegal and unsafe means. P_1's story was summed up poignantly as: "It's like we are starting a race from the back".

In P_2's personal story, the themes of lack, stagnation and slow pace of development also resonated strongly:

> Now nothing has happened, no electric – no road, no houses, no school, better school, all the children inside in the shack /…/ There is now, twenty years now of democracy, can't happen nothing in twenty years.

P_2 closed his story with resigned helplessness: "Now what we must do now, they say like me, got no power." For both P_1 and P_2, an emotional tone of powerlessness and futility characterised their stories. As facilitators of the story circle and also researchers working within a liberatory community psychology and social justice framework, our agenda was focused on using stories as a vehicle, not only to exercise voice but also to promote activism. As such, our agenda required that we do more than simply listen to the stories. Ethically and morally, we were required to balance two imperatives, on the one hand, to validate the pain, suffering and struggle and on the other, to intervene in moments of hopelessness to encourage a shift out of the struggle towards igniting agentic possibilities for hope and change. Whilst affirming suffering was necessary to empathically honour the leaders' subjective experiences, uncritically affirming a paralysing helplessness could reinforce stasis and regression. This was even more apposite in the context of challenging dominant media-reinforced narratives of Thembelihle that are squarely focused on violence and poverty (e.g. eNCA, 2015).

As facilitators and researchers cognisant of the aims of the Community Storylines project, we directly intervened in the two powerful opening stories, both of which had the potential to instill a mood of helplessness in the remaining stories to be told in the story circle. In response to P_1's story, SS (second author and facilitator) summarised the struggles for recognition highlighted in his story but also shifted the emphasis on the water system as a symbol of community resourcefulness as opposed suffering. In this manner, she drew out an alternative narrative beyond the victimisation story:

> For me, what I heard quite strongly was what you are saying about, about lack of recognition and some of the deprivation that, that still continues, that the official processes haven't quite happened in the way that that has been legitimate and legitimising for many people in the community. But I also heard you say, 'so we as the people have TRIED TO', and then you made reference to the water, for example, and that's the part that I am really interested in. How it is that the community has, has survived under those conditions that you described to us?

In response, P_1 highlighted a system of collaborative networking and problem-solving and in the process identified unity as a value system that drives the community towards collective resolution:

> Well, we are a community and we take ourself as such, you understand? So we are, as like in, in each and every community, if there is a problem that is facing that particular community, so there will be that unity. That, that inter, inter what, actions within the, the members. So to try and solve the, the problem that we are having you see.

This aspect of community survival and initiative which was obscured in P_1's story of community struggle in the context of State neglect was now foregrounded in the processes of facilitator-participant story co-construction. Picking up on the community unity aspect, SS coaxed this out further: "Can you tell us a little more about the unity that you just referred to" and P_1 offered a nuanced interpretation of community unity as that which is not drawn together by ideology ("not a unity based on a certain group of people like organisations") but rather by good "neighbour[liness]", of "people com[ing] together to solve a problem." Continuing in this co-construction, SS indicated this neglected theme as pivotal to creating a 'good' story:

> You talked about community building P_1, you talked about community building, that for me talks directly to the kinds of stories that, that you community leaders need to be, need to be sharing and saying.

Similarly, in response to P_2's story, UL (first author and co-facilitator) shifted awareness from the lens of struggle and hardship to a language of coping, and in so doing actively reframed his story from suffering to survival:

> Because you have suffered a lot in everything you know that you were saying, the lack of electricity, you are seeing so much in the community, the children suffering and everything. I wonder how, how did you cope, how did you survive where there is so much going on and such much that you see? What did you do to survive?

Assisting participants to reframe their stories required that we listen for the alternative story that was often overshadowed by a dominant storyline of suffering and hopelessness. At times, the dominant storyline persisted, despite our efforts to challenge it. P_2, for example, reiterated a story of his powerlessness in effecting change. The children, who are meant to be the symbols of hope for a lost community, in P_2's elaboration below, were described as perpetuating the same legacy of hopelessness in Thembelihle by obstinately persisting in their self-destructive ways ("smoking too much", "drinking the liquor"):

> About this child in the street, there is no listening. This child, you are talking to this child. No understand[ing], this, [they] carry on [the] same life and you say, 'No, this thing is not right, [but] still they said, 'this thing is right.'

In response to this, SS attempted to challenge P_2's stated powerlessness by offering a perspective that reinforced his strength and influence in the community. In the excerpt below, P_2 is prompted to rescript his story by "moving it forward" towards a legacy of hope and vision of community change:

> Sorry, P_2 if this was my story, then what you are saying now is exactly what I would focus on to move the story forward. So let me explain what I mean. You spoke about a life of hardship and suffering and it is really hard to listen to you talk about that because I could feel your feelings. In response to UL when she asked you, 'so what have you done to survive?' The one thing you talked about is children and what you wish to share with the younger generation in terms of the wisdom of the elder, in terms of lessons that you have learned in your own life and you know, UL was talking earlier about the legacy you want to leave behind for the, for the youth or the younger generation, and for me that is very powerful. /.../ I don't think you have no power. You might not have any power in relation to

> changing some of the, the conditions in your community but as I listen to you I hear a POWERFUL elder who, who has really invested a lot and thought a lot about what he would like to see happen for the younger people in his community so P_2, you are POWERFUL in that sense and that sense of POWER, YOUR sense of POWER, YOUR sense of what you want to do for the community.

Moving the Story Forward

In tipping these two opening stories towards "the kinds of stories" we wanted to hear, namely that of resilience, agency and power, the stories that subsequent participants shared appeared to take on a more uplifting tone geared towards activism for community change. In these subsequent stories, the participants scripted themselves as impassioned leaders fighting for the needs of the community. P_3 elaborated on his role "engaging with government to develop [the] land", P_4 self-identified with being "the spokesperson for the community", P_5 noted that he was "very, very strong for the community" actively engaged in policy work and resolving community issues, P_6 expressed his role in "motivat[ing] people to come together and fight against conditions of unemployment, condition of poverty, condition of mental slavery". Whilst these shifts may have been coincidental, we are cognisant and critical of our positions of power as facilitators and researchers, and the power these influences potentially wielded in directing this group of participants towards narrating a storyline of hope and change.

In the next section, we explore another process dimension that emerged in the scripting phases of co-creating a group story with the six community leaders. Here too, our roles as facilitators actively shaping the overarching story towards a constructive one is acknowledged. More explicit focus, however, is directed to the ways in which meaning is produced, enacted, but also challenged amongst participants. We refer to this dimension as *navigating the crises of meaning*.

Navigating the Crises of Meaning

Subsequent to P_1 and P_2's stories, the other community leaders' stories not only highlighted their activism in various spheres of community life, but also echoed themes of collectivity, unity and working together. These messages of resilience, survival, resistance and activism were in turn reinforced by SS's closing summary of participants' stories as:

> not just the hopes for the community, but your own hopes and how you could bring alive those hopes individually and then as a group too; we have been talking about moving the story forward, but also about moving the community forward.

The collective unity that was increasingly emphasised in the stories of these leaders and reaffirmed by facilitators moreover created several shifts in group processes as we transitioned from the story circle to the reflections thereof and to the scripting phase of creating a digital story. Although a group decision was undertaken to produce a collective digital story, the processes through which this emerged were not always smooth-flowing. At several junctures, as facilitators, we were required to navigate a "crisis of meaning" (Senehi, 2002, p. 43). These crises of meanings were experienced as temporary impasses that could have potentially derailed the production of a common story. Some length of time was spent tussling over various meanings of words to find those that would, from the perspective of this group, adequately capture and represent their individual and collective experiences. At some moments these exchanges were heated and tense, yet necessary to achieve amicable resolution. As Senehi (2002, p. 43) suggests, intergroup conflicts may be over tangible interests, but they "always involve a crisis of meaning". Lederach (1996), in his social constructionist stance, amplifies this point further: "conflict emerges through an interactive process based on the search for and creation of shared meaning" (p. 9). In other words, it is through dialogue and struggle that the possibilities for mutual recognition present themselves. Yet mutual recognition is not about finding or adopting a universalising view where one party unquestioningly takes on the views of the other party as the same as one's own. More importantly, it is a willingness to engage in dialogue and struggle to open up spaces to speak out and explore differences (Senehi, 2009).

Within the workshop space, a procedural decision about whether to create individual digital stories or a group digital story that united the common themes of each individual story, in effect also signaled a parallel dimension of group process. More broadly, this pivotal decision was also about whether these leaders could set aside their ideological differences and work together for the common good of the community. Creating individual stories would still highlight the plight of their community through their individual voices without necessarily having to battle out ideological differences and negotiate meanings to derive a common message and vision. Yet, for these leaders, the power of a group story was clear. It would unite their disparate voices through an effective medium and channel their activism in more cogent ways. At the outset, these differences were explicitly and unashamedly voiced. For example, in response to a question about whether the group is "relatively cohesive", is able to "work together well" and "cooperate" despite belonging to different civic and political groups, P_4 offered a categorically negative response. Elaborating on this divide amongst the community leaders, he offered an explanation of how competition trumps unity in the throes of political power:

> Um, no, I'll answer that, no. Ja [Yes], because you see South Africa, it consists of political society that everyone want[s] to own something. You see, it's not like in America where the opposition, Republic[ans] and Democrat[s], they are working together because they know that at the end working together it contribute in the development of the country, but here everyone want to monopoly, monopoly politics, that is the problem.

Moving the story forward, to borrow the aforementioned phrase from the language of screenwriting,[1] in this respect, was also about moving the community forward.

---

[1] *Moving the story forward* is outlining the necessary information or exposition to allow the reader/audience to know what is to happen next in the storyline. Although the exposition is often

In an attempt to unite the leaders' divergent voices, P_4's plea below illustrated this parallel process, wherein the creation of a group story was positioned alongside the alignment of community leadership towards a common vision:

> My plea it will be, as my comrades are here coming from different political parties and different structures, it's to combine all these struggles and make it a one struggle, the struggle of saying we don't want to see our kids moving the same direction, we don't want to see the youth, the women in Thembelihle suffering the way we have suffered, you know, and that's my plea.

Yet P_4's plea for "unity in political organisations" reignited a debate about unity and its meaning. If the meaning of unity was about good "neighbour[liness]" and "people com[ing] together to solve a problem", (as P_1) had previously offered, could unity coexist alongside the clash of political ideologies that clearly divided this group of leaders?

> Alright. I hear, you see, I hear my comrades say there should be unity in based to political. In politics there can't be unity, guys, let's not I mean fool ourselves because right now we are going towards the elections. Each and every political organisation will be contending for a seat or two, isn't it? So unity based on politics, I don't think it's something that is possible /…/ So let's look at the real issues that are affecting our community.

Navigating a decision about whether to tell individual stories or a unified group story was perhaps not simply a procedural decision about the next phase of scripting in the digital storytelling workshop. It appeared to carry with it a burden of working through difference and drawing on a common experience and vision to co-create a collective story. Whilst proposing for a group story, P_4 disputed the view that it is about seeking political unity and proposed that the group story is about building a common vision:

> Here, we are not talking about politics, I never said anything about politics, I was saying the hope that we had. Let's build, it's a foundation for the next generation.

For P_6, the story was the mechanism to moving the community forward insofar as it would transcend political ideologies to foreground the common experience and vision for the community:

> Ja, actually I believe the group story is very important because actually we must move away from political ideologies because as we are getting, as I said, the buffer zone will remain the same, even if we can try to bring the East and West together it won't happen. But if we talk of the suffering, poverty of people wishing their life to improve, we are talking of something that is in reality, that must not divide us according to political ideology.

The "buffer zone" to which P_6 referred may metaphorically capture the dual potentiality of the story itself—its divisive potential but also its potential to be unifying (Jackson, 2002). Through this process of dialogue and mediation, it was necessary to de/reconstruct language as a placeholder for meanings to unravel the commonalities of experience that united these leaders and their community towards

achieved through dialogue amongst the characters of the story (Field, 2006), for the purposes of digital storytelling, it is also created by means of the aesthetic design choices (images, sounds, transitions, etc.).

a shared vision. As we have attempted to show, "unity" as a linguistic term could not be adopted with consensus without reiterating common experiences of struggle and a common vision of hope for community change.

The crisis of meaning was, however, not just about finding a shared meaning. It was also about navigating a crisis of representation. Thus, the search for and creation of shared meaning was pertinent for this group of community leaders with different political ideologies. Yet it was also about undoing the violence of language that vilifies the community as criminal and violent through media representations (Lau & Seedat, 2017). It was also about finding a language to undo the decades of structural violence and neglect by challenging the meta-narrative of freedom and democracy, showing its failed promises in neglected communities like Thembelihle. During the scripting phase, a decision about what the group story would entail generated a series of back-and-forth changes by both participants and facilitators alike that centred on the meanings of the term development. For instance, P_4 proposed that the group story be "a message of development, the message that is to see *ama* [the] changes eThembelihle." When asked to elaborate on what development looks like, P_4 offered the following elaboration:

> The ... development that I'm speaking about is to see Thembelihle being into a formal area, being into a formal area, because I've got, at the back of our minds we all know here that there's a story of Thembelihle, why it not being developed. So if the message is clear to those [inaudible] is to develop Thembelihle. The development, the changes that I want to see is to see formal houses being built in Thembelihle.

However, this notion of development did not go uncontested. Making explicit how State tactics of relocation operate under the guise of development, P_1 argued:

> But there Comrade P_4, how, how, how do we run away from maybe the, the, you see, development can mean a lot of things to different people. Like you see, people now, they are talking about relocation,[2] that is development on its own. So how do we go about to chart on this contradiction that our message to refer and be very vividly clear to the people that we are talking about the AREA itself, not taking individuals to, to, to other places under the very same umbrella of development? /.../ Because, you see, we are playing with the, I'm sorry, political people, they twist things, you see, say this and mean that, you see that?

The "twist" in meanings for P_1 potentially derails the progress of the development of the community, an issue that is central to P_1's agenda. For P_1 the meaning of development still needed refinement to guard against its conflation with relocation. From P_1's perspective, relocation to Lehae entails an obliteration of any legitimate land ownership that existed during the period of residence in Thembelihle:

> like people, we generally know ourselves as squatters ... like, we have invaded the place, unlawful but we used to have something like the bills that we were paying before, so how

[2]As a segregation device, forced removals and relocations under apartheid were synonymous with violence, land dispossession and community destruction. Although justified in the present-day on grounds of 'development', the practice of relocation continues to strike painful resonances with the past. Relocation from Thembelihle to Lehae and Vlakfontein, both developing township areas adjacent to Thembelihle, has been offered to residents; some have willingly accepted the offer as an alternative to living in Thembelihle.

can a squatter pay a bill? So there is this mentality that if you are living in an informal settlement, you are squatter, you see, meaning that we are less

/…/

because if you move, they say if you are moving to Lehae, you understand, you lose the, what do you say, the ownership of the very piece of land you own, it's no more yours, it's been scratched (P_1).

Rather than an opportunity for (self) development, for P_1, relocation is an act of being forcefully and illegitimately dispossessed from one's original rightful home:

People they are not, they are not saying we want to be relocated but the system itself say, people they should relocate. You understand so that in that, in that sense I want, in the story you see, if that can be, can be, I mean highlighted that relocation is not just something that we, people they are just receiving this as a gift or something as, but they are forced to do it.

Despite group consensus that reference to development was specifically about development in Thembelihle itself and not about relocation to adjacent developing townships (including Lehae, for example), the issue of relocation continued to create some unease in the group. Of the six leaders of Thembelihle, two had relocated to neighbouring Lehae, but had nevertheless continued to feel passionate about serving Thembelihle as leaders. Identifying as one who had willingly chosen to relocate rather than being forced to, P_6 below expressed this uneasiness:

And then again, this, it's a reality that there are people, many who don't want to move from Thembelihle to Lehae, if we can just eh try to RECOGNISE that there are some people who are like that and there are some people WHO WANT TO MOVE to Lehae in there but they didn't register themselves with the [inaudible] subsidy and others, then the area there is full /…/ So ja, you know, it's unfortunately we are talking like this. Some of us we are in Lehae. So in other word, you are, you are talking as if we are the traitors in the community, really, but eh all in all you need to say it straight that it's TRUE that there are some people who want to move.

P_6's reference to "traitor" potentially raised tensions within the group, albeit temporarily diffused by SS below, who attempted to reunite the foundational values that seem to hold the group together. Nevertheless, in P_6's perceptions about being viewed as a "traitor" to his community reignited the crises of representation, bringing forth questions about his legitimate status to represent Thembelihle when he no longer resides in the community. Once again, divisions of political identity and issues of right to place were raised, diffused, diverted and once again put aside to work towards a common vision.

SS: Yes. So you know, when you said now about traitor and that I was surprised to hear you say that because I think we're all on the same page here. We're all saying the RIGHT to DETERMINE for yourself, the RIGHT to make certain=

P_6: No, what I'm saying is IF let's say I'm saying this, let's say it's a digital

SS: Ja, ja, story.

P_6: Then someone who's staying in Thembelihle will say, 'no but P_6 how can he can say that when he's in Thembe/You see, he can't understand me speaking about development of Thembelihle' when I'm not …

P_3: You're not staying there.

SS: Verstaan [Understand].

P_3: Ja.

SS: Okay thank you.

[Laughter amongst the group]

P_1: Okay=

SS: Sorr/sorry before you go. LK, our timekeeper is giving us a time check, right?

The shared laughter diffused the tension before P_1's attempt to interject in response to P_6. Yet, before venturing a response, SS's response to LK's (third author and timekeeper) signal that time is up shifted the group towards a light-hearted discussion about breaking for tea. Ruptures in meaning were temporarily held in abeyance.

For these leaders, once referred to as political rivals, the scripting phase as a space of dialogue was interspersed with such moments of both struggle and recognition, tenuously held throughout the facilitation space to construct a story that would be potentially cementing, rather than dividing. A least within this space, the story circle and story scripting offered a possibility that the unity of collective leadership could extend beyond the workshop space. In this respect, P_3 commented that "if we have got a clear vision of what we want to achieve with the story and what the story is all about then it's going to bring us together."

What the rupture, interruptions and tensions held in abeyance show in this exchange is that the group consensus culminating as a collective story is but a partial (re)solution in a continuing process. In this respect, whilst the collective story was materialised in the form of a digitised tool, the story nevertheless remains an unfinished one that may continue to be rescripted and re-enacted in ways that conform to or diverge from the script of the collective story. The intention here is not to ascribe specific success or failure to the digital storytelling workshop or the method of facilitation per se. To do so would re-inscript the final story, process and/or ourselves into the same colonial master script that inscribes both an ideal outcome and the norm of civilising progress (Bowden, 2011) drawn from a presupposed "model of best practices" formulaically applied across varied groups, settings and circumstances. Rather, what we attempted to illustrate within the structured framework of a digital storytelling workshop is that the unfolding process itself, in all its messiness, ambivalence and complexity, emerged as potentially valuable as the product of the story itself as a tool for social transformation.

Conclusion

As evident from this illustration, the approach we adopted to facilitating a constructive story in a group context is not one that can be applied formulaically. Rather, each unique context presents different possibilities for achieving similarly constructive outcomes. The illustration also highlights the constructed social relations that served as the site within which we employed our power as researchers to disrupt and resist the reproduction of an oppressive script, and encourage the surfacing of the less-perceptible narrative of resilience, hope and change. From the perspective of narrative research, it is in the dialogue between researchers and participants that opportunities are created, and the transformatory potential invoked through the storytelling process is shaped and enacted.

Appendix: Transcription Notations

CAPS	words spoken with emphasis/loudness
/…/	omitted text.
[ ]	inserted text/explanation
=	interruption in speech

References

Bowden, B. (2011). Colonialism, anti-colonialism and the idea of progress. In *Encyclopedia of life support systems (EOLSS)* (pp. 1–41). Retrieved from http://handle.uws.edu.au:8081/1959.7/519370

Brodkin, K. (2007). *Making democracy matter: Identity and activism in Los Angeles*. New Brunswick, NJ: Rutgers University Press.

Bussey, M., & Wise, J. B. (2007). *Trauma transformed*. New York: Columbia University Press.

Emerson, P., & Frosh, S. (2004). *Critical narrative analysis in psychology: A guide to practice*. New York: Palgrave Macmillan.

eNCA. (2015, February 27). One dead, 34 arrested following violent protests in Thembelihle. *eNews Channel Africa*. Retrieved from https://www.enca.com/south-africa/one-dead-34-arrested-following-violent-protests-thembelihle

Epston, M., & White, D. (1990). *Narrative means to therapeutic ends*. New York: W.W. Norton & Company.

Field, S. (2006). *The screenwriter's workbook: Exercises and step-by-step instructions for creating a successful screenplay* (Revised ed.). New York: Random House.

Jackson, M. (2002). *The politics of storytelling: Violence, transgression, and intersubjectivity* (Vol. 3). Copenhagen: Museum Tusculanum Press.

Lambert, J. (2013). *Digital storytelling: Capturing lives, creating community* (4th ed.). New York: Routledge.

Lau, U., & Seedat, M. (2015). The community story, relationality and process: Bridging tools for researching local knowledge in a peri-urban township. *Journal of Community & Applied Social Psychology, 25*(5), 369–383.

Lau, U., & Seedat, M. (2017). Structural violence and the struggle for recognition: Examining community narratives in a post-apartheid democracy. In M. Seedat, S. Suffla, & D. J. Christie (Eds.), *Enlarging the scope of peace psychology: African and world-regional contributions* (pp. 203–220). Cham: Springer.

Lavallée, L. F. (2009). Practical application of an indigenous research framework and two qualitative indigenous research methods: Sharing circles and Anishnaabe symbol-based reflection. *International Journal of Qualitative Research Methods, 8*(1), 21–40.

Lederach, J. P. (1996). *Preparing for peace: Conflict transformation across cultures*. Syracuse: Syracuse University Press.

Lieblich, A., McAdams, D. P., & Josselson, R. (2004). *Healing plots: The narrative basis of psychotherapy*. Washington: American Psychological Association.

Lieblich, A., Tuval-Mashiach, R., & Zilber, T. (1998). *Narrative research: A new model for classification of approaches to reading, analysis, and interpretations*. Thousand Oaks, CA: Sage.

Gubrium, A., & Turner, K. C. N. (2009). Digital storytelling as an emergent method for social research and practice. In S. N. Hesse-Biber (Ed.), *The handbook of emergent technologies in social research* (pp. 469–491). Oxford: Oxford University Press.

Meichenbaum, D. (2006). Resilience and posttraumatic growth: A constructive narrative perspective. In L. G. Calhoun & R. G. Tedeschi (Eds.), *Handbook of posttraumatic growth: Research and practice* (pp. 355–368). New York: Lawrence Erlbaum Associates.

Modingoane, N. (2010, March 3). *Peace settling in Thembelihle*. City of Johannesburg Public Liaison Department. Retrieved from: http://www.joburg.org.za/index.php?option=com_content&view=article&id=4892&catid=197&Itemid=344

Rappaport, J. (1995). Empowerment meets narrative: Listening to stories and creating settings. *American Journal of Community Psychology, 23*(5), 795–807.

Rossiter, M., & Garcia, P. A. (2010). Digital storytelling: A new player on the narrative field. *New Directions for Adult and Continuing Education, 126*, 37–48. doi:10.1002/ace.

Senehi, J. (2002). Constructive storytelling: A peace process. *Peace and Conflict Studies, 9*(2), 41–64.

Senehi, J. (2009). Building peace: Storytelling to transform conflicts constructively. In D. J. B. Sandole, S. Bryne, I. Sandole-Staroste, & J. Senehi (Eds.), *Handbook of conflict analysis and resolution* (pp. 201–214). Oxon: Routledge.

Smith, B. H. (1981). Narrative versions, narrative theories. In W. J. T. Mitchell (Ed.), *On narrative* (pp. 209–232). Chicago, IL: The University of Chicago Press.

Souto-Manning, M. (2014). Critical narrative analysis: The interplay of critical discourse and narrative analyses. *International Journal of Qualitative Studies in Education, 27*(2), 159–180.

Van Maanen, J. (1988). *Tales of the field: On writing ethnography* (2nd ed.). Chicago, IL: The University of Chicago Press.

Zingaro, L. (2009). *Speaking out: Storytelling for social change*. Walnut Creek, CA: Left Coast Press.

Chapter 13
Photovoice as Liberatory Enactment: The Case of Youth as Epistemic Agents

Nick Malherbe, Shahnaaz Suffla, Mohamed Seedat, and Umesh Bawa

Photovoice method provides marginalised populations with a platform from which to visually as well as linguistically interrogate dominant knowledges by offering a visceral, participant-centred, localised knowledge form. In the case of young people, Photovoice centralises and gives credence to the kinds of youth-generated understandings that are repeatedly ignored or silenced within dominant adult-centric knowledge-creation processes, which are exemplified within and by the academy (Shore, 2010; Suffla, Kaminer, & Bawa, 2012). If the socially transformative potential of Photovoice is to be harnessed meaningfully, it is imperative that researchers consider critically the methodology's apparent liberatory and epistemologically just enactments in ways that constrain the hegemonic impulse of dominant knowledge institutions, and allow for the emergence and situating of subaltern voice within the knowledge economy.

In this chapter, we outline the conceptual underpinnings and applications of Photovoice (see Carlson, Engebretson, & Chamberlain, 2006; Lykes & Scheib, 2015; Wang, 2006; Wang & Burris, 1997 for an in-depth overview). Drawing from

N. Malherbe (✉) • S. Suffla • M. Seedat
Institute for Social and Health Sciences, University of South Africa, Johannesburg, South Africa

South African Medical Research Council-University of South Africa Violence, Injury and Peace Research Unit, Cape Town, South Africa
e-mail: Nicholas.malherbe@mrc.ac.za

U. Bawa
Department of Psychology, University of the Western Cape, Cape Town, South Africa

Institute for Social and Health Sciences, University of South Africa, Johannesburg, South Africa

M. Seedat et al. (eds.), *Emancipatory and Participatory Methodologies in Peace, Critical, and Community Psychology*, Peace Psychology Book Series, DOI 10.1007/978-3-319-63489-0_13

a youth-centred Multi-country Photovoice Project that we facilitated in six African countries, we extract an epistemically significant moment in the project process—that witnessed the voices of marginalised youth centred in a university space—and employ it as a platform from which to critically and reflexively analyse the liberatory performances and limits of Photovoice methodology. In so doing, we illustrate how Photovoice methodology elevated constrained youth voice, yet simultaneously constrained social and epistemic justice imperatives within the project. We conclude with a call for critical reflexivity among researchers towards cognisance of the processes and arrangements that stand to compromise the methodology's liberatory potential, social action and/or enactments of epistemic justice.

Photovoice

Photovoice is a community-based participatory research (CBPR) method that seeks to expand the representational scope and the range of voices that construct and enhance people's lived realities. Since its inception in the mid-1990s (Wang & Burris, 1997), Photovoice has been applied to explore and address various social justice issues (Hergenrather, Rhodes, Cowan, Bardhoshi, & Pula, 2009), and has been implemented across diverse demographic groups—typically in marginalised communities—and geographic locations. Photovoice involves researchers and participants working together to decide on a relevant topic or photo theme that is to guide participants' photo missions in identified settings. Subsequently, participants are provided with cameras and photography training which they are to use in representing the photo theme (Wang, 2006). Finally, in an attempt to prioritise community needs, participants—either individually, as a group, or both—discuss and caption their photographs, which are usually exhibited to the public at a later stage (Foster-Fishman, Nowell, Deacon, Nievar, & McCann, 2005).

Conceptual Underpinnings

Photovoice is premised conceptually on the praxis of critical consciousness (Carlson et al., 2006), as theorised by Brazilian educator Paulo Freire (1970). From this perspective, participants are encouraged to "consider, and seek to act upon, the historical, institutional, social, and political conditions that contribute to personal and community problems" (Wang, Morrel-Samuels, Hutchison, Bell, & Pestronk, 2004, p. 911). Photovoice centres the conception that individuals have stories to be told, which are shaped by their intersecting identities and mediated by available forms of portrayal. Photovoice may then be understood as a liberatory endeavour, that is, an attempt to free the self from the control of others (Boog, 2003). By affording participants a critical, participatory and potentially transformative interrogation of their lives, the liberatory stance of Photovoice lies in its attempt to achieve freedom from power structures of oppression and exploitation (Foster, 2004). Much of the methodology's liberatory potential therefore rests on its ability to elevate participant voice, catalyse material enactments of social justice, and privilege endogenous knowledge where the latter is "always bound to a particular context determined by both social and material dimensions" and "always bears a relation to activity or behaviour" (Odora-Hoppers, 2002, p. 108). In this way, Photovoice challenges the prevailing dominance of official scientific discourse in favour of a pluriversal approach that is inclusive of local knowledges.

Photovoice reflects key principles of CBPR, including collaboration and co-learning between academic and community partners (Minkler & Wallerstein, 2009). Photovoice projects are therefore said to engender participatory competence, where a combination of attitudes, understandings, abilities and actions that are required to reshape one's community are provoked among participants (Wang, 2006). The participatory principles inherent to Photovoice construct the engagement with the researcher and the 'researched' as a partnership, with some Photovoice research referring to each party explicitly as co-researcher (see, for example, Lykes & Scheib, 2015), and the process as one of co-learning (Strack, Lovelace, Jordan, & Holmes, 2010). Photovoice researchers are thus considered facilitators rather than experts, who may stimulate participants' critical consciousness.

Voice and Epistemic Correction

Photovoice represents an attempt to resist epistemic violence. It is thus a form of epistemic correction as it attempts to promote marginalised populations' ownership, control and agency within a participatory process of knowledge construction. Teo (2010) defines epistemic violence as that which is produced when empirical data are interpreted as revealing the Other to be significantly inferior to the analyst's ingroup, even in the face of equally viable alternative interpretations. In this regard, the 'research object' becomes fundamentally othered. Epistemic violence need not be limited to the academy, and can be understood with respect to dominant discourses, representations and depictions that are circulated beyond research settings. In short, epistemic violence prescribes very particular—often stereotypical—ways of knowing and seeing onto the Other, with a socio-cultural elite most often being in possession of the mechanisms that drive these modes of knowing and seeing. Dominant knowledge forms then become oppressive as they dictate who people are and what they can be (Foster, 2004). In the context of such dominant knowledges, epistemic violence is perpetuated by denying the Other a voice with which to articulate the self and produce a counter-narrative, or to take ownership of how the self—and the group to which the self belongs—can be understood. With this in mind, epistemic violence becomes especially pervasive when dominant knowledges wield a considerable degree of influence, power and/or cultural capital.

As there is so much exploitative potential (which researchers and analysts frequently act upon) within the research undertaking, Photovoice endeavours to make visible the power asymmetries embedded in knowledge production practice, and accedes to questioning the legitimacy, basis and authority of all knowledge claims. The methodology is therefore able to disrupt dominant, epistemologically violent knowledge forms by privileging a subaltern counter-narrative, as well as participant agency. To this end, participant understandings and interpretations are made central to each phase of the Photovoice process so that researchers are able to observe the world from the view of those who do not usually have power over how the world is perceived (Wang & Burris, 1997).

Youth Voice

Across socio-economic and identity locations, young people have been noted as having diminished cultural capital, as well as less power than adults. In other words, youth voice is generally ignored, muted or silenced in preference to adult-centric, 'experienced' and 'mature' knowledge. In research, this translates into the positioning of youth as merely the 'objects' of inquiry. This is perhaps in part due to conventional notions of childhood—located in developmental or psychological theorisations—that construct young people as 'undeveloped' or 'incomplete adults' (Burman, 2008). Further, within capitalist contexts—where the generation of profit denotes power—it is adults who constitute most of the labour force. Such societies are therefore organised in ways that tend to deny youth voice and agency (Mitchell, 2015) or, at best, direct, structure and limit youth voices and agentic capacities through adult-led agendas. Resultantly, young people are seldom able to represent their experiences or construct a youth-centric counter-narrative without facing resistance from adults.

As youth voice is generally excluded from public, legislative and media-driven narratives, it is imperative that such voice is provided a discursive space within which to articulate and organise a youth-centred form of epistemic correction. In awarding authority to marginalised youth voices, young people are more likely to develop their social identites as well as their perceived level of social competence and confidence (Strack, Magill, & McDonagh, 2004). Encouragingly, there is increasing recognition of youth as knowledgeable and skilled social actors who possess the competencies to reflect upon and represent their experiences. This viewpoint has supported calls for the 'authentic inclusion' of youth voices in research (O'Sullivan & MacPhail, 2010, p. 66).

By privileging an alternative youth-centric means of knowledge-production, Photovoice acts to disrupt conventional adult-mediated understandings and claims to 'truth', representing a form of liberatory praxis. Previous Photovoice projects have shown to both galvanise youth in acting towards socially just community change, as well as facilitate behavioural change, all while enacting individual and group critical consciousness (Strack et al., 2010). Certainly, the method offers a means of harnessing the strengths and assets of young people in a manner that is able to respond to and address materially a range of community concerns (Suffla et al., 2012).

Limitations and Constraints of Photovoice

As Foster (2004) argues, effective resistance and/or liberatory praxis, no matter how slow, must involve some degree of transformation that produces change from oppressor and oppressed. It is therefore foreseeable that participants will feel dissatisfied if they are unable to effect and affect the kinds of social change envisioned and augured by Photovoice (Zuch, Mathews, De Koker, Mtshizana, & Mason-Jones, 2013). In a meta-synthesis of published Photovoice research, Catalani and Minkler (2010) found that 35% of 37 articles did not recount any kind of project-related transformation. Similarly, Sanon, Evans-Agnew, and Boutain (2014) reported that only 7 of the 30 Photovoice projects that they examined described some form of social action. It would appear then that although transformation is a theoretical pillar of Photovoice research, it remains largely absent as a project outcome.

Perhaps reports of social change are largely lacking within Photovoice studies because *change* is a fluid and experiential concept that is difficult to define, track and measure. Further, the sustainability of social change is a difficult and costly affair that requires long-term efforts from several community members, as well as researchers (Strack et al., 2010). Indeed, Photovoice studies are almost never envisioned as long-term engagements. Notwithstanding, these challenges around the realisation and enactments of social change—or lack thereof—cannot go unacknowledged within Photovoice projects. Certainly, the voices of participants become stifled, or remain partial, when projects do not consider transformation outcomes. In this manner, Photovoice has not decoupled itself successfully from the institutional arrangements that support epistemic violence, as is characteristic of the academy, that is, the very institution within which Photovoice was forged and in turn seeks to challenge.

Universities all over the world have become captured by a neoliberal agenda, where inter-departmental competition, global ranking systems, and an obsession with 'excellence' has fragmented the academy, and isolated it from the very problems—such as those relating to ontology, social justice, and public health—that it attempts to address meaningfully (Shore, 2010). Photovoice, although enacted predominantly within community settings, ultimately is owned by the academy. Beyond the photo mission and exhibition, the voice of the researcher continues to dominate interpretations of participants' work. Certainly, it is typically through the voices of researchers that those within the academy, itself an adult-centred institution, and elsewhere, come to know of participants' representations. Despite numerous attempts and influences within the academy that seek to reposition marginalised voices, Photovoice research studies are characteristically documented in a manner that mediates participants' voices, and subsumes their narrative in self-serving ways. In the main, decision-making processes within Photovoice projects—no matter how participatory these projects set out to be—ultimately rest with the researchers (Lykes & Scheib, 2015) who, as with all research, maintain an innate degree of epistemic and material power over participants throughout the project process (England, 1994).

Case Example: The Multi-Country Photovoice Project on Youth Representations of Safety

Project Narrative

In 2011, the University of South Africa's (Unisa) Institute for Social Health Sciences and its South African Medical Research Council-University of South Africa Violence, Injury and Peace Research Unit initiated the Multi-country Photovoice Project, implemented in South Africa, Mozambique, Zambia, Uganda, Ethiopia and Egypt. In seeking to be responsive to the call for the inclusion of youth voices in efforts to address the deleterious conditions to which many marginalised African youth are exposed, the project invited young people to photograph *Things, Places and People* that make them feel safe or unsafe in their respective communities. The project creates opportunities for youth to engage in critical dialogue with adults, and lead on social justice campaigns. As a community-engaged research platform, the project thereby positions young people as legitimate knowledge-producers and transformative social agents. Various photographic exhibitions that celebrated the participants' meaning-making processes and agentic capacities have been held in each country throughout the course of the project.

In 2014, participants from each country convened in South Africa to participate in Unisa's annual Research and Innovation Week (hereafter referred to as RIW). The event hosts numerous presentations and discussions from across academic disciplines in an attempt to showcase Unisa's research programmes, and promotes dialogue around a range of issues within and beyond the academy. The RIW facilitated three sites of potential liberatory praxis, the first of which was the launch of a photo book, titled *My Voice in Pictures: African Children's Vision of Safety* (Suffla, Bawa, & Seedat, 2014). The book chronicles participants' photo stories while authenticating Photovoice as an innovative approach to community-engaged scholarship. Secondly, a photographic exhibition of the photo stories was held at the Unisa Art Gallery. The exhibition was opened by Unisa's Vice-Principal, and showcased a collection of photographs taken by the participants, which reflected the contribution that young people are able to make in shaping the practices and policies affecting their lives and those of their communities. The photo exhibition offered a unique visual portrayal of the participating youth's social worlds, shared the voices and stories behind the photographs, and provided a platform for the celebration of youth knowledge and agency. Lastly, participants led a conference on African children's vision of safety, a milestone meeting opened by Unisa's Principal and Vice-Chancellor, who stated at the time that the project afforded "youth the opportunity to take their rightful place in Africa's social and science milieu, so that they may offer local knowledge, compassionate citizenship and collective innovation to the world" (Makhanya, 2014, p. 3). Presentations by the young people included a focus on the import of youth voice, use of photography skills, the experience of hosting photo exhibitions, actions resulting from the Photovoice Project, and making meaning of the project. At the conference, participants reflected on the sense of privilege, acknowledgement and the encouragement that they experienced in being invited to lead on this conference. Each of these three sites represented youth-centric, reflective and dialogic spaces that aimed to (re)position and disrupt the university's conventional adult-mediated knowledge-making mandate, and ultimately revealed the epistemic agency of the youth. Read together, the three engagements demonstrate an instance of epistemic disruption where subaltern voices were centred within a hegemonic knowledge-making space.

In 2017, as part of the project's sustainability plan, participants reconvened in South Africa for a colloquium where, among other objectives, they considered the project retrospectively as a means of conceptualising its future. The exchanges included a focus group where participants discussed the 2014 RIW. In drawing on excerpts from the discussion, we attempt to demonstrate in this chapter how Photovoice is able to function as a form of liberatory enactment by problematising dominant adult-centric knowledges and supporting participants in their disruption of epistemic spaces from which they are traditionally excluded. We then examine the importance of critical researcher reflexivity in unlocking the liberatory potential of Photovoice projects.

Liberatory Praxis

In the focus group discussion, participants reflected on their responses to the RIW, as well as instances of liberatory praxis and the limitations thereof. In noting initial feelings of excitement that he experienced at the youth-led conference, one participant revealed that "when we first arrived it was like 'oh my word! All of these people! When is it going to start? How are we going to interact with everyone?'" It would seem that this participant—as well as many others—felt displaced in this space that was foreign and largely populated by adults, leading to his feeling uncertain and, likely, othered. Such feelings are perhaps justified when considering that these events are designed by, and usually for, adults who belong to the academy. Following this, a participant noted that "it [seeing my photos] gave me courage… my picture can speak, it can let everyone know". A sense of ease in traversing this adult-mediated space was at times achieved through that which Photovoice came to signify for this participant, the currency, import and material accomplishment of youth voice. It may be said that the ability to occupy exclusionary spaces was certainly facilitated by Photovoice. In other words, for most of the participants who shared in the focus group, Photovoice was able to disrupt the epistemically skewed spaces within which it has been designed.

Although many participants stated that the presentation of their photo stories at these events granted them the confidence needed to epistemologically—and perhaps also ontologically—negotiate the very space in which their work was displayed, it seemed that for most, authentic infiltration into this space could be facilitated only by adult gatekeepers. As one participant relayed: "Thank you … for listening to us, because it's not easy for grown up people to take young people like us seriously and value what we say". Acknowledged here is the discomfort that adults are likely to experience when young people enter spaces like these; however, rather than subscribe to the assumption that it is youth who must learn from adults, a form of liberatory disruption occurs, where the speaker places the onus on adults to receive young people as legitimate knowledge producers within such an exclusionary space. Yet, within the same excerpt, the adult remains the all-knowing Other; a spatial gatekeeper who represents an object of gratitude when youth are granted access. Such access was important to participants, who conceded to ultimately feeling accepted by the academics present at the project events, with one participant exclaiming quite proudly that a professor had called her "gifted" after seeing her photo stories.

It appeared that this alienating academic space was navigated successfully only when adults engaged young people. A participant remarked that:

> When we were sitting in front and talking to professors, they were learning something from us … when someone grows [up] they tend to forget [about youth issues] so they need to be reminded by youth … they accepted the fact that they have forgotten what it feels like to be young and the fact that they respected and listen to us - it was a privilege.

For this participant, feelings of alienation from the academic space began to dissipate when the receptiveness of adults to engage—where a dialogical process is implied—and also to position young people as capable of knowledge production that is independent from adults and the academy were sensed. Epistemic correction was therefore crucial in transforming this space. Rather than attempting to disrupt the space overtly, or to capture and make it one that was entirely youth-centric, as had been attempted at earlier stages of the project, this young person experienced it as a privilege to occupy the academic space once it appeared that it was shared or co-occupied with adults. The positioning of young people as legitimate knowledge-makers through the RIW events clearly resisted their construction as foreign bodies or alien epistemic actors.

Although the events hosted by the RIW present instances where Photovoice allowed participants to appropriate exclusionary epistemological spaces, the method appeared to be somewhat lacking with regard to material and social justice outcomes, as Sanon and colleagues' (2014) and Catalani and Minkler's (2010) respective interrogations of Photovoice research remind us is typical of Photovoice applications. In returning to her home country after the engagement in South Africa, one participant claimed that:

> My brother was asking why I was being rude about everything and I was trying to tell him … "I have a job to do!" And so if the 2014 exhibition hadn't come up, my eyes would not have opened to the reality that what is in my country is actually in other countries.

Here, the participant speaks of a personal form of transnational conscientisation that occurred as a result of participation in the project, one that was misunderstood and framed as rudeness by her brother who had not shared in her experiences, implying a distance in understanding between the two siblings. The participant added that:

> We are putting in the effort to show that there are dangerous things out there but we are still tired to remove these things and abolishing all these harmful things in our societies … we only talk about it but we can't do so much.

In building on the theme of interpersonal distance or alienation suggested in the previous excerpt, here the participant describes another form of alienation which is inherent to the Photovoice method itself, that is, the inability to engage materially with what is represented by the photo stories. Interpreted further, where talk substitutes action one becomes "tired" or weary of the project's unfulfilled potential. While the liberatory theory within which Photovoice is grounded advocates for social change, it is rare that significant material change is evidenced after or even within these projects. Researchers circumscribe this issue by describing at a project's inception its liberatory potential, yet seldom privilege or appraise social change outcomes within the project itself. The Multi-country Photovoice Project presents somewhat of a long-term engagement with the participants, an anomaly within this kind of research, and gives weight to assertions that the method—like so many others that are utilised in community-engaged research—is found wanting with respect to material, observable social justice.

Some participants echoed the disappointment around social action, with one participant proclaiming: "I looked at everyone [participants at the RIW exhibition], smiling, happy, but not knowing what to do about the challenges we are facing and where we are coming from". For this participant, the pride that accompanied the display of the photo stories was somewhat diminished by his perceived powerlessness to act in the face of his and other's social struggles. A similar sentiment over the method's social action orientation was reflected—albeit somewhat more optimistically—by another participant's recollection of the RIW when he stated that:

> The first time I saw the exhibition, I was like: "I cannot believe the work that *we* [participant's emphasis] have done" … I got very emotional … it was a feeling I will never forget. I cried because of the work I can do and still have to do.

With so many other participants echoing this response, it is important that Photovoice is understood as representing a deeply emotional process for those involved. Many participants confessed to crying when they observed their photo stories on display at the RIW; however, as this participant notes, lingering over such pride was a collective sense of the work that participants "still have to do". Perhaps a noteworthy, but largely ignored, emotional moment experienced by participants within the Photovoice process is located in the hope which, although characterising the early stages of a project, tends to remain unfulfilled towards its end. Within the Multi-country Photovoice Project, Photovoice instilled a sense of pride, confidence and an increased critical consciousness among participants. However, it is apparent that the manner by which Photovoice falls short of facilitating the kinds of social change that form an integral part of its conceptual mandate needs to be addressed.

Critical Researcher Reflexivity

As referenced earlier, by assuming expertise over the lives of others, many research analyses and processes sanction epistemic violence (Teo, 2010). As researchers can never represent fully the fluid and vastly complex subjectivity of participants, an unequal power dynamic between researchers and participants will always form an inextricable part of social science research. Although such innate inequality may never be entirely extricated from research practice, we believe that a critical reflexive engagement on the part of researchers represents an immensely important means of grappling with, making sense of, and visibilising complex and unequal dynamics of power that manifest within research. It is through critical reflexivity that we, as researchers, can most effectively understand our location within Photovoice research, and indeed how we can work towards an epistemologically just kind of CBPR enactment that may allow for the optimal centring of participant voice, as well as facilitate forms of social justice.

England (1994) proclaims that reflexivity is by no means a form of redundant navel-gazing. Rather, it requires researchers to engage with an ongoing, self-critical and immensely self-conscious process of introspection. It is not enough simply to locate our interpretations and project enactments as an account that exists between the respective worlds of 'us' and 'them'. The unfamiliar must at all times be rendered unfamiliar (Pillow, 2003), and in this way reflexivity need not be shifted to the centre of research, but rather woven through it. Our experiences in the project support the argument that as researchers we need to extend our reflexive awareness by acknowledging the place of power from which our epistemological and ontological worlds construct participants, and in this sense work towards emancipating CBPR, as best as possible, from the confines and regulations of the academy. Indeed, such critical reflexivity exists outside of traditional institutional requirements and represents a nuanced and embodied extension of the 'Reflexivity' section requisite of some academic journals. Certainly, a reflexivity of this nature necessitates both vulnerability and boldness from researchers, who must acknowledge their complicity in the perpetuation of epistemic violence (Law, 2016). However, if Photovoice is to inhabit the participatory and the liberatory agenda it so explicitly espouses, researchers need to address how participant voice could be further amplified, how such voice is stifled by the researcher and/or the institution that he or she represents, and the extent to which particular projects can be detached from traditional academic institutional arrangements. This may allow participants to more fully own the project, and the possibility of real social change—whether this be reformist, policy-based, legislative, and/or revolutionary—becomes more than a mere talking point. In short, reflexivity functions to re-visibilise the researcher within CBPR so that he or she may begin to realign the methodological co-ordinates of community-engaged research in a manner that truly honours local knowledges and facilitates community-centred action.

Law (2016) maintains that in order to be genuinely reflexive, one must engage in *re-search*, that is, a practice of self-questioning around privilege and power that extends beyond data collection. It is argued that within all research practice, re-search is crucial in advocating social justice outcomes. Building on this, we believe that through critical reflexivity (a form of re-search), researchers may strengthen the enactment of Photovoice research outside of traditional institutional parameters and in a manner that is both democratic and community-driven. By reflexively facing such epistemic injustices within our work, the critical consciousness, personal development and group cohesion—which are central to participants' engagement in the Photovoice process—may begin to manifest organically, and without institutional capture, as moments of authentic and material epistemic correction and social justice.

Institutional affiliation drives how researchers feel the Other should be understood and even 'handled'. In order to challenge these shortcomings, all while recognising the researcher's political and personal need to find meaning within this sort of work, it is obvious that researchers must engage in critical reflexivity (Pillow, 2003). When optimised, critical researcher reflexivity bears the potential to identify, analyse and address the epistemic violence that is inherent to community-academy collaboration.

Referencing the above against our project and the analysis presented in this chapter, we offer below reflexive commentary—a core and ongoing feature of our engagement—to demonstrate our own epistemic consciousness in the facilitation of the project and the application of Photovoice method.

Participants were hesitant to engage in overt critique of the RIW. This may be attributed to a number of reasons, including: feeling that criticism would negate their sense of gratitude for invitation to the RIW; anxieties about the researchers misconstruing criticism for insolence; or perhaps being at the centre of events did not facilitate a critical outsider's perspective of them. Whatever the reasons, while the 2014 events epitomised and in many ways overtly honoured youth epistemic agency, in our view the events also presented a number of moments that were indicative of partial or reduced liberatory and participatory praxis. Although many of the young people expressed feelings of being heard by, and visible to the adults at the book launch, photo exhibition and conference, and shared how this in itself induced feelings of insider acceptance of the outsider, it may be said that, taken together, these feelings were relative to their contextual environment, that is, a space in which young people are almost never engaged meaningfully. In what follows, we elaborate briefly on such moments in order to address a way by which to improve the method's potential for social change.

During the youth-led conference, we observed that adult voices constantly threatened to dominate the space, illustrated by their many attempts to interrupt, clarify, interpret and—in many cases—speak on behalf of the young people. It would appear that for some of these adults, the inclusion of youth voice appeared to function merely as a form of token acknowledgment of youth participation in research. In many ways, the adults demonstrated the reclaiming of *their* epistemic space by limiting participants' discursive opportunity and attempting to restore the dialogic space to the conventions that govern traditional adult-led proceedings.

It is not inconceivable then that some of the participants' expressed despondency relates not only to the outcomes of the project, but also to some realisation that the project—throughout which their voices had been so central—did not entirely belong to them. Of course, this is not to say that project facilitators should detach from Photovoice processes and activities altogether. Indeed, it is unlikely that Photovoice projects with marginalised groups could manifest without the engagement of those affiliated to an institution of some kind. Rather, the above reflections serve as a call to Photovoice researchers and facilitators to consciously visibilise their presence and power within their work. Perhaps somewhat paradoxically then, methodological ideologies around participatory research must be more interrogative of the researcher than may be the case currently if CBPR methods are to become truly participatory. By insisting that Photovoice and other kinds of participatory research belong to the participants, the role—and indeed the epistemologically dominant presence of—the researcher stands to remain invisible, thereby stifling liberatory praxis and even social justice ambitions.

If Photovoice is to emerge from its sometimes ambiguous position as a methodology that is at once participant-centred and researcher-dominated, one that is grounded in liberatory theory yet is challenged to exhibit liberatory praxis, then the role of the researcher—exemplified in this case by the adult and the location of the academy—must be made apparent at all times. In this section, we have resisted constructing our reflections of the project along the traditional project success-project failure binary. Instead, we offer these reflexive observations as ways in which researchers can aggrandise the capacity of CBPR methods while simultaneously interrogating their theorised transformative value.

Conclusion

With the intention of catalysing social change, Photovoice seeks to centralise marginalised knowledges. By focusing on subaltern voices in an attempt to challenge epistemologically violent master narratives, Photovoice is imbued with an exciting and unique kind of liberatory potential. The method has shown to have myriad positive effects with youth participants, whose voices are usually embedded within, and marginalised by, adult-centric socio-cultural spaces. In this chapter, we draw upon a youth-centric Photovoice project on safety to illustrate the method's potential for liberatory enactment, and examine how participants' enactments within the project become stifled by the method's innately unequal power dynamics and institutional capture.

Read together, the launch of the photo book, photo-exhibition and the youth-led conference, representing a unique and noteworthy epistemic juncture within our project, sought to enact liberatory praxis and epistemic correction. In demonstration of youth epistemic agency, these three events positioned the participants as knowledge-makers and social activists who used their photo stories to convey grounded meanings of safety and the lack thereof, and enter into dialogue with adult voices that are representative of the academy about their representations and implied action. However, we contend that even as a compelling means of igniting critical consciousness and pursuing epistemic justice, the method, along with many other CBPR engagements, has to evolve further with respect to the epistemic correction of knowledge, as well as closing the gap between realised social justice outcomes and Photovoice's promise of social change. In responding to these challenges, we highlight critical researcher reflexivity as a means of shifting Photovoice from the traditional academic structures out of which it was conceived, and situating it more fully into communities where it is enacted.

Our call for critical researcher reflexivity as a means of both grappling with Photovoice's potential for supporting the epistemic status quo, and enhancing its participatory and transformative capacities presents a number of considerations for future Photovoice projects. Firstly, researchers cannot operate under an assumed, and largely false, notion of epistemic equality within these projects. Although the outcomes of Photovoice research may be considered a form of epistemic correction, the very process of Photovoice cannot neglect the method's innately unequal representational politics. Those undertaking Photovoice endeavours must reflect on the kinds of silencing devices, or self-serving rhetoric, which threaten to become acceptable within such research. Critical reflexivity on the part of Photovoice researchers is thus a crucial determinant in unlocking the method's liberatory and participatory potential, and honouring the epistemic agency of participants.

The binary between academic and community ownership of Photovoice projects must be destabilised if the methodology is to be considered a truly meaningful form of CBPR. It is at this point that participants, such as the youth in our project, may begin to arrogate Photovoice by not only working their vision of social transformation into the prescription, logic and process of the project but, importantly, by engaging the project as authoritative epistemic agents who enact social justice initiatives on their terms.

References

Boog, B. W. M. (2003). The emancipatory character of action research, its history and present state of the art. *Journal of Community and Applied Social Psychology, 13*, 426–438.

Burman, E. (2008). *Deconstructing developmental psychology*. New York, NY: Routledge.

Carlson, E. D., Engebretson, J., & Chamberlain, R. M. (2006). Photovoice as a social process of critical consciousness. *Qualitative Health Research, 16*, 836–852.

Catalani, C., & Minkler, M. (2010). Photovoice: A review of the literature in health and public health. *Health Education & Behavior, 37*, 424–452.

England, K. V. (1994). Getting personal: Reflexivity, positionality, and feminist research. *The Professional Geographer, 46*, 80–89.

Foster, D. (2004). Liberation psychology. In D. Hook (Ed.), *Critical psychology* (pp. 559–602). Lansdowne: UCT Press.

Foster-Fishman, P., Nowell, B., Deacon, Z., Nievar, M. A., & McCann, P. (2005). Using methods that matter: The impact of reflection, dialogue, and voice. *American Journal of Community Psychology, 36*, 275–291.

Freire, P. (1970). *Pedagogy of the oppressed*. New York, NY: Herder and Herder.

Hergenrather, K. C., Rhodes, S. D., Cowan, C. A., Bardhoshi, G., & Pula, S. (2009). Photovoice in community-based participatory research: A qualitative review. *American Journal of Health Behavior, 33*, 686–698.

Law, S. F. (2016). Unknowing researcher's vulnerability: Re-searching inequality on an uneven playing field. *Journal of Social and Political Psychology, 4*, 521–536.

Lykes, B., & Scheib, H. (2015). The artistry of emancipatory practice: Photovoice, creative techniques, and feminist anti-racist participatory action research. In H. Bradbury (Ed.), *The sage handbook of action research* (pp. 130–141). London: Sage.

Makhanya, M. (2014). *Address at opening of youth conference. University of South Africa Research and Innovation Week*. Pretoria: South Africa.
Minkler, M., & Wallerstein, N. (2009). Community-based participatory research for health: From process to outcomes. *Health Promotion Practice, 10*(3), 317–318.
Mitchell, C. (2015). Introduction. In K. G. Gådin & C. Mitchell (Eds.), *Being young in a neoliberal time: Transnational perspectives on challenges and possibilities for resistance and social change* (pp. 11–21). Sundsvall: Mid Sweden University.
O'Sullivan, M., & MacPhail, A. (Eds.). (2010). *Young people's voices in physical education and youth sport*. London: Routledge.
Odora-Hoppers, C. A. (Ed.). (2002). *Indigenous knowledge and the integration of knowledge systems: Towards a philosophy of articulation*. Claremont: New Africa Books.
Pillow, W. (2003). Confession, catharsis, or cure? Rethinking the uses of reflexivity as methodological power in qualitative research. *International Journal of Qualitative Studies in Education, 16*, 175–196.
Sanon, M., Evans-Agnew, R. A., & Boutain, D. M. (2014). An exploration of social justice intent in photovoice research studies from 2008 to 2013. *Nursing Inquiry, 21*, 212–226.
Shore, C. (2010). Beyond the multiversity: Neoliberalism and the rise of the schizophrenic university. *Social Anthropology, 18*, 15–29.
Strack, R. W., Lovelace, K. A., Jordan, T. D., & Holmes, A. P. (2010). Framing Photovoice using a social-ecological logic model as a guide. *Health Promotion Practice, 11*, 629–636.
Strack, R. W., Magill, C., & McDonagh, K. (2004). Engaging youth through Photovoice. *Health Promotion Practice, 5*, 49–58.
Suffla, S., Kaminer, D., & Bawa, U. (2012). Photovoice as community engaged research: The interplay between knowledge creation and agency in a south African study on safety promotion. *Journal of Psychology in Africa, 22*, 517–528.
Suffla, S., Bawa, U., & Seedat, M. (Eds.). (2014). *My voice in pictures: African children's vision of safety*. Johannesburg, South Africa: Institute for Social & Health Sciences, University of South Africa.
Teo, T. (2010). What is epistemological violence in the empirical social sciences? *Social and Personality Psychology Compass, 4*, 295–303.
Wang, C. C. (2006). Youth participation in Photovoice as a strategy for community change. *Journal of Community Practice, 14*, 147–161.
Wang, C. C., & Burris, M. A. (1997). Photovoice: Concept, methodology, and use for participatory needs assessment. *Health Education & Behavior, 24*, 369–387.
Wang, C. C., Morrel-Samuels, S., Hutchison, P. M., Bell, L., & Pestronk, R. M. (2004). Flint Photovoice: Community building among youths, adults, and policymakers. *American Journal of Public Health, 94*(6), 911–913.
Zuch, M., Mathews, C., De Koker, P., Mtshizana, Y., & Mason-Jones, A. J. (2013). Evaluation of a Photovoice pilot project for school safety in South Africa. *Children, Youth and Environments, 23*, 180–197.

Chapter 14
Critical Psychosocial Mnemonics as a Decolonising Participatory Method: Towards Reclaiming and Refiguring the Archive Through Memory, Stories and Narratives

Garth Stevens

Archives as Sites of Participatory Research and Epistemological Rejuvenation

In his seminal text, *Archive Fever*, Derrida (1998) suggests that our feverish preoccupation with archives has generated an intriguing set of possibilities and a simultaneous set of unsettling propositions. Why are archives of all sorts such crucial sites of interrogation, especially in the context of a resurgent impulse towards decoloniality across the contemporary globe? Perhaps the simplest answer to this question is that archives have a valence in the symbolic economy in relation to the construction of a politics of memory, experience, knowledge and being—that is to say, they are critical to the construction of our social worlds and the subjects within them—and therefore are sites of deep contestation between hegemonic and counter-hegemonic groups and forces. Archives are indeed places to which we compulsively return precisely because they are elusive in their definitiveness, yet never fully foreclosed, and therefore filled with possibilities.

Historically, and in the narrowest technical sense, archives are conceived of as collections of primary, "unmediated" sources pertaining to processes, events or phenomena (e.g. procedural documents, personal journals, photographs, objects of inquiry, etc.). Sometimes they are also imagined as specific institutional or organisational sites (e.g. the national archives of any country). Such a descriptive account of archives is somewhat sterile and objectivist in orientation as it presupposes collections of factual primary sources that are viewed as neutral and apolitical. This conception of archives also locates them predominantly within the purview of historians, who mine these sources to interpret and gain understandings of the past.

G. Stevens (✉)
Department of Psychology, University of the Witwatersrand, Johannesburg, South Africa
e-mail: Garth.Stevens@wits.ac.za

M. Seedat et al. (eds.), *Emancipatory and Participatory Methodologies in Peace, Critical, and Community Psychology*, Peace Psychology Book Series,
DOI 10.1007/978-3-319-63489-0_14

In contrast, Derrida (1998) makes the compelling argument that all archives and their related processes are deeply immersed within a political context, often managed by hegemonic elites for explicit or inadvertent political and ideological ends. They are a key social and political resource, given that they tend to truncate the totality of human experience by generating official histories and crafting collective memories, that in turn shape grand narratives and public discourses that frequently elide and negate the nuances of human experience. In the Derrida (1998) sense, this reflects the fact that the archive is both a place of *commencement* and *order*, that is, the archive provides a record and simultaneously determines what it is that is to be included or muted in such a record (Laubscher, 2013). Treanor (2009) similarly notes that "the nature of the 'archive' affects not only what is archived, but also how we relate to and access it. The archive also conditions the process of archiving itself and, indeed, the very nature of what is archivable … The archive is thus a filter of sorts" (pp. 289–290). This speaks directly to the sociopolitical processes surrounding any archive that come to privilege, include and exclude certain social subjects and ways of knowing in a manner that is partial, perspectival and incomplete. Historical revisionism is always associated with certain elisions in the archive, and because official histories tend to be more publicly available and overtly ideologically loaded, there is sometimes a slippage between what we understand to be the archive and official histories—a conflation of the two that requires some unpacking and disentanglement which may offer different ways of not only expanding, challenging and creating histories, but also of understanding the impact of these histories on our present and future (Mbembe, 2002; Stevens, Duncan, & Sonn, 2013).

For some, the contents in the archive are in some ways static—dead—but it is in the engagement with this archive that its contents take on a spectral or ghost-like quality, always haunting the present and thereby enlivening the archive as we witness its contents and (re)interpret them (Laubscher, 2013; Mbembe, 2002). Through this process, we of course can also determine the absences within the archive, but simultaneously recognise that every engagement with the archive is itself a contribution to that archive. Thus, the boundaries of the archive are less rigid in this conceptualisation, more permeable, and open to multiple insertions and interpretations. As such, archival research is not only about mining historical primary sources, but also about potentially contributing new sources to that archive, thereby expanding it. In addition, interpreting historical material within archives allows for research into the past, but also into the present moment of interpretation, thereby opening up a space for a liminal analytics to occur (Stevens, Duncan, & Sonn, 2013). This dynamic view of archives also suggests that they are not bound by location, they may be virtual, multiple, intersecting, and complementary in nature. Similarly, they may not be specific to particular types of collections, but can expand into multiple forms of collections (Hamilton, Harris, Taylor, Pickover, Reid, & Saleh, 2002).

In this formulation of the archive and archival research, interdisciplinarity again is encouraged as desirable, given that the same corpus of materials could be analysed in a myriad of ways and through a variety of lenses (see for example, Stevens, Duncan, & Hook, 2013b). In addition, methods that extend beyond historical mining of primary sources and genealogical analyses become possible through forms of inclusion and participation, thereby enhancing the idea of methodological pluralism. Here, writers such as Feyerabend (1975) have suggested that multiple and more complex approaches to exploring the social world are indeed necessary, and that methodological reification should be avoided both philosophically and in practice. Both interdisciplinarity and methodological pluralism and innovation help to generate new relationships to knowledge, thereby raising the possibilities for epistemological rupture and rejuvenation as we come to experience different ways of analysing and therefore of knowing, being and doing in the world. Expanding and potentially contributing to alternative readings and accounts of our histories, is a situation where we avoid reproducing knowledge that is already circumscribed and thereby revive Biko's (2004) injunction to "write what [we] like".

Psychosocial and Psychopolitical Transformation Through a Decolonial Lens

Beyond methodological pluralism and innovation, the present historical juncture has also called for deeper historical analyses of the pernicious social conditions of modernity. Certainly, the twenty-first century can be characterised as the contemporary social apex in which marginality, based on alterity, has surfaced in unsurpassed ways. Despite the homogenising influence of globalisation, distinctions between Northern and Southern contexts remain, racism continues to mutate, levels of xenophobia and anti-immigrant sentiment are on the increase, Islamophobia has returned as a mode of Othering and marginalisation, fundamentalisms of various forms have gained greater traction, and levels of proto-fascism, inequality, exploitation, violence, war and suffering are at staggering levels (Derrida, 2006). Central to an analysis of these conditions, decoloniality has emerged as a contemporary theoretical resource. While the decolonial turn epistemically is frequently cited as only emerging in the literature in the late 1990s and early 2000s, with key writings by Walter Mignolo, Ramon Grosfoguel, Sylvia Wynter, Enrique Dussel, Linda Tuhiwai Smith, Anibal Quijano and Nelson Maldonado-Torres amongst others, decoloniality as a terrain of intellectual engagement has existed for a much lengthier period of time. An impressive lineage of intellectuals have contributed to this epistemic tradition, including Aime Cesaire, Frantz Fanon, W.E.B. Du Bois, Amilcar Cabral, Patrice Lumumba and Kwame Nkrumah—all providing a significant impetus to the development of the decolonial episteme.

For Maldonado-Torres (2011), decoloniality is essentially a critique of Western modernist thought and its associated practices, that include colonisation, capitalism, racism and the modern gender system. He suggests that this entire system is embedded in violence, emerging out of European expansionism, slavery and colonialism, and constituted a colonial matrix of power that continues to shape relations of power, knowledge and being. In its sheer scale, this modernist project allowed for the emergence of global configurations of subjectivity, based on violence, alterity and exploitation (Maldonado-Torres, 2007; Taussig, 1986). As such, decoloniality is fundamentally about adopting a sceptical epistemic attitude towards Western modernity and its associated forms of knowledge, power, being and praxis.

Stevens, Duncan and Sonn (2013) and Sonn, Stevens and Duncan (2013) note that there is already a considerable body of knowledge devoted to operationalising decolonial theory into a mode of psychosocial and psychopolitical praxis (Stevens, Duncan, & Hook, 2013a)—combining theory and method to transformatively address the psychological, social and political impacts of the legacies of colonialism (see for example, Biko, 2004; Bulhan, 1985; Fanon, 1967; Memmi, 1984).

The first terrain that they identify as being impacted upon is that of history (Stevens, Duncan, & Sonn, 2013). They draw on the work of Smith (1999), who argues that the impact of imperialism and colonialism on indigenous communities implicates academic knowledge and knowledge production in the destruction of indigenous histories, and therefore motivates for projects directed at the deconstruction and reclamation of history. These alternative histories constitute alternative knowledges and open up new possibilities for knowing, being and acting in the world. Recognising this history in its totality is critical, as the consequences of colonialism imprint themselves constantly on contemporary postcolonial social formations, often in uneven material conditions, as well as within uneven social relations in the sociocultural fabric of these societies (Bhabha, 1994; Fanon, 1967; Said, 1978). Smith (1999) goes on to argue that:

> This in turn requires a theory or approach which helps us to engage with, understand and then act upon history. […]. Telling our stories from the past, reclaiming the past, giving testimony to the injustices of the past are all strategies which are commonly employed by indigenous peoples, struggling for justice … [and is] a powerful form of resistance (pp. 34–35).

The second terrain that they identify is the decimation of cultural resources amongst marginalised groups in the context of colonialism (Sonn, Stevens, & Duncan, 2013). Beyond the violence and systemised mechanisms of oppression and economic exploitation, colonialism also involved covert processes and mechanisms of control over spirituality, sexuality and culture, resulting in social relations that are fundamentally fragmented between and within both colonising and colonised populations (Bhabha, 1994; Fanon, 1967; Glover, Dudgeon & Huygens, 2005; Moane, 2003, 2009). The decolonial project must of necessity therefore be profoundly invested in the recovery of these cultural resources if the alienation of colonialism and coloniality is to be overcome, to the extent that such a recovery is indeed possible.

The third terrain of impact that Sonn, Stevens and Duncan (2013) identify is the creation and maintenance of alterity. As a fundamental mode of Othering that was a foundational element of colonialism, alterity took the primary form of racial difference through the system of racism. Quijano (2000) maintains that the shifting meanings of race must be understood in relation to the histories of empires, and this remains relevant within the context of globalisation today, where xenophobia, anti-immigrant sentiment and the rise of Islamophobia are as pernicious as the more recrudescent forms of racism directed at black populations. These forms of alterity remain important to surface as they have an enduring effect on uneven resource distribution and access at a material level in political and psychosocial life.

For decolonial researchers, practitioners and activists, moving from the broad conceptual domain to specific modes of practice are central to the operationalisation of a decolonial ethics and praxis. This includes the articulation of subaltern voices, the recovery of histories and knowledges, a deeply reflexive praxis, the translation of theoretical and philosophical work into forms of activism, and the utilisation of forms of theory that speak to the experiential and contextual dimensions of subalterns (thus potentially expanding the archive beyond the Western canon) (Sonn, Stevens, & Duncan, 2013; Stevens, Duncan, & Sonn, 2013). Martín-Baró (1994) argued that it was imperative for psychology to work alongside the oppressed in processes of deconstruction, including the recovery of historical memory, de-ideologising everyday experience (i.e. unmasking everyday realities by exposing the ways in which the status quo is justified), and building on the positive experiences of people to reconstruct community (see also Freire, 2000; Montero, 2007). With regard to reflexive praxis, Smith (1999) and Swadener and Mutua (2008) suggest that decolonising research is more about motives, concerns and knowledge brought to the research process, and is likely to be performative and enmeshed in activism, rather than being purely located within the theoretical domain (Sonn, Stevens, & Duncan, 2013). Finally, decolonising research works within the frame of other-than-Western forms of knowing that have been excluded and silenced by dominant Western modes of knowing and doing (Dudgeon & Fielder, 2006; Moreton-Robinson, 2004; Smith, 1999), thereby supporting *standpoint* methods, and highlighting that there are no value-free positions from which to engage with knowledge construction and social transformation. In addition, Reyes Cruz and Sonn (2011) suggest that the different theoretical frames within decoloniality, which include critical race studies, whiteness studies and the more general study of the social reproduction of inequality, are key to developing ways of knowing and doing that can contribute to decolonisation and liberation. Given the levels of marginalisation, exploitation, alterity, and hierarchies in relations of power that characterise the contemporary globe, a decolonial lens appears to offer much in the way of an analytics and a corpus of methods to respond to these challenges.

The Apartheid Archive Project

Writing from the specific location of South Africa, there are recent historical exemplars of the shifting nature of archives during the transition from apartheid to democracy—an apartheid archive that was initially managed and controlled to justify the racist segregation and exploitative nature of apartheid, to an archive that revealed the many horrors of the apartheid system. Here, the Truth and Reconciliation Commission (TRC) was the primary mode of rewriting and refiguring this archive. While the TRC made a critical contribution to this process of dealing with the past

(Cassin, Cayla, & Salazar, 2004; Villa-Vicencio, 2004), its focus on apartheid's gross human rights violations and atrocities meant that it effectively foreclosed the possibility of a more comprehensive exploration of the everyday manifestations of apartheid life. As a consequence, much of the commonplace details of apartheid racism have not been meaningfully assessed or publicly acknowledged (Apartheid Archive Project, 2010). Stevens, Duncan and Sonn (2013) note that it is however important to concede that the TRC played a significant role in augmenting the official record—"one that had been systematically sanitised and deliberately destroyed in some instances, between 1990 and 1994 in particular, in an attempt to conceal the machinations of the apartheid State prior to the transition to a non-racial democracy and a change in government" (p. 28). They go on to suggest that beyond extending and elaborating the apartheid archive, the TRC was however also a public national process, which advertently and inadvertently implicated itself in complex practices of memorialisation and neo-liberal nation-building. Certain events and experiences were consequently either included or excluded from the archival record, and this unfinished business of social transformation can be seen in the history of apartheid racism that continues to resonate in the present in forms of inequality, ongoing racialisation, and in its potentially pernicious future role.

The Apartheid Archive Project was initiated precisely in response to many of the above limitations, challenges and decolonising imperatives. While accepting that postcolonial contexts themselves may dynamically involve the emergence of alternative modes of subjectivity such as those articulated in concepts such as hybridity (Bhabha, 1994), creolisation (Erasmus, 2001) or entanglement (Nuttall, 2009), decoloniality is fundamentally premised upon confronting a racialised history that prevails within the contemporary material and sociocultural milieu. Central to the Apartheid Archive Project is the idea that accessing everyday stories of experiences of apartheid that have been excluded, silenced or neglected may offer us an analytic portal into how this racist history remains integral to individual and collective psyches, shapes contemporary social relations and material inequality, and is therefore critical to processes of psychosocial and psychopolitical transformation and social cohesion (Sonn, Stevens, & Duncan, 2013).

In various post-conflict and post-authoritarian societies there have been formal mechanisms and processes such as Truth and Reconciliation Commissions, symbolic acts such as formal apologies, and other types of macro- and micro-level interventions that are aimed at redressing past oppression, and laying the ground for intergroup relations based on equality and social justice (Contassel & Holder, 2008; James & van der Vijver, 2000; Rigney, 2012; Stevens, 2006). As mentioned previously, several researchers (see Contassel & Holder, 2008; Stevens, 2006) have commented on both the successes and limitations of such initiatives in different contexts to promote reconciliation and decolonisation. Furthermore, writers such as Gilroy (2010) and Goldberg (2008) also illustrate how the legacies of slavery, racism, the associated negative constructions of the black Other and even the resistances to this, continue to be appropriated into new modes of production and capital accumulation (e.g. the commoditisation of black anti-racist and aspirational values into market economies). Clearly then, a transformative praxis has to be premised on a decolonial imperative that addresses how the history of the colonial project continues to manifest in the present in overt, covert and other forms of racism, material marginalisation, intergroup conflict, constrained forms of subjectivity, and personal and collective forms of sociocultural alienation.

Stevens, Duncan and Hook (2013a), drawing on the original documents that birthed the project, note the aims of the Apartheid Archive Project as follows:

> Sixteen years ago the curtain was finally drawn on the system of institutionalised racism that the world knew as apartheid, and the memorial signifiers of its demise are writ large on South Africa's public landscape. Yet, its pernicious effects on our inner-worlds; on memory, identity and subjectivity, continue to constrain the promises of a truly post-apartheid South Africa. Trapped by a national desire to look forward rather than to the past, the everyday personal accounts of the scourge of apartheid are rapidly fading into a forgotten past … Given South Africa's apparent self-imposed, and in certain respects, carefully managed, amnesia about the apartheid era … as well as its blindness to the ongoing impact today of institutionalised apartheid racism … on inter-group and inter-personal relationships, we believe that it is important to re-open the doors to the past … [This project] will attempt to foreground narratives of the everyday experiences of 'ordinary' South Africans during the apartheid era, rather than simply focusing on the 'grand' narratives of the past or the privileged narratives of academic, political and social elites … Based, in part, on the assumption that traumatic experiences from the past will constantly attempt to re-inscribe themselves (often in masked form) in the present if they are not acknowledged and dealt with, this project aims to examine the nature of the experiences of racism of (particularly 'ordinary') South Africans under the old apartheid order and their continuing effects on individual and group functioning in contemporary South Africa (pp. 6-7).

Stated in the simplest terms, the Apartheid Archive Project is an ongoing collaborative research project that focuses on the collection of personal stories and narrative accounts from ordinary South Africans, about their experiences of racism during apartheid. Initiated in 2008 by two psychologists at the University of the Witwatersrand in Johannesburg, South Africa, the project continues to be housed at, and primarily funded by, this institution. The collected narratives, stories and related project materials are all currently stored in the Historical Papers section of the Cullen Library at the University of the Witwatersrand, and are also electronically available to the broader public (http://www.historicalpapers.wits.ac.za/?inventory/U/collections&c=AG3275/R/9023). While the Apartheid Archive Project has begun to generate its own archive of narratives and stories, it has already begun to extend its analytic gaze to existing and related archives as well (see for example, Ratele & Laubscher, 2013).

One of the primary aims of this initiative is to provide an opportunity or platform to different sectors of South African society (but particularly the politically, socially and economically marginalised, whose life stories are rarely incorporated into dominant historical accounts of the past) to reflect on and share their past experiences. These narratives, it is hoped, will offer us an array of alternative entry points into the past, in addition to the accounts of historians and other scholars. As Nora (1989) observes, narratives such as these serve as an important antidote to the "deforming, … petrifying" (p. 12) effects of dominant (homogenising) formalised histories—histories from below as opposed to histories from above, so to speak (Bonner & Nieftagodien, 2008; Thompson, 1966).

Another vital part of the initiative is to consider the ongoing effects and attributable meanings of the experiences related in the collected stories and narratives, in present-day South Africa. In this way the Apartheid Archive Project encourages both a commitment to personal and collective remembering, and a joint intellectual and political commitment to interrogating stories and narratives in their current temporal context of narrational production, rather than simply accepting them at face-value (Stevens, Duncan, & Sonn, 2013).

The Apartheid Archive Project has brought together more than 30 South African and international researchers (i.e. from Australia, the UK, the USA, etc.) from a wide range of disciplines and theoretical backgrounds in the social sciences, humanities, arts and education. Using virtual information and communication technologies, conferences, symposia, as well as public-intellectual activities, the project has been sustained as a loose association of scholars and practitioners with converging intellectual interests. This core team of researchers has pursued sub-projects of personal and collective interest (e.g. gender/sexuality and race; diasporic studies; memory studies; liberation and decolonising approaches to race and racism; and the psychoanalytics of race and racism), inducted graduate students into these research processes, and collected stories pertaining to the experiences of specifically defined cohorts (e.g. domestic workers, women, men, whites, blacks, academics, ex-combatants, etc.). The project therefore offers a richness, both in terms of who has contributed to the collection of stories and narratives, and in terms of the heterogeneity of researchers writing about the archive (Stevens, Duncan, & Hook, 2013b).

All working from the same narratives, the collaborating researchers have offered a range of analyses aimed at understanding apartheid history and its sometimes enacted and denied resonances in the present. The layering effect of scholars approaching the same corpus of texts through different conceptual lenses has produced an extraordinary depth of engagement about the past and the present (Duncan, Stevens, & Sonn, 2012; Stevens, Duncan, & Hook, 2013b).

It is also worth noting the broad range of the collected stories and narratives. In the initial stages of data collection, members of the core research team were tasked with writing their own stories, then utilising their existing networks and through a broad snowballing strategy, to recruit potential contributors to the archive. In addition, the project website also incorporates an Internet portal through which any member of the public can submit his/her narrative directly to the lead researchers of the project (www.apartheidarchive.org). Contributors were initially asked to write down their earliest significant experience of racism, with some broad reference to the temporal location of the event(s), as well as some consideration of the impact of the event(s) on their lives. This was opted for as it allowed for some degree of homogeneity in terms of the storied form which we hoped would facilitate narrative analyses, but simultaneously allowed for more personalised accounts to emerge. As the project has evolved, it has also developed more specialised sub-projects, and has been augmented with specific research questions that are of relevance to the participants being engaged with (e.g. domestic workers may very well have specific questions pertaining to their experiences of intimacy and alienation within familial spaces; and white ex-combatants are often dealing with questions of perpetration, shame, guilt and aggression at the loss of privilege). The narratives are also being generated through additional modes, such as the narrative-interview method. The task is relatively open-ended and different researchers and narrators have approached it in different ways—demonstrating the multidimensional complexity of methods of collecting storied accounts and analysing them (Stevens, Duncan, & Hook, 2013a).

Psychosocial Mnemonics, Stories, Narratives and the Politics of Memory

An intellectual and political cornerstone of the project is to contribute to a form of critical psychosocial mnemonics (Stevens, Duncan, & Hook, 2013b). Sonn, Stevens and Duncan (2013) define this as referring:

> specifically to the manner in which storytelling facilitates memory recall and its articulation, comes to restructure and shape such memories and their articulation, and indeed dialectically serves to reinforce and "create" such memories. Furthermore, the stories that are generated within such contexts may surface how subjectivities and identities are constructed, can reveal not only personal and collective social experiences of the past, but can also illuminate how the interpretation of past events within stories may be analysed to formulate certain hypotheses and attributions about the social world in the present (p. 296).

Located within the broad field of memory studies, critical psychosocial mnemonics is interested in engaging with those mechanisms and processes that facilitate individual and collective remembering (e.g. storytelling); how these memories intersect with lived experiences and histories; what they can reveal to us about the past, the present and in the future; how they reflect a convergence of the past and a changing present; how they reflect and construct the psychological and social subject, intersubjectivity and intergroup relations; and how they may allow us to make critical analytic commentaries about the social world and its psychological referents (Stevens, Duncan, & Sonn, 2013). Most importantly, critical psychosocial mnemonics is concerned with deploying such analyses in the service of questioning and subverting relations of power through deconstructing and de-ideologising them (Martín-Baró, 1994). Storytelling and narrative measures are a crucial means of transformative psychosocial practice, particularly so in the context of critical socio-political memory-work and in situations characterised by radical asymmetries of power.

The initial choice to focus on stories and narratives as the primary data source when the Apartheid Archive Project was launched, was premised on ensuring a goodness-of-fit between the political values underpinning the project and the analytic methods utilised. Lieblich, Tuval-Mashiach and Zilber (1998) note that narratives can either "be the object of research or a means for the study of another question" (p. 2). Within the context of the Apartheid Archive Project, stories and narratives are analysed both in relation to their form as well as their content, and thus serve as both objects and vehicles of study, allowing for a diverse range of analytic outcomes to be pursued.

Smith (1999) suggests that storytelling is a key method within the decolonisation project. Feminist authors (e.g. hooks, 1990b) have also highlighted storytelling as a powerful method that allows for deeper, nuanced understandings of phenomena as well as a means for disrupting the power relationship inherent in traditional modes of knowledge construction and production. Watkins and Schulman (2008) also write about the aims of decolonising research as:

> claiming resources; *testimonies*, storytelling, and remembering to claim and speak about extremely painful events and histories; and research that celebrates survival and resilience and that revitalizes language, arts, and cultural practices. Communities beset by various forms of oppression, whose members have suffered from diminished senses of themselves by virtue of racism and classism, can use research to not only nurture community understanding, but to help preserve community and cultural practices (p. 276).

Similarly, writers in the areas of critical race studies (Biko, 2004; Fanon, 1967; Ladson-Billings, 2003; Nielsen, 2011; Ross, 2000) and feminism (e.g. Bond, Belenky, & Weinstock, 2000; Mulvey, Torenzio, Hill, Bond, Huygens, Hamerton & Cahill, 2000) suggest that storied accounts promote voice and social change, as history often excludes the voices and perspectives of minority groups, and through this process of silencing and exclusion, power is justified and legitimised (Abrams & Moio, 2009; Ladson-Billings, 2003).

Extending on Scott's (1990) references to "public transcripts" and "hidden transcripts", Bell (2010) highlights four types of stories: stock stories (i.e. stories told from the perspective of the dominant group), concealed stories (i.e. stories told from the perspective of the dominated group), resistance stories (i.e. stories telling of resistance to the societal status quo and the fight for more equal and inclusive social arrangements) and emerging/transforming stories (i.e. stories to build on and amplify concealed and resistance stories and create new stories to disrupt the status quo in the service of social change). As articulated by Bell (2010, p. 18), "as we create new narratives we situate ourselves as responsive moral agents, enabling new ways of behaving in line with social justice goals".

Of course stories and narratives[1] are never "truthful" reflections of deeds, behaviours and events. They are always sites in which the investments of speakers, listeners, the invisible interlocutors who may apprehend such stories, and the influence of the social context on our interpretations of the world, converge to give rise to a constructed version of the event (Jones, 1996; Sands, 2004). Josselson and Lieblich (1995) note that the role of the researcher is in the interest of reaching a new interpretation of the raw data of the experience, not as a frozen temporal construction of the past, but as a moment of co-construction and co-interpretation within the present (Addison, 1992; Josselson & Lieblich, 1995). We can therefore learn about the social constructedness of historical experiences, social knowledges, subjectivities and identities by studying social actors' stories and narratives of their experiences.

[1] Mankowski and Rappaport (1995), Rappaport (1995, 2000) and Thomas and Rappaport (1996) have all made the distinction between stories that refer to individual representations or accounts that are unique to a person, and narratives that are stories that are common to a social group and shared through a range of social interactions.

This constructedness of stories and narratives also however highlight a range of cautions and potential limitations in relation to sociopolitical memory-work. Worby and Ally (2013) remind us of the pitfalls of establishing the retrieval of memory in binaried opposition to forgetting and thereby conflating memory with an authentic recovery of the past; Truscott (2011) highlights how this kind of retrieval in memory-work can serve as a politically reactionary mode of reproducing and ossifying the past for those who experience their decline in privilege as an insurmountable loss; Hook (2013) illustrates how memory can appear as legitimate forms of recognition about past complicities but in fact acts as a defensive mechanism precisely not to address the past; Straker (2013) points to how particular forms of articulated memory such as shame can indeed recentre former oppressors' experiences through "promiscuous" disclosures of complicity; and Eagle and Bowman (2013) stress the importance of recognising that all memory-work based on biographical accounts are also simultaneously crafted acts of self-representation with particular interlocutors and audiences in mind and are therefore always performative. These are of course all important cautions to be cognisant of, especially if the nature of the memory-work is narrowly defined as an attempt to provide a coherent "truth" about the past. However, the Apartheid Archive Project has always been premised on the idea of surfacing a range of alternative views of history, is engaged in a constantly reflexive process of self-interrogation, and views this work as constantly iterative and generative of new analytic questions. Furthermore, we developed the project with the understanding that it would constitute an open process, one that does not constitute an "end to the past" (Peterson, 2012) or an attempt to fossilise these accounts as factual. Indeed, each account that will be captured in the archive may be seen to constitute another beginning to engaging with the past, the present and the future, thereby capitalising on the liminal, non-foreclosed and provisional nature of narratives as a form of expression (see Turner, 2008)—constantly asking *why* these forms of memory emerge at particular moments in time, and also what the ideological underpinnings and political *functions* of these modes of memory-work are in moments of narrational production.

Archival Research as a Decolonial Mode of Praxis

Reclaiming the Archive

What should be apparent from the above is not a conception of the archive as an entity or record that is neutral, objective and reflective of an absolute truth. Rather, Derrida's (1998) broad conception of the archive appears more appropriate, in so far as the contents that are held within the archive are never completely transparent, unambiguous and value-free, and that "[a]n archive is rarely, if ever, black or white, true or false" (Treanor, 2009, p. 291). Instead, an archive, and especially the apartheid archive, is fundamentally related to relations of power in psychosocial and sociopolitical ways, as the archive regulates the nature of information, the formats of information, the access to information, and the hierarchies of information and knowledge in any given society. Reclaiming the archive is fundamentally about recognising these constraints imposed on the archive, that should be challenged through pushing the boundaries of the creation, maintenance, utilisation, management and control of the archive. Of course, such a task cannot be claimed as the domain of any single individual or group, nor can it be limited to a specific moment or event, but is potentially a collective process that requires hyper-reflexivity and an ongoing openness to critique, reiteration and generativity.

Stevens, Duncan and Sonn (2013) refer to this process as the "liberation of the archive". Firstly, this relates to the possibility to cast a different gaze onto the archive, so that what is sometimes concealed becomes illuminated, and what is absent becomes present through histories from below. Casting such a different sociopolitical light onto the archive opens up possibilities for detaching it from its current sociopolitical foreclosure, and for rethinking its contents historically and in the present. Secondly, it speaks to the possibility of seizing a social resource from hegemonic control, through expanding the boundaries of who may contribute to the creation of an archive, who can have access to it, and who can interpret it. Here, inclusion, democratisation and appropriation of the archive are critical elements of a decolonial praxis. Thirdly, given the probabilities of those working with the archive to re-inscribe a different set of relations of power onto the archive through determining the inclusion and exclusion of material, there is a need to encourage reflexive liberatory praxis within work in and on the archive, so as to avoid the usurping of the voices of others that so frequently occurs when archives are re-examined (hooks, 1990a).

Refiguring the Archive

Which figures and how they are reflected within an archive are as important as what is contained within the archive, as they highlight the historical and prevailing strategic relations and hierarchies of power between various subjects within a social formation (Hamilton, Harris, Taylor, Pickover, Reid, & Saleh, 2002). Within the Apartheid Archive Project, there has been an attempt to populate the apartheid archive with the figure of the ordinary South African (i.e. whites, blacks, academics, domestic workers, military veterans, etc.). The primary source of data from which analyses are conducted is in the form of the personal memories of citizens who have elected to submit their narratives—emphasising the everyday, the quotidian and their accounts of the commonplace. In this way, refiguring the archive is also about placing at the centre of the project those who have been historically excluded—the general populace and their routine experiences. In this way, the archive is not only populated by the grand figures of history, but by those who lived, reproduced and contested the nature of apartheid in the everydayness of their realities. Indeed, the invitation to participate speaks directly to this form of data when potential participants are requested to submit "stories of their earliest and/or most significant experiences of race and racism in apartheid South Africa" (see www.apartheidarchive.org)—personal accounts of ordinary individuals that epitomise a history from below, that writers such as Thompson (1966) refer to.

Nieftagodien (cited in Sullivan & Stevens, 2010) notes that:

> Personal accounts ... can become an important space in which to undermine 'grand' narratives that seem to cohere histories in neat, linear and inevitably predictable ways ... personal accounts at various points within ... narratives ... [provide] points of rupture, of discontinuity, and of possibility in expanding histories to be more inclusive of multiple voices (p. 426).

Personal memories must therefore at times be privileged, as their functions are not only related to historical expansion and inclusivity, but also to providing alternative readings of histories themselves. Similarly, Hamilton (2002), in her reflections on oral histories (as forms of personal and collective memory) in the politics of archiving, highlights the fluidity of oral histories as the precise strength of this mode of data collection. She argues that oral histories allow for a perspective that encourages us to think about history as that which can also be written by those on the outside of the formal knowledge production process, and contribute to memorialisation, reconciliation and social justice, especially in post-conflict and post-authoritarian societies (see for example, Gobodo-Madikizela & Van Der Merwe, 2009; Hamber & Palmary, 2009).

While noting the limitations of the inclusion of subaltern voices (see for example, Spivak, 1988; Vahabzadeh, 2008) that can become ideologically appropriated and re-subordinated, Bhabha's (1996) agentic view of the subaltern as one that may subvert dominant relations of power is a foundational element of the Apartheid Archive Project. Through forging and taking ownership of, and reinserting the personal memories that have been silenced, distorted, and/or eroded because of domination and colonisation (see for example, Dlamini, 2009, 2014; Duncan, Stevens, & Sonn, 2012) social experiences and categories come to be redefined and the possibilities are opened up for reimagining the nature of subject positions, identities and actions for the present and future in a refigured archive.

Generating Inter-Communal Spaces

Rappaport (1995) notes that storytelling and narratives have transformative power in building communities, and Williams, Labonte and O'Brien (2003, p. 36) argue that narratives as a form of "storytelling within group and community development work allows people to reveal and strengthen new communal narratives that challenge dominant narratives, and to (re)construct communities as empowered rather than disempowered collectives".

Within the Apartheid Archive Project, the actual processes involved in the construction of the project and its related activities have involved creating spaces within which academics and activists can promote broader public engagement with the recovery of historical memory. For those involved in the project as researchers, the project has meant the construction of an inter-communal space where people who have been and continue to be positioned differently because of apartheid and the related history of colonialism can converge to participate in the deconstruction and reconstruction of symbolic resources (Stevens, Duncan, & Sonn, 2013; Watkins & Schulman, 2008).

Thus, actual settings such as broad-based, public conferences that have become integral to the Apartheid Archive Project may be viewed as an inter-communal space. It is in this space where academics, artists, activists and members of the broader populace are afforded the opportunity to critically reflect upon their own positioning and identities and construct new ways of mobilising for social change. This is a significant opportunity because, as critical theorists have highlighted, it is imperative for those involved in the production of knowledge and cultural products to engage a range of subjectivities in order to cross boundaries and to "move toward an empathic, ethical and moral scholarship" (Ladson-Billings & Donnor, 2005, p. 298) that avoids scholarly insularity as far as possible. Such a relational approach to understanding the development and utility of intercommunal spaces foregrounds the dialectical relationship between formal knowledge production processes within the academy and the organic intellectual processes that Gramsci (1971) refers to, thereby becoming a space for decolonial praxis itself.

Fostering Public Mobilisation

Beyond the dialogical and reflexive elements referred to above, writers such as Reyes Cruz and Sonn (2011), and Sonn, Stevens and Duncan (2013) have argued that the deployment of decolonial methods must of necessity include transformative approaches to research and action with a range of potential publics—that is to say, that it has to be activating and mobilising in some way or another. The commitment to social change within the Apartheid Archive Project has meant deploying methodologies that allow for the translation of an academic project into mediums that are differently accessible to a variety of publics. This translational element has been a central component of the Apartheid Archive Project, in an attempt to breach to the boundary walls of the formal academy and to allow for much wider public mobilisation around the continued impact of our racialised past on contemporary social relations. We have already seen theatrical productions, photographic exhibitions, and literary readings, as different modes of representation within the Apartheid Archive Project, which signal the possibilities for more inclusive ways of knowing and doing as well as modes of social action (Gergen & Gergen, 2010). The mere accumulation of scientific and expert knowledge is not given primacy under these circumstances (Duncan & Bowman, 2009).

At each of the different Apartheid Archive Project conferences held in 2009, 2010, 2011 and 2014, there have been artistic performances, including photographic exhibitions, creative writing and poetry readings, dramatic enactments, as well as public discussions involving artists examining the relationships between memory and creativity. These have been significant features of the broader Apartheid Archive Project that have allowed for wider engagement in the public-intellectual space, awareness-raising about the project, and have fostered opportunities for dialogue and reflection on matters of race, identity and the connections between the past and the present. In addition, the use of social media and digital technologies have opened up different means for gathering stories, thereby expanding the potential reach of the project into various publics. These technologies can also function as tools for dissemination, and thus serve educational and emancipatory functions as well (Miller-Day, 2008).

This engagement with expressive and creative media in the project can be conceptualised as being aligned with performative social science (Gergen & Gergen, 2010) and as reflecting the possibilities this holds for what Miller-Day (2008) names as translational performances. For Gergen and Gergen (2010), performance as communication is based on the proposal that it will make research accessible to different audiences; opens up modes of representation and action; and opens up new ways of knowing and doing.

Within the Apartheid Archive Project, it has also been vital to translate the stories into resources that can be used for pedagogical purposes, both in formal educational settings and informal everyday settings such as:

> museums, the media, community organisations, advocacy groups, shadow ministries and government departments. Pedagogy in these sites is also, then, not solely a matter of explicit teaching, or of organising and imparting information. It is also something that takes place without conscious agency or engagement, through countless banal and unexamined means, words, images and practices (Hattam & Atkinson, 2006, p. 685).

Towards an Insurgent Citizenry

In the final analysis, a decolonial praxis also invariably involves a politics of contestation on which its social justice outcomes are premised. Rather than simply contributing to the active reduction of political and social instability and violence, a decolonial praxis must extend beyond dialogue, reflexivity and public mobilisation and may indeed also involve the promotion of an insurgent citizenry. Within the Apartheid Archive Project, Stevens, Duncan and Canham (2017), drawing on the work of Christie, Wagner and Winter (2001) in the terrain of peace psychology, suggest that peacebuilding is centrally connected to social justice imperatives and the eradication of structural violence, and of necessity must incorporate elements that run counter to the status quo, and therefore should encompass forms of interrogatory destabilisation and a politics of insurgency.

Here, interrogatory destabilisation refers to forms of consciousness-raising that critique the continuing ideological and material bases for structural forms of violence, inequality, privilege and power within a given social formation, especially those social formations transitioning away from violent conflict and authoritarianism

(Freire, 2000; Martín-Baró, 1994). Interrogatory destabilisation involves a repetitive critical deconstruction of the taken-for-granted assumptions and regimes of truth that suggest that power differentials and structural inequalities are normative in such societies, thereby unsettling status quos. As such, the process is deeply subjective and personally transformative, but is also a collective process of conscientisation that may potentially be socially transformative (Stevens, Duncan, & Canham, 2017).

Such a process of interrogatory destabilisation can form the bedrock for social movements that embrace a political project encouraging an insurgent citizenship and politics (Holston, 2009)—a politics of resistance or antagonism (Hook, 2014) amongst those who are precariously positioned in societies. Instead of perpetuating their positions on the periphery of society, these social movements attempt to reclaim elements of their rightful citizenship, often involving active forms of social protest and concientisation, but may also include everyday forms of social relating that run counter to what is considered as a socially acceptable form of dissent (e.g. in aesthetically provocative and confrontational social protests). As such, an insurgent citizenship and politics is a disruptive mode of engaging and living in the social world and may very well feel uncomfortably destabilising if it is mobilised politically in the service of social justice and equality, but opens up the possibilities for engaging with old and new configurations of power (Stevens, Duncan, & Canham, 2017).

Conclusion

The Apartheid Archive Project may be considered as a site of struggle and contestation that allows for a reclamation, refiguring and democratisation of history. In addition, expanding this archive allows us to examine apartheid's historical and continued effects into the present; to move beyond a mutual recognition of woundedness and entanglements; and through an actional politics, to critique the status quo along cleavages and axes of power that sustain ongoing disparities in access, power and privilege at a political, social, cultural, psychological and material level.

The Apartheid Archive Project is also an illustrative exemplar of how innovative participatory methods and novel lines of intellectual inquiry may be combined within a decolonial mode of praxis. While recognising that there are limitations to memory, storied accounts, and narratives, they are nevertheless critical to helping to foster a decolonial ethic of rupture and destabilisation, premised on historical witnessing, recognition and demands for inclusivity that challenge historical and existing relations of power, forms of knowledge and ways of being.

Acknowledgements I would like to acknowledge the work of the Apartheid Archive Project, the core team of researchers, and all those who have contributed their stories to the project. In particular, I would like to extend my thanks to Prof Norman Duncan, Prof Christopher Sonn, Prof Derek Hook and Dr. Hugo Canham—all of whom I have co-authored several publications with, and from which I have drawn upon extensively in the writing of this chapter.

References

Abrams, L. S., & Moio, J. A. (2009). Critical race theory and the cultural competence dilemma in social work education. *Journal of Social Work Education, 45*, 245–260.

Addison, R. B. (1992). Grounded hermeneutic research. In B. F. Crabtree & W. L. Miller (Eds.), *Doing qualitative research* (pp. 145–162). Newbury Park, CA: Sage.

Apartheid Archive Project. (2010). *Apartheid archive project*. Retrieved from http://www.apartheidarchive.org/site/

Bell, L. A. (2010). *Storytelling for social justice: Connecting narrative & the arts in antiracist teaching*. New York: Routledge.

Bhabha, H. K. (1994). *The location of culture*. London: Routledge.

Bhabha, H. K. (1996). Unsatisfied: Notes on vernacular cosmopolitanism. In L. Garcia-Moreno & P. C. Pfeiffer (Eds.), *Text and nation: Cross-disciplinary essays on cultural and national identities* (pp. 191–207). Columbia, SC: Camden House.

Biko, S. (2004). *I write what I like*. Johannesburg: Pan Macmillan.

Bond, L. A., Belenky, M. F., & Weinstock, J. S. (2000). The listening partners program: An initiative toward feminist community psychology in action. *American Journal of Community Psychology, 28*, 697–727.

Bonner, P., & Nieftagodien, N. (2008). *Alexandra: A history. Johannesburg, South Africa*. Johannesburg: Wits University Press.

Bulhan, H. A. (1985). *Frantz fanon and the psychology of oppression*. New York: Plenum Press.

Cassin, B., Cayla, O., & Salazar, P. (2004). Dire la vérité, faire la réconciliation, manquer la réparation (speaking the truth, reconciling and failing to offer reparation). In B. Cassin, O. Cayla, & P. Salazar (Eds.), *Vérité, réconciliation, réparation (Truth, reconciliation and reparation)* (pp. 13–26). Paris: Seuil.

Christie, D. J., Wagner, R. V., & Winter, D. A. (Eds.). (2001). *Peace, conflict, and violence: Peace psychology for the 21st century*. Englewood Cliffs, NJ: Prentice-Hall.

Contassel, J., & Holder, C. (2008). Who's sorry now? Government apologies, truth commissions, and government apologies, and indigenous self determination in Australia, Canda, Guatemala, and Peru. *Human Rights Review, 9*, 465–489.

Derrida, J. (1998). *Archive fever: A Freudian impression*. Chicago, IL: University of Chicago Press.

Derrida, J. (2006). *Specters of Marx: The state of the debt, the work of mourning & the new international*. London: Routledge.

Dlamini, J. (2009). *Native nostalgia*. Auckland Park: Jacana.

Dlamini, J. (2014). *Askari: A story of collaboration and betrayal in the anti-apartheid struggle*. Auckland Park: Jacana.

Dudgeon, P., & Fielder, J. (2006). Third spaces within tertiary places: Indigenous Australian studies. *Journal of Community and Applied Social Psychology, 16*(5), 396–409.

Duncan, N., & Bowman, B. (2009). Liberating south African psychology: The legacy of racism and the pursuit of representative knowledge production. In M. Montero & C. C. Sonn (Eds.), *Psychology of liberation* (pp. 93–114). New York: Springer.

Duncan, N., Stevens, G., & Sonn, C. (2012). Of narratives and nostalgia. Peace and conflict. *Journal of Peace Psychology, 18*(3), 205–213.

Eagle, G., & Bowman, B. (2013). Self-consciousness and impression management in the authoring of apartheid related narratives. In G. Stevens, N. Duncan, & D. Hook (Eds.), *Race, memory and the apartheid archive: Towards a transformative psychosocial praxis* (pp. 275–294). London/Johannesburg: Palgrave Macmillan/Wits University Press.

Erasmus, Z. (Ed.). (2001). *Coloured by history, shaped by place*. Cape Town: Kwela Books and SA History Online.

Fanon, F. (1967). *Black skins, white masks*. New York: Grove Press.

Feyerabend, P. (1975). *Against method: Outline of an anarchist theory of knowledge*. New York: New Left Books.

Freire, P. (2000). *Pedagogy of the oppressed*. New York: Continuum.

Gergen, M. M., & Gergen, K. J. (2010). Performative social science and psychology. *Forum: Qualitative Social Research, 12*(1), 11. http://nbn-resolving.de/urn:nbn:de:0114-fqs1101119.

Gilroy, P. (2010). *Darker than blue*. Cambridge, MA: The Belknap Press of Harvard University Press.

Glover, M., Dudgeon, P., & Huygens, I. (2005). Colonization and racism. In G. Nelson & I. Prilleltensky (Eds.), *Community psychology: In pursuit of liberation and wellbeing* (1st ed., pp. 330–347). New York: Palgrave.

Gobodo-Madikizela, P., & Van Der Merwe, C. (Eds.). (2009). *Memory, narrative and forgiveness: Perspectives on the unfinished journeys of the past*. Newcastle upon Tyne: Cambridge Scholars Publishing.

Goldberg, D. T. (2008). *The threat of race: Reflections on racial neoliberalism*. New York: Wiley-Blackwell.

Gramsci, A. (1971). *Selections from the prison notebooks*. New York: International Publishers Company.

Hamber, B., & Palmary, I. (2009). Gender, memorialization, and symbolic reparations. In R. Rubio-Marin (Ed.), *The gender of reparations: Unsettling sexual hierarchies while redressing human rights violations* (pp. 324–381). New York: Cambridge University Press.

Hamilton, C. (2002). 'Living by fluidity': Oral histories, material custodies and the politics of archiving. In C. Hamilton, V. Harris, J. Taylor, M. Pickover, G. Reid, & R. Saleh (Eds.), *Refiguring the archive* (pp. 209–227). Cape Town: David Philip.

Hamilton, C., Harris, V., Taylor, J., Pickover, M., Reid, G., & Saleh, R. (Eds.). (2002). *Refiguring the archive*. Cape Town: David Philip.

Hattam, R., & Atkinson, S. (2006). Reconciliation as a frame for rethinking racism in Australia. *Social Identities: Journal for the Study of Race, Nation and Culture, 12*(6), 683–700.

Holston, J. (2009). *Insurgent citizenship: Disjunctions of democracy and modernity in Brazil*. New Jersey, NJ: Princeton University Press.

Hook, D. (2013). On animal mediators and psychoanalytic reading practice. In G. Stevens, N. Duncan, & D. Hook (Eds.), *Race, memory and the apartheid archive: Towards a transformative psychosocial praxis* (pp. 146–162). London/Johannesburg: Palgrave Macmillan/Wits University Press.

Hook, D. (2014). Antagonism, social critique and the "violent reverie". *Psychology in Society, 46*, 21–34.

hooks, b. (1990a). Marginality as a site of resistance. In R. Ferguson, M. Gever, T. Min-Ha, & C. West (Eds.), *Out there: Marginalization and contemporary cultures* (pp. 341–343). Cambridge, MA: The MIT Press.

hooks, b. (1990b). *Yearning: Race, gender, and cultural politics*. Boston, MA: South End Press.

James, W., & van der Vijver, L. (Eds.). (2000). *After the TRC: Reflections on truth and reconciliation in South Africa*. Cape Town: David Philip.

Jones, M. O. (1996). *Studying organisational symbolism: What, how, why*. Thousand Oaks, CA: Sage.

Josselson, R., & Lieblich, A. (Eds.). (1995). *Interpreting experience: The narrative study of lives*. Thousand Oaks, CA: Sage.

Ladson-Billings, G. (2003). It's your world, I'm just trying to explain it: Understanding our epistemological and methodological challenges. *Qualitative Inquiry, 9*(1), 5–12.

Ladson-Billings, G., & Donnor, J. (2005). The moral activist role of critical race theory scholarship. In N. K. Denzin & Y. S. Lincoln (Eds.), *The sage handbook of qualitative research* (3rd ed., pp. 279–302). Thousand Oaks, CA: Sage.

Laubscher, L. (2013). Working with the apartheid archive: Or, of witness, testimony, and ghosts. In G. Stevens, N. Duncan, & D. Hook (Eds.), *Race, memory and the apartheid archive: Towards a transformative psychosocial praxis* (pp. 45–60). London/Johannesburg: Palgrave Macmillan/Wits University Press.

Lieblich, A., Tuval-Mashiach, R., & Zilber, T. (1998). *Narrative research. Reading, analysis, and interpretation, Applied social research methods series* (Vol. 47). Thousand Oaks, CA: Sage.

Maldonado-Torres, N. (2007). On the coloniality of being. Contributions to the development of a concept. *Cultural Studies, 21*(2), 240–270.

Maldonado-Torres, N. (2011). Thinking through the decolonial turn: Post-continental interventions in theory, philosophy and critique—An introduction. *Transmodernity, 1*(2), 1–15.

Mankowski, E., & Rappaport, J. (1995). Stories, identity, and the psychological sense of community. In R. S. Wyer & Jr. (Eds.), *Knowledge and memory: The real story* (pp. 211–226). Hillsdale, NJ: Lawrence Erlbaum Associates.

Martín-Baró, I. (1994). Towards a liberation psychology (a. Aron, trans.) In A. Aron & S. Corne (Eds.), *Writings for a liberation psychology: Ignacio Martín-Baró* (pp. 17–32). Cambridge: Harvard University Press.

Mbembe, A. (2002). The power of the archive and its limits. In C. Hamilton, V. Harris, J. Taylor, M. Pickover, G. Reid, & R. Saleh (Eds.), *Refiguring the archive* (pp. 19–26). Cape Town: David Philip.

Memmi, A. (1984). *Dependence: A sketch for a portrait of the dependent*. Boston, MA: Beacon Press.

Miller-Day, M. (2008). Translational performances: Toward relevant, engaging, and empowering social science. *Forum: Qualitative Social Research, 9*(2), 54. http://nbn-resolving.de/urn:nbn:de:0114-fqs0802541.

Moane, G. (2003). Bridging the personal and the political: Practices for a liberation psychology. *American Journal of Community Psychology, 31*(1–2), 91–101.

Moane, G. (2009). Reflections on liberation psychology in action in an Irish context. In M. Montero & C. C. Sonn (Eds.), *Psychology of liberation: Theory and applications* (pp. 135–153). New York: Springer.

Montero, M. (2007). The political psychology of liberation: From politics to ethics and back. *Political Psychology, 28*(5), 517–533.

Moreton-Robinson, A. (2004). *Whitening race: Essays in social and cultural criticism*. Canberra: Aboriginal Studies Press.

Mulvey, A., Torenzio, M., Hill, J., Bond, M. A., Huygens, I., Hamerton, H. R., & Cahill, S. (2000). Stories of relative privilege: Power and social change in feminist community psychology. *American Journal of Community Psychology, 28*(6), 883–911.

Nielsen, C. R. (2011). Resistance through re-narration: Fanon on de-constructing racialized subjectivities. *African Identities, 9*(4), 363–385.

Nora, P. (1989). Between memory and history: Les lieux de mémoire. *Representations, 26*, 7–24.

Nuttall, S. (2009). *Entanglement: Literary and cultural reflections on post-apartheid*. Johannesburg: Wits University Press.

Peterson, B. (2012). Dignity, memory, truth and the future under siege: Reconciliation and nation building in post-apartheid South Africa. In M. Shapiro & S. Opondo (Eds.), *The new violent cartography* (pp. 214–233). New York: Routledge.

Quijano, A. (2000). Coloniality of power and Eurocentrism in Latin America. *International Sociology, 15*(2), 215–232.

Rappaport, J. (1995). Empowerment meets narrative: Listening to stories and creating settings. *American Journal of Community Psychology, 23*(5), 795–807.

Rappaport, J. (2000). Community narratives: Tales of terror and joy. *American Journal of Community Psychology, 28*(1), 1–24.

Ratele, K., & Laubscher, L. (2013). Archiving white lives, historicising whiteness. In G. Stevens, N. Duncan, & D. Hook (Eds.), *Race, memory and the apartheid archive: Towards a transformative psychosocial praxis* (pp. 109–127). London/Johannesburg: Palgrave Macmillan/Wits University Press.

Reyes Cruz, M., & Sonn, C. C. (2011). (de)colonizing culture in community psychology: Reflections from critical social science. *American Journal of Community Psychology, 47*(1–2), 203–214.

Rigney, A. (2012). Reconciliation and remembering: (how) does it work? *Memory Studies, 5*(3), 251–258.

Ross, T. (2000). The Richmond narratives. In R. Delgado & J. Stefancic (Eds.), *Critical race theory* (2nd ed., pp. 42–51). Philadelphia, PA: Temple University Press.

Said, E. (1978). *Orientalism*. London: Penguin.

Sands, R. G. (2004). Narrative analysis: A feminist approach. In D. K. Padgett (Ed.), *The qualitative research experience* (pp. 48–75). Belmont, CA: Thomson Brooks/Cole.

Scott, J. C. (1990). *Domination and the arts of resistance: Hidden transcripts*. New Haven, CT: Yale University Press.

Smith, L. T. (1999). *Decolonising methodologies: Researching and indigenous peoples*. Dunedin: University of Otago Press.

Sonn, C. C., Stevens, G., & Duncan, N. (2013). Decolonisation, critical methodologies, and why stories matter. In G. Stevens, N. Duncan, & D. Hook (Eds.), *Race, memory and the apartheid archive: Towards a transformative psychosocial praxis* (pp. 295–314). London/Johannesburg: Palgrave Macmillan/Wits University Press.

Spivak, G. (1988). Can the subaltern speak? In C. Nelson & L. Grossberg (Eds.), *Marxism and the interpretation of culture* (pp. 271–313). Champaign, IL: University of Illinois Press.

Stevens, G. (2006). De-racialisation or re-racialisation: Truth, reconciliation and reparation in post-apartheid South Africa. In G. Stevens, V. Franchi, & T. Swart (Eds.), *A 'race' against time* (pp. 293–316). Pretoria: UNISA Press.

Stevens, G., Duncan, N., & Hook, D. (2013a). The apartheid archive project, the psychosocial and political praxis. In G. Stevens, N. Duncan, & D. Hook (Eds.), *Race, memory and the apartheid archive: Towards a transformative psychosocial praxis* (pp. 1–17). London/Johannesburg: Palgrave Macmillan/Wits University Press.

Stevens, G., Duncan, N., & Hook, D. (Eds.). (2013b). *Race, memory and the apartheid archive: Towards a transformative psychosocial praxis*. London/Johannesburg: Palgrave Macmillan/Wits University Press.

Stevens, G., Duncan, N., & Canham, H. (2017). Interrogatory destabilisation and an insurgent politics for peacebuilding: The case of the apartheid archive project. In M. Seedat, S. Suffla, & D. J. Christie (Eds.), *Enlarging the scope of peace psychology: African and world-regional contributions* (pp. 185–202). Cham: Springer International Publishing.

Stevens, G., Duncan, N., & Sonn, C. C. (2013). Memory, narrative and voice as liberatory praxis in the apartheid archive. In G. Stevens, N. Duncan, & D. Hook (Eds.), *Race, memory and the apartheid archive: Towards a transformative psychosocial praxis* (pp. 25–44). London/Johannesburg: Palgrave Macmillan/Wits University Press.

Straker, G. (2013). Unsettling whiteness. In G. Stevens, N. Duncan, & D. Hook (Eds.), *Race, memory and the apartheid archive: Towards a transformative psychosocial praxis* (pp. 91–108). London/Johannesburg: Palgrave Macmillan/Wits University Press.

Sullivan, L. G., & Stevens, G. (2010). Through her eyes: Relational references in black women's narratives of apartheid racism. *South African Journal of Psychology, 40*(4), 414–431.

Swadener, B. B., & Mutua, K. (2008). Decolonising performances: Deconstructing the global postcolonial. In N. K. Denzin, Y. S. Lincoln, & L. T. Smith (Eds.), *Handbook of critical and indigenous methodologies* (pp. 31–44). Thousand Oaks, CA: Sage.

Taussig, M. (1986). *Shamanism, colonialism and the wild man*. Chicago, IL: University of Chicago Press.

Thomas, R. E., & Rappaport, J. (1996). Art as community narrative: A resource for social change. In M. B. Lykes, R. Liem, A. Banuazizi, & M. Morris (Eds.), *Unmasking social inequalities: Victims, voice and resistance* (pp. 317–336). Philadelphia, PA: Temple University Press.

Thompson, E. P. (1966, April 7). History from below. *Times Literary Supplement*, pp. 279–280.

Treanor, B. (2009). What tradition? Whose archive? Blogs, Googlewashing, and the digitization of the archive. *Analecta Hermeneutica, 1*, 289–302.

Truscott, R. (2011). National melancholia and Afrikaner self-parody. *Psychoanalysis, Culture & Society, 16*(1), 90–106.

Turner, V. (2008). *The ritual process: Structure and anti-structure*. New Jersey, NJ: Transaction Publishers.

Vahabzadeh, P. (2008). The conditions of subalternity: Reflections on subjectivity, experience and hegemony. *Socialist Studies/Études Socialistes, 3*(2), 93–113.
Villa-Vicencio, C. (2004). Oublie, mémoire et vigilance (failure to remember, memory and vigilance). In B. Cassin, O. Cayla, & P. Salazar (Eds.), *Vérité, réconciliation, reparation (Truth, reconciliation and reparation)* (pp. 319–338). Paris: Seuil.
Watkins, M., & Schulman, H. (2008). *Toward psychologies of liberation*. Houndsmills: Palgrave/McMillan.
Williams, L., Labonte, R., & O'Brien, M. (2003). Empowering social action through narratives of identity and culture. *Health Promotion International, 18*(1), 33–40.
Worby, E., & Ally, S. (2013). The disappointment of nostalgia: Conceptualising cultures of memory in contemporary South Africa. *Social Dynamics, 39*(3), 457–480.

Index

M. Seedat et al. (eds.), *Emancipatory and Participatory Methodologies in Peace, Critical, and Community Psychology*, Peace Psychology Book Series,
DOI 10.1007/978-3-319-63489-0

The manufacturer's authorised representative in the EU is Springer Nature Customer Service Centre GmbH, Europaplatz 3, 69115 Heidelberg, Germany. If you have any concerns regarding our products, please contact ProductSafety@springernature.com

Printed and bound by CPI Group (UK) Ltd, Croydon, CR0 4YY
30/09/2026
02225651-0002